Critical
T

Critical and Creative Thinking

A Brief Guide for Teachers

Robert DiYanni

WILEY Blackwell

For Joan Weber and Carl Weber

*For my dear friends Dr. Joan Weber
and Dr. Carl Weber, who have consistently demonstrated
exemplary leadership in education and in medicine, with
generosity, grace, and compassion.*

Contents

Preface   xi

Acknowledgments   xiii

About the Website   xv

Part One   Introducing Critical and Creative Thinking

1 Essential Critical Thinking Concepts   3
   What Is Critical Thinking?   4
   Habits of Mind   5
   Why Intellectual Habits and Character Matter   7
   Overcoming Obstacles to Thinking   8
   A Model for Critical Thinking   13
   How You Know What You Know   14
   Perception and Knowledge   15
   Being Wrong   23
   Why Errors Persist   25
   Applications   27
   References   30

   Interchapter 1   Facts and Knowledge   32

2 Essential Creative Thinking Concepts   36
   What Is Creative Thinking?   37
   Seeking Alternatives and Possibilities   38
   Reversing Relationships   41
   Cross-fertilizing   42
   Shifting Attention   42

Denying the Negative 43
The Creative Habit 46
Creative Confidence 48
Creative Theft 49
Creative Crime 51
Creative Questions 52
Applications 56
References 58

Interchapter 2   Sustaining Curiosity 60

Part Two   Practicing Critical and Creative Thinking

3 **Becoming a Critical and Creative Thinker** 65
Becoming a Critical Thinker 66
Intellectual Standards as Guidelines for Critical
   Thinking 67
Language and Thought 67
Reports, Inferences, and Judgments 69
The Prevalence and Power of Metaphor 74
Innovating through Analogy 78
Becoming a Creative Thinker 79
Developing the Creative Habit 80
Focus 83
Solo and Group Creativity 85
Concepts as Cognitive Tools 87
Applications 90
References 95

Interchapter 3   Embodying Experience 96

4 **Critical Thinking Strategies and Applications** 101
The Nature of Argument 102
Claims, Evidence, and Assumptions 102
Evidence: Claims and Warrants 105
Inductive and Deductive Reasoning 106
Sherlock Holmes as a Logical Thinker 109
Syllogisms, Enthymemes, and Argument 112
Argument and Authority 113
Argument and Analogy 114
Argument and Causality 116

Causality, Coincidence, and Correlation 120
Further Causal Consequences 122
Applications 123
References 129

Interchapter 4   Blending Art and Science **130**

5 **Creative Thinking Strategies and Applications** **133**
Imagination First 134
Imagination, Creativity, and Innovation 135
The Limits of Imagination 136
Capacities for Imaginative Thinking 137
Why Ideas Are Important 139
How to Get Ideas 140
Creative Whacks 147
Being Practical/What Iffing 153
Combining Things 156
Using Paradox 157
Thinking the Unthinkable 160
Applications 161
References 164

Interchapter 5   Combining Connections **166**

Part Three   Applying Critical and Creative Thinking

6 **Decision Thinking: Making Critical Decisions** **173**
Making Decisions 174
Affective Forecasting 180
Achieving Insights that Affect Decisions 184
Institutional Decisions 186
Incentives and Decisions 188
Decisiveness 189
Making Tough Decisions 192
Making Group Decisions 194
Applications 195
References 198

Interchapter 6   Embracing Ambiguity **200**

7 **Ethical Thinking: Making Ethical Decisions** **205**
Basic Ethical Concepts 206

Contents

Ethics, Values, and Virtues   209
Ethical Imagination   213
Cosmopolitanism and Global Ethics   218
Technology and Ethics   220
The Ethics of Information   222
Ethical Decisions   224
Ethical Provocations   225
Applications   227
References   231

Index   233

Preface

When we think about thinking, we often think first of "critical" thinking. The world at large values critical thinking highly—and for good reason. Critical thinking involves analysis and evaluation, interpretation and judgment. Critical thinking is essential for making sense of the world and for understanding ourselves.

To limit thinking, however, only to critical thinking is reductive, even dangerous. To supplement and complement critical thinking, we need "creative" thinking, the kind of imaginative thinking that leads to new ideas, to creativity and innovation. Creative thinking is also highly valued in the world at large. Creative thinking completes and fulfills critical thinking. Either without the other is inadequate. Whole-minded thinkers generate new ideas creatively and evaluate them critically.

Learning to think critically and creatively can make a difference in your personal and professional life. Developing your critical and creative capacities can increase your confidence, deepen your understanding, and improve your performance. Thinking well broadens your perception and enriches your intellectual and emotional well-being.

Not thinking well, on the other hand, reduces the range, depth, and intensity of your lived experience. Not thinking well limits your potential accomplishments. This book can help you overcome such limitations.

Combining critical and creative thinking, this book explains a set of approaches and offers a series of opportunities to think about a wide range of issues and topics. It includes both general guidelines and specific techniques to improve your thinking and the thinking of your students. Drawing from and consolidating a wide range of sources, it summarizes and synthesizes key ideas and presents them for your consideration.

A few words about the book's structure. Part One introduces essential concepts for critical and creative thinking. Part Two provides opportunities to practice them. Part Three applies critical and creative thinking to decision-making and questions of ethics. Six interchapters identify essential strategies for developing higher order thinking. Each strategy is associated with a thinking habit of Leonardo da Vinci.

It is one thing to learn about the various ways of thinking that this book provides; it is another, however, to develop skill in using them. To benefit most from what the book offers, you should work through its varied applications. Select a few for your reflections in writing.

There is nothing more vital than developing your capacity to think well about complex issues and questions. This book is designed to help you do just that, while developing your critical and creative thinking powers. These thinking powers can make a difference in how you perceive yourself, how you understand others, and how you experience the world. And they can help you make a similar difference in the lives of your students.

Acknowledgments

I would like to acknowledge and thank a number of people for encouraging me on the path that eventuated in this book: Bob Boynton and Peter Stillman of Boynton/Cook who published my first book, *Connections*; Kathleen Hulley, who hired me to teach Critical Thinking at NYU; Pat C. Hoy II, former Director of the Expository Writing Program at NYU, who has long been a powerful influence on my own thinking about writing and its relationship to thinking. Bill Costanzo, Distinguished Professor of English at Westchester Community College, SUNY, who has given me much good advice; John Chaffee and Richard van de Lagemaat, two fine critical thinkers with important books on the subject; Nancy Willard Magaud, of the English Language Schools Association (ELSA) in France, who reviewed the manuscript and made helpful suggestions for revision.

At various stages of this book's development, including its many drafts, I received thoughtful and productive responses from a number of reviewers. I would like to thank the following for their input:

Roseanne Abbott, Australia Teacher of the Year in 2013, English Teacher and Department Chair, Callaghan College, New South Wales, Australia.

Jack Bartholomew, Chair of Science, Morristown Beard School, Morristown, New Jersey.

David Blagbrough, former Director of the British Council and of Inspire, a non-profit organization in London that works with at-risk students.

George Ewonus, Director, Advanced Placement Program, Canada.

Terence Young, Head of English, St Michael's University School, Victoria, British Columbia, Canada.

At Wiley Blackwell, I have had the good fortune to work with Jayne Fargnoli, who believed in this book from the beginning and who supported its development unstintingly. Mark Graney orchestrated the reviewing process expeditiously, and Julia Kirk managed the books production expertly. Thanks also to all the other Wiley Blackwell staff and freelancers involved in the production of this book. *None of these good people should be held accountable for any errors contained in this book. Any errors are mine alone.*

My final and most important acknowledgment of appreciation is to my wonderful wife, Mary Hammond DiYanni. Mary is a critical and creative thinker *par excellence*. I am fortunate beyond measure to have enjoyed her steadfast love and splendid companionship for more than four decades. My toughest critic, Mary has also been my most ardent supporter. I owe her not less than everything.

About the Website

Please visit the companion website to view additional content for this title at

www.wiley.com/go/diyanni/guidetocriticalcreativethinking

Available to Instructors Only:

- Detailed lessons, written by the author as well as other teachers, that make thinking visible and call upon students' critical and creative thinking faculties and targeted at middle school, high school, or first-year university students.

Part One

Introducing Critical and Creative Thinking

1

Essential Critical Thinking Concepts

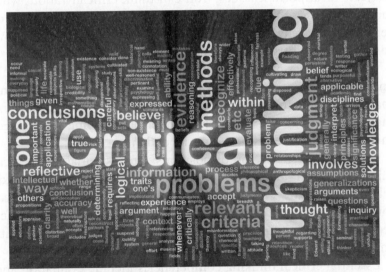

Figure 1.1   Critical thinking. © Keng Guan Toh/Shutterstock

No problem can withstand the assault of sustained thinking.

—Voltaire

Critical and Creative Thinking: A Brief Guide for Teachers, First Edition. Robert DiYanni.
© 2016 John Wiley & Sons, Inc. Published 2016 by John Wiley & Sons, Inc.

What Is Critical Thinking?

Critical thinking is a type of thinking in which you reflect and analyze when making decisions and solving problems. Based on logic and careful reasoning, critical thinking is purposeful thinking guided by reasoned evidence. It defines problems, identifies competing arguments, uses relevant data, raises key questions, and uses information effectively to make reasoned judgments. The word "critical" derives from the Greek work *kritikos*, which means "judge." Critical thinking involves rationality and convergent thinking.

Critical thinking does not necessarily involve criticizing ideas (although sometimes, being "critical" in this way can be an aspect of thinking critically). Nor is critical thinking used only for serious subjects or important issues. You can think critically about what kind of popcorn to buy or what hat to wear, whether to marry or remain single, whether you should go to graduate school or move to a foreign country.

Characteristics of critical thinking include noticing perceptively and establishing careful connections; asking probing questions and making meaningful distinctions. Critical thinking involves analyzing, interpreting, and evaluating evidence; applying knowledge; thinking independently and interdependently.

Certain tendencies, or dispositions, are essential for critical thinking. Among them are open-mindedness, honesty, and flexibility; perseverance; reasonableness, diligence, and focus. Critical thinkers reconsider ideas and sometimes change their minds. They recognize the legitimacy of alternative views, embrace ambiguity and remain open to continued learning.

Essential critical thinking competencies include evaluation and self-direction. Evaluation through informed and sound judgments, and through considering values, is central to the process of critical thinking. Self-direction includes self-awareness and self-regulation—managing your thinking and your motivation for thinking. Critical thinking also involves asking productive questions. Asking the right kinds of questions is as important as answering them. Essential significant questions include those shown in Table 1.1.

Table 1.1 Essential critical thinking questions

What do you know?	What have you assumed?
What questions can you ask?	What does it mean?
What is the evidence?	What are the criteria?

Underlying these questions is the fundamental critical thinking question: "How do I know what I think I know?" And, "What evidence do I have for what I think I know?"

Critical thinkers constantly challenge their thinking and the thinking of others. They exhibit a stance of deliberate skepticism, refusing to accept assertions without evidence to support them. They also try to consider their own ideas from the perspective of others who might see things differently. The following questions, which have been adapted from Richard Paul's and Linda Elder's (2002) *Critical Thinking*, offer guidance in doing this.

Guiding questions for critical thinking

1. What are the purpose and goal of the thinking?
2. What question or problem is being addressed?
3. What is the point of view or perspective?
4. What claim or idea is being advanced, and why?
5. What facts, information, or data support the claim or idea?
6. What assumptions are being made, and which of those assumptions might be questioned or challenged?
7. What inferences are being made, and what conclusion is drawn from them?
8. What implications and consequences can be inferred?
9. What concept or theory guides the thinking?

Habits of Mind

Your intelligence is the sum of your habits of mind—how you use those mental habits to think and solve problems. This book is designed to improve your current productive habits of mind while helping you modify or eliminate bad thinking habits. The Institute for Habits of Mind identifies and recommends the following thinking habits: (1) applying past knowledge to new situations; (2) remaining open to continued learning; (3) posing questions and identifying problems; (4) taking intellectual risks; (5) developing and sustaining curiosity; (6) thinking independently and interdependently.

Applying past knowledge to new situations

Using what you already know, you make connections between prior knowledge and new situations. American philosopher John Dewey reminds us that we learn by reflecting on our experiences. Thomas Edison claimed that he never made mistakes, but rather kept learning what didn't work in the process of figuring out what might.

Remaining open to continued learning

You continue learning all your life, which involves identifying opportunities for continuous learning everywhere. Being "open" to learning opportunities includes being willing to consider other perspectives and ideas, to possibilities for intellectual growth and development wherever they can be found.

Posing questions and identifying problems

Asking productive questions and identifying problems are essential for quality thinking. Socrates asked probing questions, pushing those he questioned ever deeper into inquiry, often to the point of exasperation and an acknowledgment of their ignorance. Questions invite answers; considering answers to thoughtful questions helps you discover the limits of your knowledge.

Taking intellectual risks

Taking risks with your thinking, moving outside your comfort zone prods you to think in new and interesting ways. Taking risks involves the chance of failure; it involves being frustrated by uncertainty. Progress, however, depends upon taking chances. Being willing to fail, and even to embrace failure, is essential for invention and discovery.

Developing and sustaining intellectual curiosity

Curiosity is the motivation for all learning. Children are immensely curious about all sorts of things. Many people, unfortunately, lose that curiosity during their years of schooling. One of the greatest thinkers of all time, Leonardo da Vinci, considered curiosity fundamental to his life as an artist, scientist, and inventor. He repeatedly acknowledged curiosity as his most important habit of mind.

Thinking independently and interdependently

Although necessary, independent thinking is only part of the story; also necessary is collaborative thinking. The process is reciprocal: you link your thinking with the thinking of others. You feed off the ideas of others, who then feed off yours. Both independent and interdependent thinking spur progress and spark innovation.

Why Intellectual Habits and Character Matter

To become truly useful, these habits of mind need to be actualized as things you do regularly. In making these kinds of thinking habitual, you develop what Ron Ritchhart (2004) has called "intellectual character," a cohesive way of thinking that is distinctively your own. His notion of intellectual character includes habits of mind, along with patterns of thinking and general dispositions about thinking that reflect how you think. Developing an intellectual character requires building on positive thinking dispositions, such as persistence, patience, and perseverance. Your intellectual character defines you as an individual thinker; it reflects your particular way of engaging the world mindfully.

David Brooks (2014) echoes and extends these ideas with a set of "mental virtues" he believes are embedded in character, virtues necessary for quality higher-order thinking. Among these mental virtues are intellectual courage, which Brooks defines as the "willingness to hold unpopular views." Firmness and autonomy require an ability to hold to your ideas in the face of opposition. They involve a balancing act between flaccidity and rigidity, and between respect for authority and tradition on one hand, and the ability to depart from those influences, on the other. Brooks adds generosity and humility to the mix, recognizing others' ideas and acknowledging the limits of your knowledge and understanding. Thinking well requires resisting vanity and laziness, pushing against the need for certainty, resisting the urge to avoid painful truths. In short, good critical thinking for Brooks is a "moral enterprise," one that requires "the ability to go against our lesser impulses for the sake of our higher ones."

Enhancing your ability to think critically can have a pronounced effect on your behavior as well as on your attitude toward learning and the thinking of others. Taking intellectual risks can make you both a more daring thinker and a more interesting one. Being open to the possibility of failure can lead you to a more experimental and exploratory frame of mind, permitting you to try different options with the knowledge that some won't work out. Risk-taking demonstrates a kind of intellectual courage necessary for eventual creative breakthroughs.

Learning to think interdependently enriches your intellectual experience, with opportunities for you to bounce ideas off others and to share in the pleasure of figuring things out together. It also provides practice in the necessary skill of collaboration, which is critically important in today's workplace. Being open to others' ideas and perspectives and willing to change your mind helps to develop skills in negotiation and conflict management, while enhancing your reputation as a reasonable and flexible thinker.

Overcoming Obstacles to Thinking

To develop productive intellectual habits, you need to overcome various obstacles that can block your thinking. In *Conceptual Block-busting*, James L. Adams (2001) discusses blocks to thought, including perceptual blocks, cultural blocks, intellectual blocks, emotional blocks, and polarizing blocks.

Perceptual blocks to thinking

Perceptual blocks inhibit your ability to make sense of what you are looking at. They interfere with what you can see. To overcome perceptual blocks you keep looking until you can make sense of what you are seeing.

In looking at Picasso's painting *Guernica*, for example, you notice distorted human figures. You can find Guernica on many Internet sites, including http://www.pablopicasso.org/guernica. jsp.

You see a horse with an open mouth, its tongue a spike, in what appears an agonized scream; you see an extended arm and a hand holding a light. You see distorted human arms and legs, hands and fingers and feet in contorted postures. You see a head thrown back with its mouth open, a person with arms extended upwards, and a hand clutching a sharp object.

Making sense begins with careful noticing. It involves relating the details you see, considering why they have been put together. It involves asking questions about what you observe. In the process you arrive at an understanding of the significance of what you are looking at.

Besides doing your own noticing, you can also ask colleagues or friends what they see and what sense they make of *Guernica*. You can also do some research into what Picasso attempted with this painting, and why he created it. Knowing something about the historical events that inspired Picasso to paint *Guernica* and learning something about the painting's varied contexts can deepen your understanding and enhance your appreciation.

Learning to see ably requires patience, effort, and practice. You prepare yourself to see; you learn how to look. One crucial element for improving your thinking, then, is to become more observant—to broaden and deepen your perception.

To notice the special features of Chartres cathedral, to appreciate the moves of basketball star LeBron James, or the skills of actors, such as Leonardo DiCaprio and Cate Blanchett, you have to know something about architecture, basketball, or acting, respectively. One pillar of observation is knowledge. The more you know about something, the better you see it, understand it, and appreciate it. You may take pride in your knowledge of architecture, basketball, movies and acting, a pride earned through a deepening of knowledge. That deepened knowledge enables you to see more and to see better than those who lack such knowledge. You can overcome perceptual blocks to thinking, then, in a variety of ways. Seeing more and seeing better, and knowing more are some productive perceptual blockbusting strategies.

Cultural blocks to thinking

Cultural blocks develop from ingrained thinking habits. Cultural blocks to thinking derive from ethnic, racial, national, and intellectual traditions, as well as from your gender and social class. Italians and Norwegians, Latinos and Native Americans, Japanese and Singaporeans, men and women, the wealthy and the poor, bankers and poets, have different life priorities largely because of their different experiences and their differing social and cultural, political, and economic backgrounds. Similarly, people of different religions are committed to varied ideas about the role of children or animals in society, or the degree of respect given the elderly, or to educators, for that matter. Your perspectives on issues, including your way of seeing the world, are influenced by such factors.

Cultural blocks inhibit thinking. Recognizing cultural blocks is the first step toward avoiding them as an impediment to thinking. Being aware of your cultural filters enables you to better understand why you see the world as you do and why others may see it differently. It's a first step toward recognizing those other ways of seeing and acknowledging their legitimacy and value. This acknowledgment validates your own cultural background, perceptions, and filters, while also recognizing the legitimacy of other ways of seeing things, of other cultural perspectives.

Intellectual blocks to thinking

Intellectual blocks involve knowledge and its limitations. You may sometimes find yourself unable to solve a problem because you lack information or because the information you have is incomplete or incorrect. In buying a car, for example, you may not know the performance ratings of various models, or of their differing repair or safety records. You may have only information provided by dealers and their sales reps. If you lack a knowledge of cars, you will lack confidence when purchasing one.

On the other hand, you may know quite a bit about a particular subject yet lack the skill to express your ideas effectively. How often have you said to yourself, "I really knew what I wanted to say, but I just couldn't find the right words?" To break through an intellectual block, you need to acquire additional information or to deepen your understanding. You may have to think more deeply and more broadly about what you know—to consider other ways your knowledge can be applied or valued.

Emotional blocks to thinking

Emotional blocks to thought occur when feelings interfere with thinking. Emotional blocks include your fears and anxieties, with perhaps the biggest emotional block to thinking being the fear of being wrong. You may be concerned about how people perceive you, especially what they might think if you are mistaken. Consequently, you may be reluctant to advance ideas you are unsure of. "What if I'm wrong?" you might wonder. "What if people think my comment is stupid?" Such emotional blocks can inhibit your ability to explore ideas; they impede your thinking. The solution is to allow yourself the luxury of being wrong, to forgive yourself for your mistakes. Mistakes are necessary for intellectual development. Not always knowing the answers is normal; error can lead to discovery, as the history of science and technology repeatedly demonstrates. The invention of Kevlar, for example, which is used in bullet-proof vests, was developed after a serendipitous lab experiment that didn't work out; the failed experiment led to the discovery of a fiber that was five times stronger than steel and many times lighter, one that has saved thousands of lives. Such knowledge can alleviate your fears about being wrong and overcome emotional blocks to thinking.

Another emotional block to thinking is an inability to tolerate confusion, uncertainty, and ambiguity. Periods of uncertainty are often necessary for breakthroughs in thinking. A toleration of chaos in thinking, however temporary, can be critical. In writing a report, for example, you shouldn't expect to decide on your idea, plan the organization, and write the ideal version in a single attempt. Exploring a subject, entertaining ideas, experimenting with different organizational structures, and writing some messy drafts is common, even for professional writers. The esteemed American writer E. B. White took six drafts and 25 hours of work before he was satisfied with a single paragraph that he published about the moon landing in *The New Yorker* magazine in 1969. Few successful thinkers and writers get things just right the first time, even masters of their craft like E. B. White.

Polarizing blocks to thinking

To polarize is to see things as opposed—"polar opposites" we call them, such as "us" and "them," liberal and conservative, fashionable and unfashionable. Polarized thinking is "black and white" thinking, "either–or" thinking. Such thinking creates mutually exclusive categories that avoid compromise. Polarized categories, such as the following, inhibit thinking:

Yes/no	Friend/enemy
Win/lose	Diligent/lazy
Strong/weak	Intelligent/stupid

Avoid limiting your thinking with these and other polarized categories; seek instead, the middle ground between them. Think, for example, about being "for" or "against" some plan, project, or idea. Consider how such a limited forced choice often misrepresents the complexity of your feelings. You might create a continuum that permits gradations between the opposing perspectives. You may want to say, in such a case, "Hold on. I am for this part of the plan, but I'm against that part." You may favor curtailing health care costs, for example, but that does not necessarily mean that you support the President's latest plan for health care reform. Conversely, opposing the President's plan doesn't mean that you are against controlling the costs of health care. You may favor a particular economic stimulus package—just not the one that either Barack Obama or his opposition favors. Perhaps you support elements of each of their plans, but don't support either totally. "Yes but" and "No but" provide a structure for avoiding black-and-white, all-or-nothing polarized thinking.

Asking "to what extent" or "to what degree" is more productive than seeing a situation as "all or nothing." To avoid "black and white," "either–or" thinking, ask yourself the following question: "To what extent" is an idea acceptable, a book interesting, a film entertaining or provocative? Considering degree or extent pushes you to make distinctions, to explore and consider possibilities and

Table 1.2 How to overcome obstacles to thinking

Obstacles to thinking	Ways to overcome obstacles
Perceptual blocks	Practice observing and noticing.
Cultural blocks	Become aware of cultural perspectives.
Intellectual blocks	Study. Review. Research.
Emotional blocks	Conquer fear of mistakes.
Polarizing blocks	Identify the middle ground.

shades of difference. It encourages listening to others' views and perspectives, thinking interdependently, and ultimately developing better critical thinking habits of mind (see Table 1.2).

A Model for Critical Thinking

In *Theory of Knowledge*, Richard van de Lagemaat (2006) presents a cyclical model for critical thinking: Question—Clarify—Support—Evaluate—Reflect. The model is cyclical, such that after the final stage reflection, the cycle begins again. According to this model, you begin with what you know—or think you know. And then you cycle through the following actions:

- *You ask questions*: What questions can you ask about this knowledge?
- *You seek clarification*: What does this knowledge mean for you?
- *You consider available support*: What is the evidence for this knowledge?
- *You evaluate*: What are the criteria by which you evaluate this knowledge?
- *You reflect*: What have you assumed and what can you consider about this knowledge?

The circularity of the process suggests continuity; it never really ends. You continue to question and clarify, to seek evidentiary support. You keep on evaluating and reflecting on what you know. In the process, you deepen your understanding and extend your critical thinking capacities.

How You Know What You Know

Underlying Richard van de Lagemaat's model of critical thinking—or indeed any model of thinking—lies a basic question: "How do you know what you know?" "Where does your knowledge come from?" Essentially, you learn things in three ways:

1. through your individual experience of the world;
2. through reading and hearing from others;
3. through figuring things out for yourself.

Experience, or empirical knowledge, comes through your senses—what you observe, feel, hear, smell, taste, and the like. Learning from others involves accepting authority, taking on faith what experts say about a subject. Figuring things out involves using your reasoning powers to understand and arrive at conclusions. Some philosophers posit a fourth way of knowing, a kind of intuitive understanding independent of experience. This kind of knowledge is somehow already there inside you; it is innate, or inborn; you simply have to discover it.

Each of these ways of knowing, however, can lead you astray. Empirical knowledge cannot always be trusted, for sometimes you don't observe things accurately. Taking the word of others can also lead you into error when others are untruthful or mistaken. Using your reason can be problematic if you don't reason logically, or if you base your reasoning on false premises or erroneous information. And intuitive understanding might not be corroborated by empirical experience.

Another challenge to knowledge concerns models of how the world works, because models are often vastly oversimplified when they are not simply wrong. As Nate Silver (2012) points out in *The Signal and the Noise*, inaccurate models magnify error because mistakes about complex systems are measured not by degrees or small margins of error, but by large orders of magnitude—the difference of a single zero between, say, 1,000,000 and 10,000,000, or the difference in a political forecasting error large enough to swing an election to one candidate rather than another. Perhaps the best known example of how small divergences in initial conditions can lead to divergent outcomes is the so-called

"butterfly effect," in which it a massive storm on one conti-
nent can result from a distant butterfly flapping its wings on
another.

One complication with our knowing things is that particular
facts change over time. In *The Half-Life of Facts*, Samuel Arbesman
(2012) suggests that facts have "half-lives" in the same way elements do. He explains that we can understand the rates at which
facts are created and the rates at which they are disseminated.
Facts in the aggregate can be predicted in systematic ways. We
can classify the ways facts emerge and are replaced by other more
accurate facts. Some facts are in constant flux—the weather and
the stock market, for example. Others change exceedingly slowly—
the number of continents and oceans, for example. And then there
are facts whose rate of change is somewhere in between, "meso-
facts," as he calls them. Examples include the number of planets
in the solar system; the number of chemical elements in the peri-
odic table; the ways we store, process, and disseminate information. Knowledge is not inert; it does not stand still. Changes in
our knowledge—in what and how we know—occur all the time in
large and small ways. This kind of knowledge variability is the rule
rather than the exception.

Perception and Knowledge

Perception is more complex than it typically appears. It involves
more than a simple kind of "seeing." Perception involves interpretation, and hence understanding; it reflects what you think you
know and not just what you think you "see."

The art historian E. H. Gombrich (1960) has suggested that
we cannot separate "what we see from what we know." This is so
for three reasons. First, you can't know more than you can see.
That is, you can't understand something until you "see" it either
literally or figuratively (as when you "grasp" or "see" an idea). Second, your ability to see (and understand) anything is grounded in
your prior experience. Your understanding is based on this prior
knowledge and on the expectations that derive from it. And third,
your knowledge and seeing are linked because they are based on
the conceptual categories you "think" with. You always see something "as" something that can be categorized, something that you

know from experience or from general knowledge. The categories you use to see things enable you to see them yet, at the same time, limit your ability to see them in other ways, or to see other things. Categories work as perceptual filters that enable your seeing while, paradoxically, constraining it.

Seeing is also a kind of thinking, and "observation is also invention," as another art historian, Rudolf Arnheim (1969), has argued. When you see something, you make sense of it by making inferences about it, guessing what it is and adjusting those guesses to conform to your changing perceptions. Seeing, thus, is an active, selective, and interpretive process; it is not simply an automatic, objective absorbing of external reality.

How does this process of seeing work? When you see something, you begin "editing" it. Your brain highlights particular features of what you are looking at and suppresses others. Without the brain's editing of visual stimuli, you would not be able to make sense of what you see. By selecting, classifying, and relating details, your brain enables you to see something rather than a confused jumble. When viewing an object rooted in the ground, its trunk rising and proliferating in branches festooned with leaves, you see it "as" something—in this case as a deciduous tree. If your brain did not isolate particular features and highlight them, you would register, as American psychologist William James has noted, "a blooming, buzzing confusion."

Up till now, we have been emphasizing how we see via our sight. Perception, however, refers more broadly to an awareness of things through the other senses as well. Perceiving through your senses provides a knowledge and experience of the world and of others. Sight, for example, is essential in critical ways for scientific observation, for historical investigation, including eyewitness accounts, and for every aspect of architecture and the arts of painting, drawing, and sculpture, as well as for work in mathematics and music, language and literature—and much more. Hearing is essential for music, of course, and for theater, but it is also important for the study of literature—poetry especially—as well as for work in political science and rhetoric. Careful listening attunes us to nuances of meaning and implication, especially in social circumstances, especially when they involve unfamiliar cultural norms and values.

Figure 1.2   Train in perspective. © Oleksiy Mark/Shutterstock

Perceptual illusions

One of the dangers of perception is that sometimes things you see appear different from the way they really are. Artists have long known how to make things appear "realistic"—the way they seem to us in everyday life—by using linear perspective. That's why the photograph of the train in Figure 1.2 seems right to us.

Look now at the three silhouette shapes in Figure 1.3. Things look a bit strange because the figures have not been scaled. The figures are actually the same size—though the one in the rear looks larger than those in the middle and in the foreground. Your eyes and brain tell you that the figures differ in size, but a measurement will confirm that all three are indeed the same size.

Figure ground and perception

In looking at objects, you focus on some aspects or details rather than on others—on the "figure" and not on the "ground." Reading these words, for example, you ignore the white background in favor of the black printed letters. You ignore, too, the spaces between the words—withoutthespacesthereitwouldbehardtoreadthewords.

Figure 1.3 Figures in perspective. © Darq/Shutterstock

Some images can be confusing because they can be "read" in more than one way at the same time. Such figures or images are unstable and ambiguous. You can use figure and ground to look at the two images in Figures 1.4 (Goblet/faces) and 1.5 (Letter/number). In looking at Figure 1.4, focusing on the white part of the figure while keeping the black area as the (back)ground, you see two faces staring at each other. In switching the figure and ground, focusing now on the black figure with the white as background, you can see a goblet. In Figure 1.5, Letter/number, you can see either the letter B or the number 13. These unstable images, rife with visual ambiguity, suggest that things can be seen in more than one way–though not at the same time.

Perception and expectation

Expectations influence what and how you see. Read the following signs:

We go	Oh how
to	I love
Miami	Paris
in the	in the
the winter	the spring

Did you read "We go to Miami in the Winter" and "I Love Paris in the Spring"? Or did you read them as "We go to Miami in the

Figure 1.4   Goblet/faces. © astudio/Shutterstock

the Winter" and "Oh How I Love Paris in the the Spring"—which is what is actually written. Most people miss the second "the" in each case because that is not what they expected.

You see what you expect to see, and you don't see what may be in front of your nose if you did not expect to see it. In a striking set of psychological experiments, Christopher Chabris and

Figure 1.5   Letter/number

Daniel Simons (2010) had participants watch a video showing two teams, one dressed in white, the other in black, as they bounced a ball back and forth. The participants counted the number of bounces made by the white-clothed players. During the experiment, a person dressed in a gorilla costume walked in front of the camera. In one experiment the "gorilla" went by quickly; in another, the "gorilla" stood for a few seconds before moving out of camera range. The psychologists asked the participants whether they saw anything unusual during their viewing of the video. Half saw only the teams bouncing basketballs, completely missing the "gorilla." It didn't matter whether the "gorilla" walked by quickly or paused briefly. Some participants, in fact, refused to believe that the "gorilla" was there at all—even after being confronted with the evidence on film. They simply did not believe they could have missed something so obvious. In fact, however, they didn't see it. You can find the original and subsequent examples of this selective attention test on YouTube.

Rolf Dobelli (2013) in *The Art of Thinking Clearly* calls his phenomenon "the illusion of attention." He suggests that we vastly overrate our ability to attend to things—especially when doing or seeing two or more things simultaneously. It is not so much that you miss every extraordinary event that streams past your visual plane. What you fail to notice remains unrecognized and unvalued. You may have no idea what you missed; you don't know what you don't know. This is dangerous because when you think you are perceiving everything of importance, you aren't. The reality may be distinctly otherwise.

Perception and culture

One additional filter of perception is culture. Your cultural background enables you to see things in certain ways. However, it also prevents you from seeing things in other ways. Or at least it makes it more difficult to see things from a different cultural perspective. That is one reason there is so much misunderstanding and conflict in the world. And it's one of the prime reasons a capacity to consider perspectives other than your own, other ways of seeing and understanding—other ways of describing "reality"—is so important.

Roger von Oech (1986), who has written and consulted widely on thinking, tells a story about differing perceptions and understandings that result from differing cultural expectations. During World War II, American soldiers dated English women. Because of differing cultural expectations about dating, each accused the other of being sexually aggressive. The confusion resulted because of differently interpreted signals regarding kissing. According to American cultural norms of the time, kissing is about five on a sequence of thirty courtship steps leading to sexual intimacy. In the American sequence of events, kissing signals early romantic interest.

In pre-World War II England, however, kissing was more like step twenty-five of thirty. Kissing, from this perspective, was a much more serious event, and one that came considerably later in the courtship process. So when an American GI, dating an English woman decides, after a couple of dates, that it's time to kiss her to let her know he's interested, she is astounded. She thinks: "This isn't supposed to happen until much later." She might even feel cheated out of the remainder of the courtship rituals that, from her perspective, should have preceded the kissing. However, she must make a decision: either cut this relationship off, or get ready for intercourse, since, in her mind, it's only a few steps away. The American soldier, of course, is equally confused, since if the English woman backs off after the first kiss, he doesn't understand why. Conversely, if she turns on the heat, he wonders whether she's being overly aggressive. The result is culture shock for both of them.

Look at Figure 1.6 (Marine scene). What do you see? How do you think would someone from a culture with very different social values would describe what they see? Look again at the picture and consider how an American student and a Chinese student might describe it.

In an experiment in which they were asked to describe the picture, people of western backgrounds emphasized the fish swimming in the foreground. According to them, the picture was about the fish. People of Asian cultural backgrounds saw it somewhat differently. They placed more emphasis on the environment in which the fish were swimming. For them, it was less about the fish than about the relationship among all the elements of the environment, the fish being only one part. How people from these different

Figure 1.6   Marine scene. © Audrey Armyagov/Shutterstock

cultural groups look at the picture—or, more precisely, what they see when they do—differs significantly.

What's interesting about this experiment is the ways it reflects how western cultures emphasize the individual, whereas Asian-Confucian cultures emphasize the group. For westerners individual will trumps the will of the group, for the most part. Of course, every individual has to negotiate his or her own self-expression and self-placement within a series of larger group contexts. But in the west, the development of individual talent takes precedence. Asian-Confucian countries tip the balance the other way, with subordination and restraint outshining boldness and assertiveness. An American proverb has it that "the squeaky wheel gets the oil"; in Japan, a proverb with the opposite implication carries more weight: "the nail standing up gets hammered down."

Cultural bias provides another related way that culture filters perceptions. If you prize your cultural heritage, you probably tend to see mostly the good in it while downplaying its less attractive features. You will likely be attentive to its achievements and contributions while ignoring its less savory aspects. Cultural biases include pride in your ancestry, your language, your country, geographical region, city or town, and neighborhood.

Gender, race, and religion also serve as perceptual filters. What you see and understand is influenced by your experience as a male or female, as a member of a particular racial group, and by the beliefs you hold about the world. With such varied and powerful perceptual filters affecting what you see and think, you need to be alert to their shaping influence. In striving for the open-mindedness necessary for critical and creative thinking, you need to recognize the complexity of perception and its relation to knowledge and to other ways of thinking.

Being Wrong

In her book, *Being Wrong*, Kathryn Schulz (2011) identifies a number of reasons why we are often wrong, especially on occasions when we are convinced we are right. Primary among these is "error-blindness," which is, necessarily, invisible. Even though other factors contribute to error—arrogance, insecurity, stubbornness, and egocentrism, for example—blindness to false beliefs seems to trump them all. Part of the reason for the power of "error-blindness" is that we are not really able to feel that we are wrong, even when we are clearly in error. Since we can't see our mistakes, we conclude that we are right. Once we do see our mistakes, Schulz suggests, we consider them as our past mistakes—what we once thought or believed but which we no longer accept as true. Thus, they are no longer part of our perceptual apparatus, no longer part of what we believe.

She cites an example presented by Sigmund Freud in *The Psychopathology of Everyday Life*, a classic study of why people make mistakes. Freud describes a time when he could not recall the name of a patient he had treated, even though he had seen her for many weeks not long before his instance of forgetting. It turns out that Freud had misdiagnosed the patient as suffering from hysteria when in fact she was suffering from abdominal cancer, which soon killed her. Freud's lapse of memory was a direct consequence of his need to forget such a horrible outcome, for which he blamed himself. She also provides an example from her own life when she made a mistake in pronouncing the name of the German poet Goethe (GER-tah) and had to be corrected by a professor. Her mistake, though embarrassing, was something etched in her memory, unlike Freud's, which was something to suppress. And who knows more about suppression and repression than Sigmund Freud, who, ironically, did the very thing he identified as a general behavior of others?

Another series of explanations for error is offered in *Thinking, Fast and Slow*, in which Daniel Kahneman (2011) identifies numerous biases that skew thinking, arguing that we overestimate how much we understand about the world and, conversely, underestimate how little we actually know. He adds that our confidence, actually an over-confidence, is increased by what he calls "the illusory certainty of hindsight." We behave as if we know that we are right because we feel that we are, even when we are incontrovertibly wrong. This state of affairs he calls "theory-induced blindness," which is "an adherence to a belief about how the world works that prevents you from seeing how the world really works."

Thinking, in Daniel Kahneman's view, functions as two parallel mental systems. The first, which he calls "System I," operates quickly and automatically, even effortlessly. The second, "System II," involves effort and thought. System I thinking occurs fast without second thoughts. System II thinking takes time; it involves concentration, judgment, and analysis. You mostly operate with System I thinking habits in full force. That's the default. The ease of this kind of nearly effortless thinking is seductive; it involves the "blink" thinking in contrast to the cognitive strain and mental effort involved with "think," or deliberate thinking. "Just stop and think about it," you sometimes have to tell yourself (or someone else, when ready to make a decision). "Have you (or I) really thought this through"? In such instances, "System II" thinking is in effect. Both of these thinking systems are necessary. We need to understand the limitations of each and develop an awareness of when, where, and how to use thinking fast, and when, where, and how, to use thinking slow.

Daniel Kahneman uses the acronym WYSIATI to stand for "What You See Is All There Is." In believing WYSIATI, you are likely to make judgments and decisions on insufficient information, on a too-small sample, on inadequate evidence. The result, often, is a mistake. WYSIATI errors are related to overconfidence in a detected pattern, a pattern you believe to be of value and importance, one that explains things with predictive accuracy. However, WYSIATI understanding is less a matter of fact than a matter of faith. Faith in WYSIATI simply confirms your prior beliefs; it reinforces your hopes; it reflects a perceptual problem identified as confirmation bias, which involves looking for evidence that sanctions what you believe and ignoring evidence that contradicts that belief.

Why Errors Persist

In considering another kind of related error—the failure of predictions and forecasts—Nate Silver, in *The Signal and the Noise*, offers three common reasons for the their persistence. First, you focus on signals, on information and details that convey a story or embody a picture of the world less as it is, than as it is believed to be. Second, you exaggerate positive potential outcomes while wildly downplaying risks, all the while ignoring risks that are hardest to measure. Third, you make assumptions about "reality"—the world as it is—that are typically far rougher and cruder than what is really the case. Uncertainty and ambiguity are distasteful even when inescapable; they are an intractable part of understanding complex occurrences.

A different explanation for errors and mistaken understandings is provided by Satyajit Das in his essay, "Impossible Inexactness," where he argues that inexactness cannot be escaped; Das (2013) sees it as a "profound beauty [that] transects science, mathematics, method, philosophy, linguistics, and faith." He suggests that inexactness undermines certainty and scientific determinism. All knowledge of the world is inherently and inescapably inexact—incomplete, uncertain, and contingent.

Inexactness, moreover, constrains measurement and limits the usefulness of causal explanation. Experiments can only prove what they have been structured or designed to demonstrate—nothing more. Causal explanation, based on knowledge of the present and allowing for prediction of future consequences, is false because knowledge in and of the present is ineluctably inexact. Predictions about future results, thus, suffer from inevitable uncertainty.

Another consequence of error is that once we are shown false information, it is difficult to erase it from our minds. As Daniel Levitin (2014) explains in *The Organized Mind*, it is "difficult to hit the cognitive reset button." Erroneous information has staying power as original knowledge. That's why lawyers often plant the seed of false information in the minds of judges and jurors. They know that false information will persist in jurors' minds.

This phenomenon is especially strong with respect to faulty social information—malicious gossip, for example. Nicholas Epley (2014) in *Mindwise* argues that we remain unaware how our beliefs are formed, that we just don't know how we come to believe or think what we do. This "belief perseverance" makes it very hard to eradicate false accusations and assertions about others that we hear about. Those false notions insinuate themselves into our consciousness such that even when evidence is shown that discredits them, we persist in believing those first inaccurate errors.

Other problems leading to error include something that Samuel Arbesman (2012) in his *The Half-Life of Facts*, calls "change blindness." In this error syndrome, you simply filter out facts you find uncomfortable or inconvenient. One example is how old information sticks even when new information has clearly displaced it, a form of "factual inertia." In everyday life this kind of error behavior affects only individuals and mostly in small ways. However, when extended to more significant scenarios of scientific research, "change blindness" and "factual inertia" can have more serious consequences. The physicist Max Planck once remarked: "New scientific truth does not triumph by convincing its opponents and making them see the light, but rather because its opponents eventually die, and a new generation grows up that is familiar with it." Such is the human reality that accompanies scientific research and advancement.

As another example of how error can permeate scientific studies, Samuel Arbesman summarizes the work of a researcher, John Ioannidis, who has found that significant clinical trials of new medical procedures, which are initially found to have significant benefits, upon repeated study, are later discovered to have negligible effects and sometimes no beneficial effects at all. The outcome, essentially, of more testing is a better understanding such that we can trust less and less in what was initially found to be the case.

Arbesman summarizes the key points that Ioannidis makes about scientific studies:

1. The smaller the study, the less likely the research yields true results.

2. The smaller the size of the effect, the more likely the findings are false.
3. The greater the number of tested relationships in experiments, the more likely that some results are due to chance.
4. The more flexibility in the design, definition, and outcome, the less likely the research findings can be replicated.
5. The greater the financial and other biases, the less likely the research yields accurate and useful results.
6. The hotter a scientific field, the less likely the research findings are to be true.

Errors abound, even when it looks like scientific studies are being done to show how something is the case, when on closer inspection, they prove that it is not. To sum up: error leads not away from the truth, but toward it incrementally, a little at a time.

Applications

1-1. Which of the traits of intellectual character described by Ron Ritchhart and David Brooks do you think are most important? Which, for you, are the most difficult intellectual traits to acquire and develop? Why?

1-2. Choose something to look at that has been difficult for you to really see. It could be a work of art, something in nature, a person, a place in your neighborhood, even a room or portion of a room in your home, school, or workplace. Make an effort to look really closely and patiently and to discover at least three elements you had not noticed or appreciated before.

1-3. Identify two cultural blocks to understanding and thought that, if removed, would promote tolerance, improve social relationships, or enhance one of the environments in which you live or work.

1-4. Describe a time when you were fearful of presenting an idea or of volunteering for a project. Looking back on it now, consider what you might have done to overcome or at least minimize your fear. Consider, too, why you may have experienced that fear—and the extent to which it was a legitimate fear.

1-5. Choose one of the following sets of polarized terms. Draw a continuum, as shown in the example for love/hate. Identify 3 or 4 intermediate terms and place them on your continuum.

Example: Hatred ... Love

Hatred Enmity Animosity Disaffection Indifference Affection Fondness Love

    Heroic ... Cowardly

    Proud ... Humble

    Speech ... Silence

    Spiritual ... Secular

1-6. Apply Richard van de Lagemaat's critical thinking cyclical process to a topic with which you are familiar but not an expert. Perform the tasks at each of the stages associated with his cycle of actions—to question, clarify, support, evaluate, and reflect.

1-7. Give an example of a time when you were in error because of sense experience, being misled by others, reasoning from false premises or erroneous information, or discovering that a self-evident truth you believed was contradicted by empirical knowledge.

1-8. Why do you think so many participants failed to see the "gorilla" in the experiment done by the psychologists Christopher Chabris and Daniel Simons? Do you think you would have seen it? How confident are you about that? Why?

1-9. How do you respond to the "kissing" scenario described by Roger von Oech? What do you think the woman should have done? Why? Was there a way for her to have avoided the possibility of misunderstanding?

1-10. Describe a time when one aspect of your cultural background and experience influenced, or perhaps even caused you to see, experience, and/or understand something very differently from someone else. What did you perceive? What did the other person perceive? How did the difference in perception affect your discussion or relationship?

1-11. Which of the following advertisement slogans do you think would appeal to Americans and which to Koreans? Why?

    1. Seven out of ten people are using this product.

2. The Internet isn't for everybody. But then you are not everybody.

1-12. Select two of the following questions for reflection.

1. To what extent can we trust our perceptions? To what extent is perception a reliable source of knowledge?

2. How can we prepare ourselves to see things from the perspective of others? To what extent is this possible?

3. How does our description of what we see (or someone else's description of it) affect how we see it and respond to it?

4. How can we minimize the role our emotions play in perception? And should we try to do this?

1-13. Identify a current television comedy or movie you have seen that turns on some kind of error or mistake. Explain what is amusing about that error and what the actors and director make of it. To what extent do you agree with Kathryn Schulz that error can be useful, beneficial, and productive?

1-14. Why do you suppose that Freud could not remember his patient's name and that Schulz seems unable to forget her mistake about pronouncing the name of Goethe? To what extent do you think the forgetting and remembering are related to the seriousness of the incident?

1-15. What benefits can we take away from Daniel Kahneman's analysis of our propensity to overestimate our knowledge and our ability to predict what will happen in the future? How useful do you find his discussion of WYSIATI? Of his idea that we are "blind to our own blindness?"

1-16. What does Nate Silver add to your understanding of the challenges that confront us as we attempt to understand how things work in the world?

1-17. How do you respond to Samuel Arbesman's discussion of "factual inertia" and "change blindness" and to the idea that error leads us closer to truth?

1-18. How does the criminal justice system use epistemology in asking a jury to determine a defendant's guilt or innocence? What is the jury actually asked to do in a criminal trial? (That is, how does "doubt" factor into their decision? What place does "doubt" play in their verdict?)

1-19. In his *Theory of Knowledge,* Richard van de Lagemaat proposes that we think of belief and knowledge in terms of a continuum—a spectrum—that ranges from the impossible through the possible and on to the certain:

<->10	<->5	0	+5	+10
Impossible	Unlikely	Possible	Probable	Certain
		(*Belief*)		(*Knowledge*)

Put the following different beliefs on the continuum:
1. Eating six walnuts a day is good for your heart.
2. American astronauts planted the American flag on the moon.
3. Other universes exist; aliens exist in some of them.
4. There is life after death.

1-20. How do you respond to the suggestions about the persistence of erroneous thinking made by Daniel Levitin and Nicholas Epley? To what extent do you recognize in yourself a tendency to retain errors you received as original knowledge? What might you do to combat or otherwise compensate for this tendency?

References

Adams, James L. 2001. *Conceptual Blockbusting.* New York: Basic Books.

Arbesman, Samuel. 2012. *The Half-Life of Facts.* New York: Penguin.

Arnheim, Rudolf. 1969. *Art and Visual Perception.* Berkeley: University of California Press.

Brooks, David. 8/29/2014. "The Mental Virtues." *The New York Times.*

Chabris, Christopher and Daniel Simons. 2010. *The Invisible Gorilla.* New York: HarperCollins.

Das, Satyajit. 2013. "Impossible Inexactness." In *This Explains Everything.* Ed. John Brockmanm. New York: Edge Foundation, Inc.

Dobelli, Rolfe. 2013. *The Art of Thinking Clearly.* New York: Harper.

Epley, Nicholas. 2014. *Mindwise.* New York: Knopf.

Gombrich, E. H. 1960. *Art and Illusion.* Princeton: Princeton University Press.

Kahneman, Daniel. 2011. *Thinking, Fast and Slow.* New York: Farrar, Straus, and Giroux.

Levitin, Daniel. 2014. *The Organized Mind.* Toronto: Penguin Canada.

Paul, Richard and Linda Elder. 2002. *Critical Thinking.* Upper Saddle River: Financial Times, Prentice Hall.

Ritchhart, Ron. 2004. *Intellectual Character*. San Francisco: Jossey-Bass.

Schulz, Kathryn. 2011. *Being Wrong*. New York: Ecco.

Silver, Nate. 2012. *The Signal and the Noise*. New York: Penguin.

Van de Lagemaat, Richard. 2006. *Theory of Knowledge*. Cambridge: Cambridge University Press.

Von Oech, Roger. 1986. *A Kick in the Seat of the Pants*. New York: Harper.

Interchapter 1

Facts and Knowledge

Great value is attributed to facts. Getting at true facts, however, is harder than it seems. There are many false facts floating
around, pseudo-facts, and other forms of erroneous information
masquerading as "facts," often in the form of "data," which carries
with it an aura of power. Data, however, is often raw. Data needs to
be analyzed and interpreted to become useful information. Facts
need to be confirmed and verified.

Information, too, is not quite enough. It is important to have
good information, accurate information. But information needs to
be networked, vetted, and validated to become productive knowledge. Information requires analysis and interpretation, just as raw
facts, or data, do. And when data and information are tainted or
mis-taken, so will interpretations based on them. In those cases,
error rather than true knowledge results.

To become useful knowledge, information requires a conceptual framework. Facts and data only make sense and become part
of knowledge when they can be related to other things you know. A
conceptual framework is necessary for true understanding. Without it, facts float untethered, where they are eventually lost and
forgotten.

Be vigilant about the information that comes your way. Be skep-
tical about it. Sift it, sort it, examine it, question and challenge it.

Critical and Creative Thinking: A Brief Guide for Teachers, First Edition. Robert DiYanni.
© 2016 John Wiley & Sons, Inc. Published 2016 by John Wiley & Sons, Inc.

In their book *Blur*, Bill Kovach and Tom Rosenstiel (2011) propose using following questions:

1. Where did this information come from?—(the *sources*).
2. What is the evidence for it?—(evidence versus *assertion*).
3. Why is this information important to know?—(its *value*).
4. What's missing?—(*completeness*).

In *When Can You Trust the Experts? How to Tell Good Science from Bad in Education*, Daniel T. Willingham (2012) suggests the following process for analyzing any claim, especially a scientific claim.

First, "strip it." Eliminate extraneous detail and language to better see the actual claim.

Second, "trace it." Identify who is making the claim and what others have said about it.

Third, "analyze it. Consider why you are asked to believe the claim, how it squares with your experience, and what evidence is given to support it.

Fourth, consider whether you should adopt (or accept) what is being proposed, advocated, or claimed.

As Michael Gelb (2000) has noted, Leonardo da Vinci was a stickler about what information came his way. He trusted only empirical, or sense-based evidence. When he put his observations together to formulate a hypothesis, Leonardo tested those hypotheses in a version of what would later become scientific methodology.

Leonardo wanted to know how things work; he wanted to see evidence with his own eyes. In his notebooks, Leonardo writes, "Anyone who relies in discussion upon authority uses not his understanding but his memory." While respecting the ancient thinkers, he did not depend upon them as authorities. Instead, he investigated nature through his own studies and demonstrations. As the physicist Richard Feynman (Feynman and Robbins 1999) was fond of noting, there is a big difference between knowing the name for something and understanding how it works. To define "friction" or "inertia," for example, is very different from understanding what actually happens when a toy car is rolled on a carpet or a wagon with a load of bottles is pushed forward from a standing position. Leonardo was an early advocate of understanding how things work based on careful observation.

Leonardo referred to himself as a "disciple," or follower of experience. He tested the ideas of others through his own experience. He valued learning by example, from models, but only if those models measured up and what they proposed was confirmed by his observations and experiments.

Some people argue that in the Internet age learning facts and amassing knowledge are no longer important. "You can look it up," they say. To some extent, of course, they are right. But there's more to finding things out. First, much of what is available on the Internet is simply wrong. Unless you are equipped with a method of sifting out errors, you are in real knowledge trouble. Second, even when you can find useful information, doing so the easy way, by surfing the Web rather than researching in more strenuous ways, leads to a belief that knowledge acquisition is always easy. All you have to do is make a few clicks on your devices. This is a dangerous misconception.

So, too, is the notion that you don't need to have facts at your fingertips. Consider, for example, how knowing with confidence the times tables from one to twelve makes it easy to estimate numbers, products, percentages. If you never learn those number facts because they are readily available at the click of a mouse, you will never be able to estimate with ease and confidence. You need to know things—as many things as you are able to absorb and retain. Knowing more about many things allows for the opportunity to combine them in surprising and unexpected ways. That way innovation lies.

Applications

1. What experience of learning have you had that made a powerful impression on you? What was unusual or memorable about that experience? To what extent was it based on observation?
2. To what extent have you learned from the example of others—as good or bad models or what to do or not to do? Think of one example of a positive or negative model that has changed the way you understand some aspect of your experience—or changed how you yourself think and/or act in one area of your life.

References

Feynman, Richard and Jeffrey Robbins. 1999. *The Pleasure of Finding Things Out*. New York: Perseus.

Gelb, Michael. 2000. *How to Think Like Leonardo da Vinci*. New York: Dell.

Kovach, Bill, and Tom Rosenstiel. 2011. *Blur*. New York: Bloomsbury USA.

Willingham, Daniel T. 2012. *When Can You Trust the Experts?* San Francisco: Jossey-Bass.

2

Essential Creative Thinking Concepts

Figure 2.1 Thinking out of the box. © amasterphotographer/ Shutterstock

To cease to think creatively is but little different from ceasing to live.
—Benjamin Franklin

Discovery consists of seeing what everybody has seen and thinking what nobody has thought.

—Albert Szent-Gyorgyi

Critical and Creative Thinking: A Brief Guide for Teachers, First Edition. Robert DiYanni.
© 2016 John Wiley & Sons, Inc. Published 2016 by John Wiley & Sons, Inc.

What Is Creative Thinking?

Creative thinking is imaginative thinking directed toward innovation. It is based on questions that ask "what if," "why" and "why not"; "how" and "how else"? Creative thinking is grounded in the consideration of alternatives, possibilities, other ways of imagining and doing things. The key to creative thinking is imagination, which American philosopher John Dewey defined as looking at things "as if they could be otherwise." Its goal is to develop new insights, novel approaches, fresh perspectives.

Some characteristics of creative thinking include being open to new ideas; believing that alternatives exist; deferring judgment; generating multiple approaches to problems; trying novel ways to generate ideas. Creative thinking is associated with imagination, innovation, originality, lateral thinking, and divergent thinking. Creative thinkers exhibit fluency and flexibility of thought; they use metaphor, analogy, and visualization to make connections and explore ideas.

Creativity has been defined as the ability to make something from nothing; it has been described as thinking of a common idea in an uncommon way. It involves the ability to take a concept, task, idea, or product and move it in new directions. Creativity has been considered under the aspect of problem solving and as a type of improvisation in the manner of jazz musicians together creating something that did not exist until they performed it in their unique manner. Richard Florida (2012), in *The Rise of the Creative Class Revisited*, locates creativity at the "intersection of novelty, utility, and surprise."

Dispositions that foster creative thinking include patience and perseverance, along with a speculative sense of wonder. They include curiosity, playfulness, and a positive frame of mind. Creative thinking requires self-direction, initiative, and a "can-do attitude." It is less concerned with argument and proof than with inquiry and exploration. Creative thinkers view mistakes as opportunities to learn; they welcome challenges and difficulties; they are willing to follow their intuition and instincts.

Creative thinking provides a necessary complement to the analytical, rational, and logical powers of critical thinking. You need both kinds of thinking skills to make full use of your mental capacities.

Among the core creative thinking skills are observing and noticing deeply; asking thoughtful questions; envisioning and visualizing; wondering and speculating about possibilities; engaging with problems patiently and persevering with them. A key factor in creativity is satisfying constraints. Limitations imposed by constraints release the imagination, as when a chef creates a new dish from limited ingredients, an employee finds effective ways to work with fewer resources, a poet works within the confines of a highly constraining literary form such as the haiku or the sonnet.

In his book, *Creative Intelligence*, Bruce Nussbaum (2013) describes a "social dynamics" of creativity. He argues that creativity is facilitated by intense social connecting and networking, along with an environment in which small groups of people who trust each other can engage in risk-free forms of play. Creativity involves both cognition and social context. Research on creativity, in fact, follows two streams—one focuses on cognition, on how the brain works; and another focuses on culture, asking questions such as "What are the social conditions that lead to creativity?" And: "How does creativity emerge from collaboration?"

One of the great social and collaborative creative environments has long been Bell Labs, which has been dubbed "the idea factory," for the large number of technological innovations invented there. At Bell Labs, engineers and other experts represent a talent pool with diverse skill sets. The culture at Bell Labs embraces failure as a necessary step on the road to success. The Bell Labs culture rewards risk takers who try new things rather than remain satisfied with the status quo. Among the many inventions created at Bell Labs was the vacuum tube, the first of the major breakthroughs of the electronics revolution. The vacuum tube found its first major use in radio, but was later found to provide sound amplification for television, radar, sound recording, amplifiers as well as boosting the capacity of other technologies, including radar and microwave ovens. In large part, ideas flow freely and copiously at Bell Labs through a continuous exchange of ideas, shared, challenged, refined, and improved.

Seeking Alternatives and Possibilities

One general definition of creativity is the purposeful generation and implementation of novel ideas. Examples include recently developed products, some still in development, such as computer watches and Google glasses, driverless cars, and brain implants that enable us to do things we couldn't do without their enhancement. Gene therapy advances promise medical interventions targeted to an individual's specific genetic endowment.

Creativity involves the ability to think of a common idea in an uncommon way, the ability to take a concept, idea, or product and push it in new directions. With creativity, something new and useful is generated, developed, and implemented.

Creative thinking can be illustrated by considering different ways to categorize objects, as for example, thinking of different uses for a brick or a metal clothes hanger. You might approach such a task by describing features rather than functions, or by identifying elements or aspects rather than according to an object's primary purpose. Open-minded thinking considers how common tasks might be performed in an unconventional order—preparing a sandwich, for example, in an unconventional way. Researchers have found that such mental exercises develop "cognitive flexibility."

A creative thinking mindset seeks alternatives, looks for different ways of understanding a situation, arriving at a judgment, making a decision, or solving a problem. In such cases, you choose the best solution from a number of options. However, you first need to generate the options or possibilities from which to make your choice. Cultivating the habit of seeking alternatives and possibilities is an essential first step.

Establishing a quota of alternatives

You can seek alternatives by establishing a quota, a set arbitrary number of alternatives. In deciding how to solve a problem or undertake a project, avoid settling on the first approach that comes to mind. Rather, set yourself a quota—four or five possibilities, perhaps—before deciding. In considering whether to go on a cruise, for example, you might do Internet research, talk to friends who have had cruise experiences, read the publicity brochures by various cruise lines, and consider alternative vacations.

Using a quota strategy to generate possibilities provides a chance to come up with something better (or at least different) from an initial idea. Perhaps you want to open a small business, but you aren't sure just which business is best for you. You consider catering, or perhaps selling something you make online; or you offer your services walking dogs or running errands for busy people. Perhaps you can give music or ski or technology lessons. In the event that your first thought is actually the best one, there is the comfort of having considered alternatives and found them less valuable. Even if you select your first idea, thinking through other possibilities might influence the way you develop the initial idea, possibly extending or enriching it in an unforeseen way. Maybe that catering business you want to start can include a musical component, perhaps a solo pianist or guitarist you hire to play while the food is prepared and served where the event happens.

You can practice applying the quota-of-alternatives technique by considering the following scenario:

> Each weekday morning, a woman takes the elevator in her office building to the tenth floor. She gets out there and walks up the sixteenth floor, where her office is located. After work, she enters the elevator on the sixteenth floor and rides down to the first floor. She then exits and heads home.

One explanation for the woman's behavior is that she uses the restroom on the tenth floor, the only floor between 10 and 16 with a restroom. Another is that she stops to meet her supervisor, who works on the tenth floor. Consider some other explanations for the woman's elevator-riding behavior. Set yourself a quota that includes a few very likely possibilities and some others that are more far-fetched.

Why might it be useful to consider alternatives and different approaches to a question or problem? The main reason is that you often find more and better ideas when you consider such alternatives. Considering alternatives enables you to see more than one or even two "sides"; it pushes you beyond simple and too easily satisfied explanations; it increases choices and encourages you to see more shades and shadows, to consider issues and ideas, problems and solutions, along a wider spectrum of possibilities. This simple tool stretches your thinking beyond what is typical, easy, or comfortable. It broadens your perception.

Reversing Relationships

Another strategy for considering alternatives is to reverse relationships, which involves, essentially, considering another person's point of view. One way to do this is to consider the opposing arguments for and against a public policy—first from say a liberal (or Democratic) perspective and then from a conservative (or Republican perspective). One example might be the legalization of illegal immigrants currently residing in the United States. This kind of mental shifting can aid in understanding the "logic" of an opposing viewpoint. It can foster understanding "the other side," even if only to find ways to better support counter-arguments you can make against arguments for the other side. Reversing relationships might also have the benefit of enabling you to see that even though you may disagree with someone who presents another perspective, you can begin to see at least some merit in that position and some reasons for the thinking that led a person to that opposing point of view. In the process, you become a more reasonable thinker.

In the best of circumstances, reversing relationships spurs reconsideration and rethinking. It broadens your perspective so that even if you wind up adhering to your initial point of view, you begin appreciate other viable and reasonable ways of considering the issue. Moreover, reversing relationships can, on occasion, lead to new and deeper insights about a topic, or to better ways to solve a problem.

Consider, for example, the way ancestral humans once were preoccupied with getting to the water hole. At a later stage they reversed this relationship to get the water to themselves, a decisive shift. Or consider how, in creating a work of art, you might normally think of building it up, adding materials, as in constructing a sculpture. Michelangelo reversed that direction when he "subtracted" his *David* from a huge block of Carrara marble. Michelangelo envisaged his *David* as being contained in the marble block. His artistic task was to free him, to release the figure imaginatively envisioned as imprisoned with the marble.

Reversing relationships can spur creative thinking by helping you break away from conventional ideas and rigid ways of thinking. Like setting a quota of alternatives, reversing relationships generates surprisingly different perceptions that lead to new ideas.

Cross-fertilizing

A related creative thinking strategy is cross-fertilization, which applies the ways of thinking about one kind of activity to another. For example, you might use the vocabulary of basketball to talk about business (achieving a "slam-dunk" with a product, for example), or the vocabulary of war to talk about football (throwing a "bomb," for example, or staging a "blitz.") You might take concepts from the graphic arts—color, line, pattern, texture—and apply them to music, literature, or fashion, or perhaps take a concept from physics—for example the concept of centripetal force or a force field—and apply it to a problem in economics or social psychology.

Cross-fertilization is a special kind of analogical thinking, a way of seeing relationships between things that are not normally related, and may even be "far-fetched." Like other creative thinking techniques, cross-fertilization involves an act of imagination. Its method, essentially, is to force what Michael Michalko (2011) has described as "conceptual blending," by combining elements from different realms, domains, and areas of reference. Cross-fertilization shakes up conventional thinking patterns and pushes thinking in new and unexpected directions. Closely related to analogical and metaphorical thinking, cross-fertilizing makes connections among disparate things.

Shifting Attention

Yet another strategy to develop your capacity for creative thinking is to shift attention from one facet of a situation, one aspect of a problem, to another. In writing a report about the effects of excessive drinking, for example, you might consider large-scale social effects, such as the impact of alcoholism on work productivity and its cost to businesses, or its impact on the cost of health care nationwide. A shift of attention from this kind of macro consideration to a smaller-scale micro aspect could help generate additional ideas.

For example, you might consider the costs of alcohol abuse to a drinker's family and friends—to his or her personal relationships. And you might consider the effects on the drinker himself or herself, both physically and psychologically. You can make still another shift from the effects of alcoholism to its causes. Considering causes pushes your thinking in another direction; it generates new ideas by coming at the topic or problem from a different angle. You might ask yourself why people turn to alcohol in the first place. Whether all these aspects are eventually included in your report hardly matters. What is important, however, is to generate a variety of ideas to consider.

Michael Michalko refers to this kind of shift as a change in "perceptual positions." He suggests that your perceptual positions influence and even determine how you see things. Rotating your perceptual positions to see things from multiple perspectives is an especially useful habit to develop. Michalko offers the following thought experiment as an example.

Suppose you have the opportunity to reduce the human error associated with hospital procedures, including mistakes in diagnosis, medicine dosages, and hospital-induced infections. Consider how different experts, such as a football coach, a prison warden, an airline pilot, an orchestra conductor, and a priest, might approach this challenge.

In *The Checklist Manifesto*, a book that includes a solution to this last problem, Atul Gawande (2011) explains how using a checklist for hospital operating room procedures eliminated deaths from hospital-induced infections. The improvement was due primarily to introducing a checklist of sterilization procedures, including scrupulous and frequent hand sanitizing. Assiduous enforcement of the checklist procedures by nurses improved results dramatically. And those results were people's lives: results, clearly that matter greatly.

Denying the Negative

If critical thinking tends toward evaluating and ultimately rejecting ideas, creative thinking inclines more toward encouraging them. Some kinds of thinking say "no"; other kinds of thinking say "yes." For example, instead of thinking of approaches to a problem as not being workable—as unrealistic or inadequate, silly or

Table 2.1 Basic creative thinking strategies

Seeking alternatives and possibilities
Establishing a quota of alternatives
Reversing relationships
Cross-fertilizing
Shifting attention
Denying the negative

---

stupid—think more positively. Say "yes, perhaps," rather than "no, never." Deny the negative. Pursue the possible.

Be careful not to reject an idea out of hand, regardless of how unpromising it may at first appear. A poor idea taken seriously can lead to a better idea, even when the lesser idea is rejected and a more suitable idea developed. Reaching a dead end on an idea for developing a new product or process, for example, might lead to a different approach. Asking "what if" and "why not" can help you pursue possibilities and discover promising options.

Changing the way you speak to avoid negatives and emphasize positives can influence what you feel and how you think. Basic creative thinking strategies are shown in Table 2.1.

Scamper

SCAMPER is a creative thinking strategy—really a suite of techniques. Letter by letter, SCAMPER stands for the techniques shown in Table 2.2.

SCAMPER is based on the idea that everything new is based upon something that already exists. Michael Michalko notes how petroleum derives from chemical feed that becomes synthetic rubber that eventually winds up as car and truck tires, which can become the soles of sandals.

Substitution is an essential technique. When you don't have what we need at hand, you search for something to use in its place. You can substitute people and processes, rules and materials, locations and times.

Combining things is another essential principle—perhaps the fundamental principle of all creative thinking. You can combine

Table 2.2 Scamper thinking strategy

S = *Substitute*—What can be substituted?

C = *Combine*—How can it be combined with other things?

A = *Adapt*—How can it be adapted?

M = *Magnify, minimize, modify*—How can it be enlarged, reduced, altered?

P = *Put to other uses*—To what other uses can it be put?

E = *Eliminate*—What aspects or elements can be eliminated?

R = *Rearrange and reverse*—What can be rearranged, perhaps reversed?

---

purposes and units, appeals and uses, people and programs. Combinations include alloys (metals), blends (wines), assortments (candies), and ensembles (musicians), among many other combinatorial kinds.

Adaptation is the essence of survival. Without adapting to changing conditions and circumstances, survival is jeopardized. Some questions to ask include: What else is like this? What parallel does the past suggest? What different contexts can be considered? What direction might be taken?

Magnification and minimization—making it larger or smaller. Can some aspect of your idea be exaggerated or weakened, enlarged or shrunk? Instead of developing a new teaching unit, develop an entirely new course. Or to go in the other direction, instead of asking an entire department to participate in a teaching experiment—team teaching, perhaps—ask for one or two teaching pair volunteers to pilot a new unit or a new course.

Putting the idea to another use involves changing the context. How many uses can be found for the common red brick? How about for a peanut? George Washington Carver discovered more than three hundred uses for the humble peanut.

Eliminating, subtracting something from the idea can be useful. Whether pruning trees or pounds, trimming or cutting can result in renewal. Spotlighting an aspect and backgrounding other elements can eliminate distraction. Key questions: What can be understated, simplified, reduced, cut? What is not really necessary? How can it be condensed or streamlined?

Rearranging things is another type of combination. All the elements are already in the idea or product or service, unlike combination, where something is added. Baseball managers shuffle lineups; basketball coaches run players in and out of games; composers rearrange music for different instrumental combinations. Key questions: What components can be interchanged? What sequences can be adjusted? What schedule or pacing changes can be made?

Reversing a perspective helps us see things in new ways. Asking about opposites can clarify what we are looking at. Yin and Yang: Dark clarifies light; losing amplifies winning; positive spin counters negative spin. Key questions: Can you flip it; spin it; turn it around, upside down, inside out? Can you reverse roles?

The Creative Habit

Creativity and creative thinking can be approached in a deliberative, intentional manner. In *The Creative Habit,* dancer and choreographer Twyla Tharp (2003) argues that creativity can be developed through habitual effort. She suggests making creativity a habit, without claiming that you can become a creative genius like Leonardo and Michelangelo, Mozart and Beethoven, Tolstoy and Dickinson, Nijinsky and Balanchine if you do. Twyla Tharp does suggest, however, that by focused attention and sustained concentration over time, you can dramatically increase your creative capabilities.

She provides guidelines and practices for doing so, along with personal examples and stories of creative breakthroughs, which are informative, entertaining, and inspirational. She advocates a number of principles to foster what she calls "the creative habit." Among them are rituals, creative DNA, memory, the box, and scratching. A few words about each of these will show just how richly varied a set of practices she provides.

1. *Rituals.* Creativity requires preparation, and the best and most consistent kind of preparation is ritual. Twyla Tharp suggests employing rituals in preparation for creative thinking and activity. She describes how the great cellist Pablo Casals began each day by playing a prelude and fugue from Bach's solo keyboard work, *The Well-Tempered Clavier.* She herself begins her days by hailing at

cab at 5:30 am for her trip to the gym, where she routinely does a two-hour workout as preparation for her dance and choreography work.

2. *Creative DNA.* She believes that we are all born with a *"creative code* hard-wired into our imaginations." That creative code conceals a talent for something that brings out your uniquely expressive creative powers. It might be the way you dribble and shoot a basketball, or the way you handle a needle and thread, how you prepare and cook a meal, solve problems in mathematics or science, arrange flowers, plan a vacation, express yourself verbally, musically, or physically. Your creative DNA marks your uniquely special way of being in the world; it exhibits your sense of style, your particular way of walking, talking, writing, and thinking.

3. *Memory.* A well-stocked memory can be a solace in times of difficulty, provide entertainment in times of boredom, and lend coherence and meaning to life. Twyla Tharp describes different kinds of memory you can harness and develop. One type is a kind of muscle memory that dancers exhibit in physical movement and musicians display when performing on their instruments. Another is "virtual memory," which projects into the past to re-capture and re-experience former emotions, and into the future to visualize a successful outcome for a project or course of action.

4. *The box.* For every creative project, Twyla Tharp gathers materials for potential use and deposits them into a file box. She labels her boxes with the project name. Into each box go slips of paper with random ideas, clippings from magazines and newspapers, CDs, videotapes, photographs, pictures of artworks, books, excerpts from books, and anything else of potential value. Using such a box is a practical and functional way to keep connected to a project.

5. *Scratching.* In answer to the question "where do you get your ideas," she suggests "scratching," a form of inquiry that involves looking around for a spark, for any bit of energy to jump-start thinking. Scratching begins an improvisation, the hunt for the scent of inspiration. A writer might scratch by recording a snippet of overheard conversation. Scratch around in various places. Put yourself in motion. Take a walk. Visit a museum. Look around. Talk with a friend. Listen. Some productive thinking can come of it.

Creative Confidence

When creative thinking is intentional, deliberative, and habitual, it is rooted in confidence. The practice of creative thinking, moreover, strengthens creative confidence. In their coauthored book, *Creative Confidence*, brothers Tom and David Kelley (2013) claim that having confidence in your ability to be creative is fundamental to improving your creative capacity. They claim that creativity is a muscle than can be strengthened with disciplined and regular practice. You can nurture your creative potential with effort and through experience.

According to the Kelley brothers, creative confidence improves your ability to make better choices. It enables you to more easily push yourself in new directions. It enables you to become a better problem solver, to collaborate more productively, and to approach challenges with confidence.

You can choose to be creative. You can get beyond just "trying" and, as the Nike ad asserts, "Just do it!" Instead of waiting, you can act, get moving, do something to become at least a bit more creative. Tom and David Kelley have the following suggestions for getting started.

1. *Choose a project or activity you are interested in doing,* and break it down into small steps. Take the first small step. Tackle a doable piece.
2. *Lower the stakes.* If your project or activity requires significant investments of time and/or money or other resources, scale it down. Also, in starting work at it, consider what you do initially as only an experiment.
3. *Establish a milestone,* or series of milestones, that you can celebrate once reached.
4. *Set multiple mini-deadlines* for small segments of the project or activity.
5. *Don't worry about perfection at first.* Just produce something to get your creative juices flowing. Revision and refinement can come later as you make progress.
6. *Seek help from others.* Create a support network.

Ed Catmull (2014), in his book *Creativity, Inc.*, suggests that you learn to accept and deal with uncertainty and instability, with the unpredictable and unanticipated, including fear and failure, and perhaps most importantly the fear of failure. As he says, "The attempt to avoid failure makes failure more likely." From early in your life, you have been told to avoid failure, that failure is bad, that it's for losers, that it is shameful to fail. If you are like most people, you don't want to fail in part because it stains your self-image; you find it embarrassing, humbling, mortifying.

And yet failure has also been necessary, essential in fact, for much of your learning—from learning to read and to ride a bike, drive a car; swim, ski, play a musical instrument. You took the risks to learn those things—and many others—to speak your native language and perhaps a foreign language as well, all along accepting the inevitable mistakes, errors, failure that were part of the learning process.

It is the same with developing your creative thinking powers, your capacity to be innovative. If you avoid risk and fear failure, you will likely achieve less, innovate less, and be less creative. If, on the other hand, you can learn to accept failure as a necessary, inevitable part of learning and of creating, you will find that you will become more productive and very likely more interesting as well. Embrace failure rather than avoid it; fail early and often, and accept failure as both a condition for and as evidence of learning. Give failure a try. What have you got to lose?

Creative Theft

In *Steal Like an Artist*, Austin Kleon (2012) advocates stealing ideas and influences wherever you can find things worth the stealing. His premise is that nothing is original, that everything new derives from something that already exists. Remixing and reimagining are key concepts, as is the notion that originality is a burden to be shed. Originality can be replaced with influence. To be creative, find and steal from what you love, for as Johann von Goethe said, "We are shaped and fashioned by what we love."

You might single out a particular writer or artist, filmmaker or architect, philosopher or musician. It doesn't matter, as long as that individual's work means something to you. Study his or her body of work; get to know it deeply and thoroughly. Then go on to discover two or three individuals that your hero loved. Study those influences in the same way you deepened your knowledge of and appreciation for your primary influence. In this way, you become part of a creative history, a creative lineage. That lineage will inspire you to do your own creative thinking and creative work.

In his painting *Triple Self-Portrait*, the artist Norman Rockwell depicts himself painting his self-portrait while looking into a mirror. Alongside the upper edges of his canvas, he has placed little portraits—self-portraits actually—of famous artists who excelled at painting themselves. Among them are Albrecht Durer, Rembrandt van Rijn, Vincent van Gogh, and Pablo Picasso. It is likely that he included those little self-portraits as inspiration for his own triple self-portrait. Those artists are his lineage; they set a standard for him to aspire to. In the same manner, you can find and celebrate, copy and emulate your standard setters, those whose work you admire and wish to emulate.

You might have some qualms about copying the work of others. But you shouldn't. One of the most common ways of teaching and learning is to copy and imitate what others do, how others work. Manual trades educate this way. And so too, for centuries, was rhetoric taught and learned this way. When William Shakespeare and John Milton were in school in their respective sixteenth and seventeenth centuries, they copied the words and works of other authors, the better to see how those words worked, and how those works were constructed. And they wrote their own pieces imitating the style of the writers they studied.

It is not only artists and writers who copy and imitate. Musicians copy; filmmakers copy; athletes copy. Beethoven began by writing symphonies and string quartets that sounded much like those of Haydn and Mozart. Along the way, and before long, he began sounding different—like himself. Paul McCartney has said that he imitated a number of early great rock musicians, including Buddy Holly, Little Richard, Jerry Lee Lewis, and Elvis Presley. He and his songwriting partner John Lennon went on to become one of the greatest and most distinctive of songwriting teams.

In an interview, the filmmaker Francis Ford Coppola of *Godfather* and *Apocalypse Now* fame has said: "We want you, at first, to steal from us, because you can't steal. You will take what we give you and you will put it in your own voice and that's how you will find your voice." And he goes further in saying: "Don't worry about whether it's appropriate to borrow or to take or do something like someone you admire because that's on the first step and you have to take the first step."

Los Angeles Lakers basketball star Kobe Bryant has said that he watched tapes of his heroes to copy their moves, since he believes that every basketball move derives from an earlier move done by a previous player. He notes, though, that he couldn't pull off the moves he was copying from other players because he didn't have the same body type as they did. He had to adapt their moves. In the process he developed his own moves. But he started by copying and imitating. And now other young players imitate and adapt Kobe Bryant's moves on the court.

Creative Crime

You may very likely have heard the name Philippe Petit in conjunction with one or another of his high-wire feats—crossing on a wire between the towers of Notre Dame cathedral in Paris in 1971, between the two north pylons of Sydney Harbour Bridge in Australia in 1973, and perhaps, most famously, walking a wire across the twin towers of the World Trade Center in 1974. His book *To Reach the Clouds* (2003), and the Oscar award winning film based on it, *Man on a Wire*, describe his feats and the creative preparation that went into each of them. Philippe Petit's walks, of course, were illegal. Technically speaking, they were crimes, violations of the law. (He was not punished for them, with NYC, for example, letting him off the hook when he gave a wire-walk performance for children across a pond in Central Park.)

In *Creativity: The Perfect Crime*, Petit (2014) explains how he planned and executed his famous feats of high wire derring-do. And he extrapolates from them a set of principles and guidelines that describe his personal approach to creativity. He then uses the notion of the crime as a metaphor for creativity, offering a set of recommended beliefs, attitudes, and practices for the rest of us. Among his practices and recommendations are that you accept the inevitable chaos that accompanies any initial creative effort, that you not over-plan and expect to figure everything out from the start. Learn to be patient with chaos; don't begin imposing order until order begins to show hints of emerging without being forced. Watch and wait patiently and persistently.

Another suggestion is to create a sense of urgency about your creative project. Get started right away. Don't wait for all the conditions to be right to begin. Set yourself a schedule of things you will do, small steps you need to take as the process develops. Create a map—not a rigid outline, but a rough guide to your creative goal. And don't be afraid to alter the map and to revise your schedule. But make every attempt to adhere to each new timetable you set for yourself, even knowing that there will be inevitable interruptions and delays. Just keep moving in the directions of your goal, however minimally, however incrementally.

And finally, he suggests that whatever your creative project, from designing a product to walking a high wire, from planning a presentation to making a pitch for a job, you need to do three things: practice, practice, practice. Rehearse, retry, redo; revisit, re-imagine, re-conceptualize.

Creative Questions

Effective thinking involves asking questions. The kinds of questions are important, as are the ways initial questions lead to subsequent ones. Good questions direct thinking, encourage exploration, and open your mind to unimagined possibilities. Creating useful and productive ones enlivens curiosity, provokes thinking, and excites the imagination.

What are the characteristics of good questions? Good questions are open ended; they admit of more than a single answer. Good questions generate other questions; they lead beyond themselves. Good questions produce rich and varied answers; you can judge a question by the kinds of answers it evokes. Good questions jump-start thinking—they stimulate, engage, and provoke. Neil Postman (1995), in *The End of Education*, puts it this way: "The value of a question is determined by the specificity and richness of the answers it produces and by the quantity and quality of the new questions it provokes."

Here are some examples of questions that meet these criteria:

- What do we mean by a fact? Is a biological fact different from an historical fact or a mathematical fact? Can facts change? Can something once considered a fact be dethroned and shown to be a fact no longer?

- What is the relationship between fact and truth? How would you begin to answer that question?
- How should science be taught in the high school curriculum? How many sciences? In what order? To what extent should teaching and learning the sciences be integrated with one another. To what extent should science be integrated with technology? With other subjects? Which ones? Why?
- Is history a science? Is dance a language? What is a saint? What counts as an experiment? How would you go about answering these questions?
- How do you know what you know? How can you compensate for the limitations of reason, the inaccuracies of perception, the reliability of what you read and hear?

Learning to ask useful questions is a skill, even, perhaps an art. The better your questions, the better chance to develop your capacity for critical and creative thinking, since questioning is a key element of all thinking.

In *The Innovator's DNA*, Jeff Dyer, Hal Gregersen, and Clayton M. Christensen (2011) have found that innovators routinely use a plethora of questions to discover what had been previously overlooked. Among their questions are "what-caused" questions to get at what lies at the root of the way things are. For example, instead of asking, "How can I build a better x, y, or z," you can ask: "What is happening with x, y, or z," or "Why is x, y, or z not as effective as we would like it to be?" These generic questions can be applied across the board to why a heart stent isn't functioning optimally to why a project you are working on is not up to snuff, from why your workout routine isn't yielding the results you hoped for to why your relationship with a friend, spouse, or boss is sub-par. As Dyer *et al.* indicate, once you have learned to ask productive questions, "relevant and appropriate and substantial questions," you have, essentially, taught yourself how to learn and continue learning.

Questioning is at the heart of innovation; it is a creative driver for innovative behaviors. The authors distinguish between what they term "what is" *descriptive* questions and "what if" *disruptive* questions. They argue for asking both kinds of questions repeatedly to identify what currently is (and how it came to be that way) and what might be in the future. The goal of *descriptive* questions is to gain a deeper understanding of "what is"; the traditional journalistic investigatory questions of "who," "what," "when," "where," "how," and "why" are the descriptive questioning workhorses. *Disruptive* questions, on the other hand, tend more toward "Why?" and "Why not?" and include "What if?"

The authors suggest that it is important to drill down with these questions, particularly with "why" questions. They recommend a fivefold sequence of asking "why" in order to uncover chains of causal links that identify the stages or processes of how things have come to be as they are. They argue that persistent "why" questions lead naturally to "why not" and "what if" questions, and they suggest that multiplied "why" questions move from description to disruption, from explanation to innovation.

Among the strategies they recommend are these:

- *Engage in group-question-storming sessions in which only questions are allowed* in the process of thinking through a problem. No solutions or explanations are permitted. Just questions—as many as forty or fifty. Record the questions on a chart or a whiteboard so that everyone can see each one as it is written out. After collecting the questions, prioritize them. Select the most promising area for further discussion, analysis, and evaluation.
- *Cultivate a questioning frame of mind.* One way to do this is to identify a number of key problems in the form of statements and then to recast those problem statements as questions. The interrogative mood opens up problems; it stimulates consideration of "possibility thinking," as well as encouraging active responses to problems and prospective solutions.
- *Keep a notebook of questions for daily consideration.* After accumulating a batch of questions, analyze them to detect prevalent patterns and question types. Identify those question types that yield unexpected insights, the kinds of questions that challenge assumptions, stir strong feelings, and generate other questions.

Questioning routines

One productive approach to questioning involves a set of inquiry strategies developed in conjunction with Project Zero at Harvard University, a wide-ranging initiative to improve teaching and learning, with an emphasis on critical and creative thinking. One part of the Project Zero program, "Visible Thinking," emphasizes the use of "thinking routines" connected with four ideals for thinking: *understanding, truth, fairness, and creativity*. Two of the visible thinking routines focus on "thinking for understanding": *See, Think, Wonder;* and *Think, Puzzle, Explore*.

The first of these thinking routines, "See, Think, Wonder," is particularly useful for thinking about visual art and images. In using this routine, you ask yourself, "What do I *see*"? You take some time looking so as to notice as much as possible. Then you follow with another question: "What do I *think* about what I see"? Here you consider your perspective, or stance, toward what is being viewed. These initial thoughts are followed with yet another question: "What do I *wonder*" when looking at this object? Here you let your mind wander toward notions that emerge. This wondering offers less of a firm grounding and clear direction than the original question, but it can lead your wondering-wandering mind to further connections and insights.

The second thinking routine, "Think, Puzzle, Explore," is designed to deepen thinking. In using this thinking routine, you first consider what you think you know about the object, issue, topic, or problem. You take stock. Then you ask yourself what is puzzling about it. What questions do you have about it? What don't you understand? What might be confusing? And finally, you consider how to explore the object, issue, topic, or problem further. You consider what might be done to extend and deepen your thinking and understanding. Both thinking routines are explained and exemplified in *Making Thinking Visible* by Ron Ritchhart, Mark Church, and Karin Morrison. Table 2.3 summarizes important approaches to developing your creativity.

Table 2.3 Enhancing creativity

Creative habit—Twyla Tharp
Creative confidence—Tom and David Kelley
Creative theft—Austin Kleon
Creative crime—Philippe Petit
Creative questions—Neil Postman
Prolific questions—Jeff Dyer *et al.*
Questioning routines—Ron Ritchhart *et al.*

Applications

2-1. For each of the following, provide three alternative explanations or approaches.

Discouraging people from driving their cars into the center of a city.

Encouraging people to donate money to charity.

Dealing with a school bully.

Incentivizing students to work hard in school.

Meeting deadlines for work projects.

2-2. Set yourself a quota of alternatives for one of the following: improving your salary, saving money, losing weight, increasing the amount of reading or exercise you do.

2-3. Consider how the following paradoxes illustrate reversing relationships: To save your life you must first lose it. To rise you first must fall. To lead you need to follow.

2-4. Take one of the following pieces of "common sense," and reverse it.

Example: If something's worth doing, it's worth doing well.

Reversal: It's OK to do it poorly—at least at first. If you insist on doing it well, you may never do it at all. Worrying about how well you're doing anything can prevent you from stretching yourself and trying new things—which you probably won't do very well in the beginning.

Patience is a virtue.

Haste makes waste.

Business before pleasure.

Too many cooks spoil the soup.

Curiosity killed the cat.

2-5. Explain how each of the following cross-fertilizations might work—what the idea is for each analogy.

School as entertainment; school as confinement

Shopping as an addiction; shopping as socializing

Moviegoing as escapism; moviegoing as intellectual stimulation

Work as play; work as fulfillment of an obligation

Marriage as a partnership; marriage as an adventure

2-6. Use a shift of attention to solve the problem presented in the following story, a version of which can be found in Edward de Bono's (1968) *New Think*.

A merchant owed a large sum of money to a moneylender who was attracted to the merchant's beautiful daughter. The moneylender offered to cancel the debt if the merchant would allow him to marry his daughter. The moneylender proposed that they allow chance to determine whether this should happen. He suggested that a black pebble and a white one be placed into an empty bag. The girl would pick one of the pebbles by reaching into the bag. If she picked the black pebble, she would become his wife and the debt canceled. If she picked the white pebble, she would remain with her father with the debt also canceled.

When the merchant agreed, the moneylender bent down to select the two pebbles for the bag. The girl noticed that he chose two black pebbles instead of one black and white pebble. With the two black pebbles in the bag, the merchant asked the girl to pick out the pebble that was to decide her fate and that of her father. What should she do?

2-7. For part of one day—a morning, afternoon, or evening—record how often you hear people using the negative, how often they deny and reject ideas, options, and possibilities. Notice, too, how often you do this yourself. On at least one of these occasions, consider how what is being denied may be possible after all. Let the unpromising possibility sit for a while; then consider some ways it might be a viable possibility—perhaps by making some adjustments using one of the other creative thinking strategies: quota of alternatives, reversing relationships, using analogy, shifting attention.

2-8. Choose some aspect of your workplace or home that you would like to improve. Use SCAMPER to generate ideas for improving it. You might try using SCAMPER with an existing product or service, such as e-book readers, mail delivery, department meetings, professional development.

2-9. Choose one of Twyla Tharp's five strategies for developing the creative habit. Consider how you could apply and adapt her suggestions to prepare yourself to be more creative, to develop your creative potential more fully. (Rituals, Creative DNA, Memory, The Box, Scratching.)

2-10. To what extent have you victimized yourself by believing in a fixed mindset about your abilities, including your creative abilities? To what extent are you made hopeful and do you find helpful what Tom and David Kelley (2013) suggest about your creative potential. Which of their suggestions do you find most promising, and why?

2-11. Of the four sets of tools for creative thinking—SCAMPER, Creative Habits, and Creative Confidence—which do you think might yield the best results for you? Why?

2-12. Provide an example of a time when a chance meeting, an accidental encounter, or otherwise unplanned connection started you thinking in a new way—gave you an idea that you made use of, perhaps helped you solve a problem, or create a new approach to a problem.

2-13. How do you respond to the advice Austin Kleon gives regarding "stealing"? To what extent do you agree with what Francis Ford Coppola advises about getting started on a creative project?

2-14. Which of the various pieces of advice offered by Philippe Petit do you find most interesting, most surprising, and most useful? Why?

2-15. Which two of Neil Postman's questions interest you most? Why? How would you begin to answer them?

2-16. Which of the approaches to questioning from *The Innovator's DNA* appeals to you most, and why? How might you go about implement this questioning approach for a particular project or assignment you are working on or will soon need to work on?

2-17. Use one of the Project Zero thinking routines to think about one of the following: a painting, photograph, sculpture, or work of architecture; a poem, story, novel, play, or movie; a scientific or mathematical discovery; a historical figure or event; a religious or philosophical problem; a musical or theatrical work; an ad or commercial; a TV show of any genre; a political, social, or economic idea or theory.

References

Anderson, Ariston, interviewer. 2011. "Francis Ford Coppola: On Risk, Money, Craft & Collaboration." 99u.com/articles/6973/francis-ford-coppola-on-risk-money-craft-collaboration, accessed March 28, 2015.

Catmull, Ed. 2014. *Creativity Inc.* New York: Random House.

de Bono, Edward. 1968. *New Think.* New York: Avon.

Dyer, Jeff, Hal Gegersen, and Clayton M. Christensen. 2011. *The Innovator's DNA.* Cambridge, MA: Harvard Business Review Press.

Florida, Richard. 2012. *The Rise of the Creative Class.* New York: Basic Books.

Gawande, Atul. 2011. *The Checklist Manifesto.* New York: Metropolitan Books.

Johnson, Steven. 2014. *How We Got to Now.* New York: Riverhead.

Kelley Tom and David Kelley. 2013. *Creative Confidence.* New York: Crown Business.

Kleon, Austin. 2012. *Steal Like an Artist.* New York: Workman Publishing Company.

Michalko, Michael. 2011. *Creative Thinkering.* San Francisco: New World Library.

Nussbaum, Bruce. 2013. *Creative Intelligence.* New York: HarperBusiness.

Petit, Philippe. 2008. *To Reach the Clouds.* 2003. London: Faber and Faber.

Petit, Philippe. 2014. *Creativity.* New York: Riverhead.

Postman, Neil. 1995. *The End of Education.* New York: Random House Vintage.

Ritchhart, Ron, Mark Church, and Karin Morrison. 2011. *Making Thinking Visible.* San Francisco: Jossey-Bass.

Tharp, Twyla. 2003. *The Creative Habit.* New York: Simon & Schuster.

Interchapter 2

Sustaining Curiosity

Curiosity is a driving force in thinking and learning. Children are innately curious; their curiosity spurs their continued learning. For adults, curiosity sparks continued personal and professional growth. In extending the boundaries of your curiosity, you expand the parameters of your knowledge and broaden your realm of experience. In the process you become more interesting.

Creative thinking begins with curiosity—with wondering why something is the case, how something came to be, what might happen if something else could be done.

How might sound be carried great distances? How might books and newspapers and magazines be delivered electronically? How might humans orbit the planet and land on the moon? How might polio be prevented, malaria and tuberculosis treated?

In *Curious*, Ian Leslie explains how curiosity is foundational for higher order thinking, especially for creative thinking. He suggests that in addition to the human drives for food, sex, and shelter, a fourth drive, curiosity, distinguishes humans from all other species—and also from computers. Though computers are "smart," they are not curious. Only humans are.

Curious learners, as Ian Leslie (2014) notes, go both deep and wide. They are hedgehogs, who know one big thing deeply and

Critical and Creative Thinking: A Brief Guide for Teachers, First Edition. Robert DiYanni.
© 2016 John Wiley & Sons, Inc. Published 2016 by John Wiley & Sons, Inc.

well. They are also foxes, who know lots of different things. Charles Darwin, whose singular big idea, evolution by means of natural selection, is a hedgehog thinker. Yet Darwin was also a fox, a voracious reader curious about many things. It was Darwin's reading of Thomas Malthus on population growth that sparked his thinking about species competing for resources, which led him to an idea about how their survival might occur.

Is it better to know one big thing well—to have expertise in one discipline—or to know many things across diverse areas of knowledge? Neither, of course, is better. Both approaches to knowledge are highly valuable. The curiosity that drives the deep learning of the hedgehog also stimulates the broad knowledge of the fox. Today's employers want people with specific knowledge and deep expertise. But they also want quick learners who can adapt and collaborate with others who know many different things. They want hedgehogs and foxes. They seek employees who have "T-shaped knowledge," with the vertical line of the "T" indicating depth and its horizontal line, breadth.

Curiosity is essential for innovation and progress. The inquiring minds of individuals constitute the most valuable asset of any society. But curiosity isn't valuable only because of what it can do. Curiosity possesses intrinsic value; it fulfills, enlivens, and makes you more interesting to yourself and to others. You can choose to be curious—or not. And since curiosity expands one's intellectual and cultural range, why wouldn't you decide to be curious?

Curiosity drove Leonardo da Vinci's inquiries. He was fascinated by many aspects of life and exhibited an intense interest in both the natural and human worlds. Sir Kenneth Clark (1989) has described Leonardo as "the most relentlessly curious man in history." His interests took him into human anatomy, geometry and geology, mechanics, the flight of birds, plant and animal biology, optics and hydraulics, art, architecture, engineering—and music.

Leonardo's vigorous curiosity was driven by an unquenchable thirst for knowledge. "Iron rusts from disuse," he wrote, "stagnant water loses its purity and in cold weather freezes; even so does inaction sap the vigor of the mind." Exercising curiosity keeps your intellectual muscles in shape. Leonardo contended that we come to love the things we learn; "Great love is born of great knowledge," he noted.

Curiosity begins with questions—useful questions, productive questions, questions that lead to other questions. It is the right questions more than the right answers that stimulate successful critical and creative thinking.

In his book on Leonardo, Michael Gelb (2000) also suggests asking "awkward" questions—the kinds of questions that cause difficulty or discomfort—or at least questions that provoke thinking. Some examples: Why is this a problem? Why is it done this way? Who says we are required to do it like this? In general, asking questions that begin with "What If" and "How," with "Why" and "Why not" tend to yield fresh thinking.

Applications

1. Of the following pairs, which is a hedgehog thinker and which a fox? Plato and Aristotle. Shakespeare and Milton? George W. Bush and Bill Clinton? Steve Wozniak and Steve Jobs?
2. Develop a set of questions—perhaps a dozen—about a subject that interests you or is important to you. See where your curiosity leads you. Begin to think about some answers for five of those questions.
3. What are some of the most challenging questions you have ever asked? What are some of the most challenging questions you have ever been asked? How were they answered? With what results?

References

Clark, Sir Kenneth. 1989. *Leonardo da Vinci*. New York: Penguin.
Gelb, Michael. 2000. *How to Think Like Leonardo da Vinci*. New York: Dell.
Leslie, Ian. 2014. *Curious*. New York: Basic Books.

Part Two

Practicing Critical and Creative Thinking

3

Becoming a Critical and Creative Thinker

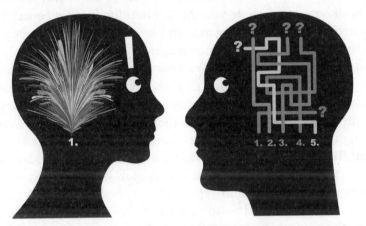

Figure 3.1 Facing heads. © Sangoiri/Shutterstock

We are shaped by our thoughts; we are what we think.

—The Buddha

When the mind is thinking, it is talking to itself.

—Plato

The rational mind is a faithful servant and the intuitive mind is a sacred gift.

—Albert Einstein

Critical and Creative Thinking: A Brief Guide for Teachers, First Edition. Robert DiYanni.
© 2016 John Wiley & Sons, Inc. Published 2016 by John Wiley & Sons, Inc.

Becoming a Critical Thinker

How can you develop your critical thinking skills? What do you need to do regularly and consistently to become a critical thinker? You can work on developing the following intellectual traits, which are among those identified by Richard Paul and Linda Elder (2009) in their book *Miniature Guide to Critical Thinking: Concepts and Tools*.

Intellectual integrity has to do with honesty, with facing facts as they are and not as you might wish them to be. Integrity of thinking involves adhering to strict and rigorous standards of evidence and proof both for your own views and those of others.

Intellectual humility requires that you recognize that knowledge is often complex, issues are often complicated, and you don't always know as much as you think. Humility in intellectual matters involves avoiding arrogance and egocentrism, while recognizing the limitations of your knowledge.

Intellectual perseverance requires sticking with tough problems and difficult questions, and not giving up when a problem doesn't admit of a quick and easy solution. It requires persevering through confusion and frustration, and being willing to work through complex challenges over extended periods.

Intellectual courage requires a commitment to your ideas and the evidence that supports your beliefs even when those ideas and beliefs are unpopular and represent a minority, perhaps even a highly singular view. It also requires acknowledging ideas even when those ideas are uncomfortable for you, or otherwise differ from or challenge your customary ideas and beliefs.

Intellectual empathy requires an appreciation of the perspectives and point of view of others, even when you disagree with them. Being empathetic intellectually involves seeing an issue through the eyes of another; it requires an ability to listen with an open mind and to understand how and why others think and feel as they do.

Intellectual autonomy refers to the capacity of doing your own thinking, thinking for yourself and taking responsibility for your thinking. It requires that you not only know what you think but why you think as you do—how you have come to your ideas, what evidence you have to support them, and what reasons you have for holding them.

Intellectual Standards as Guidelines for Critical Thinking

The following standards, modeled on those of Richard Paul and Linda Elder (2009) from their *Miniature Guide to Critical Thinking: Concepts and Tools*, are useful for assessing your own or another's thinking.

1. **Clarity**: Is the reasoning clear? Can it be further elaborated or detailed? Would an example help?
2. **Accuracy**: Are the reasoning and evidence in its support accurate or true? How can the accuracy of reasoning and the truth of evidence be verified?
3. **Precision**: Is either the claim and is the evidence supporting it overly general? What specific details might be provided to clarify the claim and strengthen the supporting evidence?
4. **Relevance**: Are all statements relevant to the claim or idea being considered? How do the statements relate to or bear on the issue under consideration?
5. **Depth**: Is the question or issue under consideration being addressed only superficially? What complexities are being considered or are being overlooked?
6. **Breadth**: Is the question or issue being treated too narrowly and from a restricted point of view? What might be done to broaden the perspective?
7. **Logic**: Does what is being argued make sense? Do the evidence and examples follow logically? Are there any contradictions or gaps in thinking?
8. **Fairness**: Is the argument developed honesty and fairly, and with respect for alternative perspectives? Are there any distortions or unfair characterizations of alternative explanations or arguments?

Language and Thought

Language is inextricably connected with thought. The connotations, or associations, of words, for example, affect your perception of things. Moreover, connotations imply attitudes and feelings. Metaphors enable us to take your thinking in unexpected directions. The language of metaphor aids in understanding things in different ways and conveys ways of seeing and understanding to others.

Your mind, as John Searle (1999) notes in *Mind, Language, and Society*, is linguistically structured. For all but the very simplest thoughts, language is necessary to think your thoughts. If thought involves language, so too, does language involve thought. You think in your native language, which filters the way you see and experience the world. (And if you speak other languages, you actually see and experience the world in somewhat different ways because of the way those other languages carve up and filter your experience of the world.) This philosophical notion is based on the concept that reality is constructed rather than simply absorbed. From this constructivist perspective, each individual experiences reality differently. And yet each person also experiences reality in concert with others, based on the language you speak and the culture of which you are a part. How far this idea of cultural and linguistic relativism holds, and what implications this idea actually has, remain in dispute among linguists and cultural historians.

For example, if a language lacks a future verb tense, does that mean that its speakers have no sense of the future—no concept of futurity? This is unlikely. Just think about English, which can be used to express a future notion without a "will" or "will have" verb. "I am going there tomorrow," we might say, and use the present tense verb "am" and the present participle "going" with the word "tomorrow" to convey future time. Or, to take another example, since the German language has a very tightly organized logical structure, does that mean that German speakers are more logical and more organized thinkers than speakers of Swedish, French, Hindi, or Swahili, for example? What about languages that have many more words for colors than others? Does a speaker of one of those color-rich languages see a painting by Van Gogh or Matisse differently from a speaker of a color-poor language?

In *Through the Language Glass*, Guy Deutscher (2011) considers these and other questions about the relationship between languages and the ways people think in, with, and through different tongues. Challenging the notion people think pretty much the same no matter what languages they speak, he contends that different languages can and do lead their speakers to different ways of thinking.

Different languages (and cultures) name the rainbow in different ways; thus, their speakers see the rainbow differently. Different languages also classify things differently, and even sex them differently. It makes a difference whether the word for "sea" or "moon" in a language is masculine, feminine, or neuter. The different genders of the moon and the sea lead speakers of different languages to perceive the moon and sea differently.

In *The Language Hoax*, John McWhorter (2014) roundly rejects this idea, contending that the influence of language on thought is negligible, and that language reflects culture rather than the other way around. Language does not control or influence the way people think; rather, language serves their thoughts, enabling them to express those thoughts in the different ways languages have evolved to enable speakers' to express ideas through them. Thought is wider and richer than language, which expresses only part of what is known and how it is understood.

Every language has ways to conceptualize "reality," and all languages develop relationships between specific and general, concrete and abstract. They just do not all make those connections the same way.

Reports, Inferences, and Judgments

In his classic book, *Language in Thought and Action*, first published in 1930, S. I. Hayakawa (1991) distinguishes usefully between reports, inferences, and judgments to highlight the ways language intersects with thinking. A **report** is a declarative statement that can be verified. It's a statement of fact. Report statements, or reports for short, can be right or wrong, correct or incorrect; their intent, nevertheless, is to identify something noted and believed. To test a report you attempt to verify it; you check its accuracy. If you hear that the price of gasoline increased throughout the country in the past week, you could verify that statement by checking with agencies that monitor that kind of information. Given the proper resources, if a statement can be verified—proven true or false—it's a report.

An **inference** is an interpretive statement about the unknown based on what is observed. An inference is the recognition of an implication, what is implied or suggested by something noticed.

You infer one thing on the basis of something else. For example, you might infer that someone is afraid of spiders based on the following observations. She screams when she sees one. She faints if she notices one crawling on her. She stammers when she tries to say the word "spider." Those last three statements are reports, in Hayakawa's terms; they are declarative statements that can be verified. In considering the implications of those three statements, our inference that she is afraid of spiders seems quite reasonable.

You make inferences all the time; it's virtually impossible not to do so. You might infer the wealth of a person from the cut of his or her clothes, from the kind of watch or jewelry worn, from his or her address, job title, and the like. You might be wrong or right; the more information on which you base your inferences, and the more accurate the information, the likelier it is that your inferences will be correct. It's important to know that you are making inferences when doing this, so as to avoid confusion between inferences and reports, or statements of fact. The quality of an inference is directly related to the quality of the reports or facts upon which it is based.

A **judgment**, in S. I. Hayakawa's terms, is a conclusion. Judgments are often expressed as opinions with the added element of approval or disapproval. Judgments can cloud our thinking, as we tend to jump to conclusions—to judge quickly with very little evidence in support. To confuse judgments with reports is a major obstacle to clear thinking. In saying, for example, that "the Apple iPhone6 is a great device," or that "the iPhone4 was a dud," you are making a judgment. To say: "the iphone4 contained a more powerful camera than earlier models and a unique shared video feature" is a report; so is "the iphone4 had a wrap-around antenna that dropped calls more frequently than other iPhone models." These statements can be verified, can be checked and shown to be correct or incorrect, which makes them reports, declarative statements about what is observed.

On the other hand, to accuse someone of being a "liar" or a "thief" is to make a judgment (and also a prediction that he or she will lie or steal again). It's an opinion expressed with a strong dose of disapproval. In order to verify any of these accusations, you would have to acquire some facts. You would need to uncover information, such that what the person said contradicts what all other have said, and/or that it contradicts what his telephone records show. Or that he has been convicted twice for theft, and has served a year in prison on those convictions. (Of course, he might have been wrongly convicted; the evidence may have been planted, and so on. But even so, the decision to convict was based on reports. In some cases those reports are either erroneous or deliberately falsified.) All these matters of fact and falsity, of course, complicate the effort to know what is true and to make reasonable inferences and fair judgments based on factual evidence, or reports.

The biggest danger of judgments is that when they are made prematurely, without accurate evidence, they can be wrongheaded, even dangerous. Judgments typically stop thought because judgments are essentially conclusions. When you come to judgment (or conclusion), your mind has been made up.

Without acknowledging these distinctions among reports, inferences, and judgments, your thinking becomes muddled.

Reports, inferences, judgments, and the Kitty Genovese story

You have probably heard the story of Kitty Genovese, who was murdered in 1964, in Kew Gardens, Queens, New York, as she returned home from work late one night. According to newspaper reports, about 3:00 am, Miss Genovese had parked her car and headed toward her apartment when a man assaulted her. She screamed for help, and some neighbors in the apartment building adjacent to the parking lot turned on their lights. A few came to their windows to see what was happening. One yelled, "Let that girl alone!" Some, thinking it was a lovers' quarrel, returned to bed. Frightened by the commotion, the attacker ran off, but not until he had stabbed her a number of times. When the neighbors turned off their lights and went back to bed, he returned and stabbed her again, repeatedly. She cried for help again, and once more lights went out and the attacker ran off. Bleeding profusely from her wounds, she made her way into the vestibule of a neighboring building. The attacker found her there and continued his assault. Finally, one of the neighbors called the police. But it was too late, and Kitty Genovese was pronounced dead at the scene of the crime.

This incident sparked considerable public interest. It received extensive press coverage, with newspaper and magazine articles appearing for months afterwards. The primary question in the minds of most who hear about this murder is: "Why didn't some-body help her? Why didn't someone at least call the police from the start?

You can find out more about the incident and the press response from the New York newspapers for March 14, 1964 and from a *New York Times* article, "Thirty-Eight Who Saw Murder Didn't Call the Police," by Martin Gansberg, published on March 27, 1964. A book by A. M. Rosenthal, *38 Witnesses*, was published that year, as well. The 1975 movie, *Death Scream* and a 1996 *Law and Order* episode, "Remand," were based upon the incident, as was a 2000 book, *Acts of Violence*. For now, however, we will look at the headlines from three newspapers—the *New York Times*, the *New York Herald Tribune*, and the *New York Daily News*. Here are the first two of these headlines:

New York Times: Queens Woman Stabbed to Death in Front of Home
New York Herald Tribune: Help Cry Ignored, Girl Dies of Knifing

What do you notice immediately about these two headlines? Which headline relies more on the denotation of words—the dic-tionary meanings, and which chooses words that have stronger connotations—personal associations? How, for example, do the connotations of "girl" differ from those of "woman"? Do you think the difference today might be greater or less than the difference between the connotations of those words in 1964? What is the difference in "stabbed" versus "knifing?" How does each head-line make you feel about the victim? Which headline "grabs" you more—affects you more deeply, emotionally?

Here, now, is the headline from *The Daily News*:

Queens Barmaid Stabbed, Dies

What does the word "barmaid" imply—that is, what do we infer from it about Kitty Genovese? To what extent does it alter your response to her? What is implied in the *Daily News* headline about Kitty Genovese that is not implied by the language of the other two headlines from the *Times* and the *Tribune*? Which of these head-lines seems the most "objective" and neutral in how it refers to the incident?

Is the *New York Times* headline the fairest in this respect? If so, why? And what of the emotional charge generated by the other headlines from the *Daily News* and the *Herald Tribune*? Though they differ in what each suggests about Kitty Genovese, in how each portrays her, they do share a common feature: they both rely on heavily charged language, on words that carry very strong connotations—and, in the case of the *Daily News* headline, a strong negative judgment.

Suppose you had read only one of these headlines. What would your perception of the event have been? Having read three headlines, what is your perception of the event now?

Here, now, are the first lines of each of the articles that follow the headlines for the three newspapers. First, the *New York Times* article's opening sentence:

> A 28-year-old Queens woman was stabbed to death early yesterday morning outside her apartment house in Kew Gardens.

That sounds fairly neutral, doesn't it? It uses words with a low connotation quotient, words that are direct and factual. The sentence conveys information, pretty much in the style and manner of the *New York Times* headline quoted above.

Here are the *Herald Tribune*'s first sentences:

> The neighbors had grandstand seats for the slaying of Kitty Genovese.
> And yet, when the pretty diminutive 28-year-old brunette called for help, she called in vain.

That's much more engaging, isn't it—a lot more emotionally charged? You might ask a number of questions about this sentence. Among them: Why is the victim described as "pretty"? Is that relevant? Why is she referred to as a "brunette"? How necessary is that detail? (Have you ever read an account of a man's murder in which information about his hair color or physical attractiveness was included?)

What do you make of the first detail: the neighbors watching from "grandstand seats"? What is implied about the neighbors with that detail? And what is the effect of the words "called for help" and "called in vain"? Would the news article have been more effective if it had read that when she "cried for help, she cried in vain?"

And, finally, here is the first sentence of the story printed in the *New York Daily News:*

> An attractive 28-year-old brunette who had given up a more pro-saic life for a career as a barmaid and residence in a tiny Bohemian section of Queens was stabbed to death early yesterday.

How does this article's opening sentence reinforce the negative judgment made by the *Daily News* headline: Queens Barmaid Stabbed, Dies? What words, in particular, convey a negative view, a critical judgment, of the victim?

The Prevalence and Power of Metaphor

In addition to connotation as a rich and powerful linguistic resource, language is indelibly metaphorical, using various forms of comparison to see and say one thing in terms of another. To see how prevalent metaphorical expression is in your life and how persistently metaphor appears, consider the following examples of how people talk about love. They have been adapted from *Metaphors We Live By*, a book by George Lakoff and Mark Johnson (2005).

- I could feel the electricity between us.
- They gravitated toward one another.
- Her eyes drew him to her.

These ways of talking about love see love as a physical force. What about these next examples? How do they talk about love?

- This is a sick relationship.
- We've been getting back on our feet.
- The children have never fully recovered from the divorce.

In these, love is described in terms of a medical condition, an illness.

In his book, *Metaphor,* Denis Donoghue (2014) suggests that when you say that someone is something else—you compare a woman to a gazelle, for example—you think of it (in this case her) in a new way. You emphasize her grace and elegance, for example. If you think of money as a form of speech (think "Money talks") you activate the concept of money as a form of power. Figures of speech we might say are also figures of thought. Metaphor is not mere description or ornament; it is a way of thinking, specifically in fact, a way of imagining.

When you read a novel or a poem rich in metaphor, it expands you, broadens you in the same way that the characters in a novel or the speaker in a poem are expanded through metaphor. "Metaphors offer to change the world," Denis Donoghue contends, "by changing one's sense of it." Our sense of things is altered, as Kenneth Burke has noted through what he calls "perspective by incongruity," through bringing together two things normally unrelated into a new and surprising conjunction. The bolder and more audacious the metaphorical connection, the more striking and memorable is the metaphor.

Metaphor and ideas

Another aspect of metaphor is the way metaphors can help to generate ideas. One way to do this is to think of metaphors that involve some kind of action. Think, for example, of how solving a problem might be like interpreting a poem or organizing a dinner party. Consider how giving a presentation might be compared with skiing down a mountain or planting a garden. How might managing a project be similar to planning a vacation? Thinking of a challenge you confront at work, in school, or at home, as an obstacle course presents a very different scenario than seeing that challenge as a game or as an opportunity. Seeing a weight-loss plan as a military campaign directs your thinking one way; seeing it as an opportunity to become a more creative cook and a chance to discover new foods and tastes results in very different dieting experiences.

Metaphors matter. Our metaphors affect and direct the way we experience the world. We all make connections; we are all metaphor makers.

In an essay "Metaphors are in the Mind," Benjamin Bergen (2013) claims that metaphorical language rather than being haphazard is, instead, "systematic and coherent." He suggests that it's mostly abstract things that are described with metaphors, the metaphors making the abstract more concrete and specific. Political campaigns are "horse races." Silence is "golden." Morality is being "clean." Understanding something is "seeing" it. "I see what you mean," you might say; and: "Let's shed some light on the problem."

You don't just talk metaphorically, you think metaphorically. Speaking of understanding in terms of seeing enacts thinking of understanding as seeing. Thinking about morality in terms of cleanliness equates morality with cleanliness. Understanding *is* seeing. Morality *is* cleanliness. Benjamin Bergen argues that metaphorical speaking indicates metaphorical thinking. It is the thinking with metaphors that drives the use of metaphor in speech. Metaphor is more than a way of comparing one thing with another and much more than a decorative aspect of language. It is essential for communicating and for thinking and for communicating what you are thinking.

Metaphors of reading

Let's now consider some of these implications of metaphor for reading. What metaphors might be used to think about the implications of reading—the meanings it might have for us?

Let's begin with a familiar notion, that reading is a form of acquiring information. You read to learn, and so reading is a kind of search. That's one useful but rather limited metaphor of reading. Extend the concept a bit to consider just what you are searching for. If you substitute—or add—a search for "experience" to the search for information, reading takes on a new kind of meaning. In the search for experience, reading becomes something more and other than a kind of pragmatic searching. In this larger search for experience, reading itself becomes an "experience"—the experience of reading, which brings with it particular kinds of rewards and pleasures that transcend the simple acquisition of information. Reading is a kind of mining, a way of searching for metaphorical "gold," for valuable information and ideas, for exceptional experiences.

We can open up our metaphors of reading further by considering different kinds of things we "read" in everyday experience—or different kinds of things than can be read. In talking about reading, you usually talk about reading texts—words on a page or a screen. But people also read each other, especially their faces and gestures, their postures and moods. The natural world is "read" as well—waves and clouds, landscapes and animals. You read paintings and films, buildings and battlefields, ballparks and other public spaces.

Astronomers read the sky, architects read the land on which a house will be built; card-players read one another's gestures; parents read their children's faces for signs of joy and fear. Lovers read each other's bodies, and doctors read the bodies of their patients. Fortunetellers read tea leaves, tortoise shells, birds, stars, and lines in hands. Scientists read tree rings, laboratory slides, graphs, charts, and data patterns.

All these kinds of reading and more involve looking at things, noticing them, and making sense of them based of what is observed. All these kinds of reading are forms of analysis and interpretation. Through these and other kinds of reading, you make the world intelligible, and you make yourself intelligible to others. You live in the light of what and how you read. And you read in the light of what and how you live. The processes are reciprocal.

In reading as in life you get out of it what you put into it. Reading, like life, is never really finished until you are no longer capable of doing either—reading or living. Reading, too, requires a blending of research and imagination—of looking for knowledge and of imagining knowledge, of making meaning for yourself from what you learn. Reading is most effective when it zigs and zags between seeking contextual information and imagining yourself in the contexts you discover.

Metaphors of teaching

Different metaphors of teaching carry with them very different kinds of implication for envisioning, understanding, and engaging in the practices of teaching. Is teaching more like wrestling or more like dancing? To what extent is teaching comparable to setting things on fire—ideas and minds, perhaps? Is teaching more like work or more like play? How is teaching related to performance? To demonstration? To communication? To discovery and invention? To exploration and adventure?

There is a scene in the movie *Sister Act* in which Whoopi Goldberg, playing the role of Sister Mary Clarence, is invited to conduct a small group of nuns in choir practice. Sister Mary Clarence takes the baton from another nun who has been responsible for this work, but who has not had much success with the choir.

What Sister Mary Clarence does at that point is instructive, particularly with respect to successful teaching practices. The first thing she does is to put down the baton—that symbol of the conductor's directorial authority. She then asks a few questions of the nuns—which ones are sopranos, which altos and basses? With this information, she makes some changes; she moves the singers to different positions, placing the sopranos with sopranos, altos with altos, basses with basses.

Sister Mary Clarence observes patiently and notices things. Her attentiveness allows her to single out one nun who sings too loud and another who sings too softly. She takes each one aside individually, and with a few swift interventions, has them both improving almost instantaneously. The loud singer, she compliments, but reminds her that she is drowning out the other nuns with her "powerful instrument." The soft singer, she brings up close and pushes a finger into her diaphragm, in the process startling the quiet voiced singer into a brief loud burst of music. She then instructs the little nun about how to project her voice.

Sister Mary Clarence's teaching is efficient and individualized. It is targeted to what is needed by each individual and for the group. She makes the group sing a simple single note—an A, and then a second note and a third. When the nuns can sing the chord harmoniously and in unison, she compliments them. But only up to a point, since they have only made a small, even though important, accomplishment. In the process she makes them listen to each other—not just to themselves.

Finally, she inspires the singing nuns. She does this primarily through metaphor, when she tells them that they are singing to God. Their singing, she implies, is a form of prayer.

Innovating through Analogy

Metaphor exemplifies the larger concept of analogy and represents a particular type of analogical thinking. Analogy is often considered simply a way to explain an idea, to clarify it by linking the unfamiliar with the familiar, what's being learned with what is already known. But analogy's power extends to generating ideas and not just explaining or elaborating them.

In a *Wall Street Journal* article, "See the Analogies, Change the World," John Pollack (2014) suggests that many of the greatest breakthroughs in invention and discovery were sparked by and generated by analogy, by seeing and considering the implication of parallels between disparate things. Pollack's examples include Darwin's theory of evolution by natural selection, the Wright Brothers' flying machine, the assembly line, and the computer "desktop," envisioned respectively by Henry Ford and Steve Jobs a century apart.

Each of these innovations is grounded in and founded on an analogy. Darwin was inspired both by animal and agricultural breeding to creative modifications better suited to survival and by geological change over time, the way a stream can over millennia carve out a canyon. The Wright Brothers approach to flight was influenced less by birds flapping their wings than by how they propelled themselves and retained their balance and forward momentum, the way bicycles, which the brothers had already built, were kept in motion through propulsion, control, and balance. The assembly line for assembling cars was created via an analogy with butchers carving up cattle carcasses as they moved by on a system of pulleys overhead, and the computer desktop by the top of an actual desk with its place for files and assorted business tools.

Itself a concept, analogy works to identify the concept within and the principle behind a way of doing something that can then be appropriated and adapted to something else. Therein lies its power. Analogy thus can be used as a conceptual tool to generate fresh thinking and develop new ideas and their application.

Becoming a Creative Thinker

Creative thinkers cultivate particular attitudes and mental habits; they employ specific tools and strategies. You can use the guidelines shown in Table 3.1 to develop your creative thinking capacities.

Table 3.1 Creative thinking guidelines

- Develop the habit of seeking alternative explanations, additional possibilities for how something can be done. Ask: "How else might I do this?" "What other ways are there to do what's needed?"
- Cross-fertilize your thinking by seeing how a problem, challenge, or idea might be explored from different academic disciplines. Ask: "How would a scientist or artist, an architect or a poet, an engineer or a psychologist, a mathematician or a philosopher approach this topic?"
- Develop the analogical habit. Learn to look at things through "as if" spectacles. Ask: "What is this situation, scenario, challenge like?" "What can it be compared with?"
- Broaden your perception. Extend the reach of your thinking. Ask yourself: "What else can I imagine? What else is interesting?" "What else is possible?"
- Create your own rituals and practices to foster creative thinking. Keep a diary of your thinking. Try out your ideas on teachers and classmates, friends and family. Develop your own thinking habits.
- Release your imagination. Read books and magazines. Watch films and YouTube videos. Listen to concerts and conversations. Look, listen, and learn. Let your imagination take off from what you observe and experience.

Applying creative thinking tools and techniques

You can also develop a creative thinkers toolkit—a set of tools and techniques to generate ideas, cultivate and foster our creative thinking potential. Table 3.2 presents a few tools and techniques you can use.

Developing the Creative Habit

In Chapter 1 you were introduced to dancer and choreographer Twyla Tharp (2003), whose book *The Creative Habit* identifies a series of practices that enabled her to develop a habit of thinking creatively. Here are five more of her suggestions for making creativity a habit.

1. *Accidents.* Like many others who write about creativity, Twyla Tharp values the potential for accidental discovery—for times

Table 3.2 Creative thinking tools and techniques

1 ***Be curious about everything***. Cultivate your curiosity as if it were a rare and precious species of life.

2 ***Ask questions upon questions upon questions***. Imagine yourself a child full of questions—whether or not satisfactory answers are available for them.

3 ***Identify patterns***. Observe patterns of sight and sound, image and idea, experience of knowledge. Patterns of habit and patterns of error. Patterns of success.

4 ***Make connections***. Determine how things are related to one another. Relate what you study to your life. Connect what you are learning with what you know. Always connect. View nothing in isolation.

5 ***Get into the flow***. Find your Zone. Identify something you love to do such that when you are doing it, you lose all sense of time and place. Doing it provides a heightened awareness with intrinsic value of and for itself.

6 ***Break the rules. Have fun. Be like a child.*** Avoid constraints, except those that provoke fresh thinking.

7 ***Embrace ambiguity, complexity, and uncertainty***. Life is volatile, fast changing. The only constant, it has been said, is change. Accept volatile change as the new normal. Recognize that issues, ideas, and values are complex and that uncertainties abound. Learn to live with and value those complications. Revel in uncertainty; celebrate complexity; embrace ambiguity.

when errors and mistakes can lead to productive results. And like those others, she also advocates the necessity to be prepared to take advantage of such happy accidents. You have to be prepared to be lucky; you have to learn to recognize an opportunity, to keep your eyes and ears and mind open and receptive, and then to seize that opportunity when it appears. Tharp gives the example of the creator of the General Electric advertising slogan, which conveys the idea that GE makes things that make life good. Playing with this concept and thinking of different ways to express it enabled the copywriter who created the GE slogan to be prepared himself to recognize what was eventually created: "We bring good things to life."

2. *Spine.* By "spine," Twyla Tharp means the core idea for a work or project, the essential notion that motivates and animates

it. The spine is your goal, your intention, your central concept or idea. For Buster Keaton's slapstick comic routines it was to get the last laugh. For Michael Jordan shooting a basketball, it was to jump up above the defender. For French novelist Gustave Flaubert, it was to get the words of his novel *Madame Bovary* exactly right. It's easy to drift from that spine as you gather material for a project, as you explore it and work out its implications. It's important to keep reminding yourself of what you are trying to do, then to evaluate the project in light of its "spine," and revise it according to its essential purpose and goal.

3. *Skills.* Acquiring the skills to perform a work and the knowledge to develop a project demands effort and practice. Skills and knowledge are a necessary foundation, an essential pre-requisite for any creative output. Although necessary, they are not sufficient; something more is needed. But you won't make progress unless the fundamentals have been developed solidly and confidently. You can't compose an intricate piece of music, perform a complex series of dance movements, produce an emotionally powerful film, or create an exceptional four-course meal, without mastering the fundamentals of music, dance, film-making, or cooking. Learning and disciplining yourself to develop those fundamental skills, practicing them, and keeping them sharp and fresh—these provide the essential baseline and foundation for working passionate creative magic. Combining skill with passion is the very essence of the creative life.

4. *Failure.* Failure is painful, humbling, dispiriting. It can also be instructive, illuminating, inspiring. Twyla Tharp suggests that failure is unavoidable, especially for creative efforts and attempts. You failed in the past, and you will almost inevitably fail again in the future. But that simple fact should reveal that you are trying new things, attempting things you have not yet done or cannot quite do—yet. Without romanticizing failure, you need, as people say, to simply "get over it." And then get on to the next new thing. That's Twyla Tharp's sound, sane, sagacious advice.

It is also important to consider what causes failure. Is it a failure of nerve? A failure of judgment? A failure of skill or of concept? Perhaps, the failure stems from denial—a denial to listen to the good advice of others, or to your own best instincts. And once you determine the cause of failure, it's then time to do something to fix it, change it, address it, remedy it—and then get beyond it.

5. *The long run.* By "the long run" Tharp means the arc of creative development, the creative trajectory of one's life and career. Although creative thinking and creative production have been shown to peak in the prime years of middle age—after the rich learning curve of youth and before the decline and trailing off of creative energy in later years—there are exceptions to that pattern. Exemplary creative individuals continue to produce fresh and original work all their lives, with their late work as vibrant and original as their earlier masterpieces. Such a catalogue includes Mozart and Schubert (both of whom died young), Verdi and Wagner (who lived much longer), and many who lived the normal life-spans for their times, Rembrandt, Dostoyevsky, Yeats, Cezanne, Picasso, Matisse, Kurosawa, Balanchine.

Focus

Although most people don't think of focus as a creative act or strategy, it almost always can be. One of the benefits of focus is that it targets and directs thinking. Another is that it directs attention to small matters that others haven't bothered to consider, such as the Black & Decker "Workmate," a workstation for using power tools. While a number of people focused on improving the company's power tools and creating new power tools, the inventor of the "Workmate" focused on the place the tools could be used. Also of interest is the variable-speed windshield wiper, whose inventor focused on varying the speed of the windshield wipers rather than on improving their wiping ability.

Another aspect of focus concerns the necessity of "paying attention" to one thing at a time. As Daniel Levitin (2014) notes in *The Organized Mind*, "attention is a limited-capacity resource." You are limited in what you can focus on at any one time.

The human brains, he suggests, has evolved to focus on one thing at a time, to stay on task. Multi-tasking obstructs the ability to sustain attention and focus; multi-tasking is the enemy of focused attention, one that exacts a significant "cognitive cost," which research shows are significantly greater than the cognitive loss suffered from smoking pot.

In reality, multi-tasking is a cognitive illusion, even a delusion, since when you think you are multi-tasking, you are doing no such thing. In reality, you are switching rapidly back and forth between and among tasks. In the process you diminish the quality of attention to each task and decrease your effectiveness. To manage your time efficiently and effectively, focus on one task at a time; avoid splintering your attention with distractions. Success in any task involves sustained and concentrated attention and effort.

General area focus and purpose focus

Deciding on a focus is very important because if you have the wrong focus, you solve the wrong problem and waste a lot of time and energy, and perhaps money as well. Edward de Bono proposes thinking about focus in two ways: (1) around a general or "area" focus, and (2) on a more specific "purpose" focus.

For a general or area focus it's enough to ask for "some new ideas about" something—restaurants, for example, or coffeemakers, or dormitory housing, or hotels. This general or area focus can be broad or narrow. Here are some examples of a general focus:

- We need some ideas in the area of organizing a school.
- We need some ideas on organizing a middle school.
- We need some ideas on inquiry-based learning in the school.

The virtue of this way of asking for ideas is that it keeps the idea pathways open. The ideas don't necessarily have to be purpose driven, practical, or feasible. The only constraint is the general direction of the thinking as it is defined. You can see the difference if we recast the request for ideas this way: "We need ideas to improve efficiency in organizing our department." This is also a useful direction for thinking—a useful focus. But it differs in being more specific and targeted; it is also directed toward a particular purpose—improving efficiency in organization. Sometimes, however, we want to consider broader ways of organizing or even "improving" our target focus. It's not that one kind of focus is better than the other; they are simply different and yield different kinds of thinking results; we need both.

Here are some examples of the more specifically directed purpose focus for creative thinking:

- We need ideas on improving traffic flow on our campus.
- We need ideas to improve test scores.

- We need ideas to increase the effectiveness of the evaluation process.
- We need ideas to increase participation in strategic planning.
- We need ideas to improve morale in our district and in our schools.

There is much more that de Bono (1993) includes in his discussion of focus in *Serious Creativity* and elsewhere. For our purposes, however, the critical point is to think about the focus of our thinking—exactly what we are thinking about and why.

Solo and Group Creativity

In their respective books, *Group Genius: The Creative Power of Collaboration*, and *Quiet: The Power of Introverts in a World That Can't Stop Talking*, Keith Sawyer (2007) and Susan Cain (2012), respectively, emphasize group and individual creativity. Sawyer argues that every major innovation and many minor inventions involved more than a single individual. Examples include Charles Darwin's discovery of evolution through the mechanism of natural selection, which was triggered by Darwin's reading of Thomas Malthus on population. Sawyer cites the development of the board game, *Monopoly*, which was invented by a group of Quakers, extended to other players, offered to Parker Brothers, the game company, and eventually codified with a set of rules and a standardized board and set of pieces (the game moving pieces—thimble, hat, iron, etc., owing to their humble Quaker origins). The frisbee and the mountain bike, radio and television, the Internet and social networking—all involved multiple people working together and apart.

Susan Cain emphasizes, instead, the need for individuals to spend time in isolation thinking things through before they can advance knowledge and spark innovation. She laments the contemporary emphasis on brainstorming, on group activities, excessive collaboration, and the design of workspaces so open that they impede contemplation, reflection, and considered thought. She stresses the link between an emphasis on group activity and extroversion, claiming that American business prides itself on the collaborative nature of creative thinking leading to innovation. What is ignored, or at least downplayed, according to Cain, is the extent to which creativity begins with an individual working obsessively on something he or she loves. Cain argues that those introverted types need to return to their private places to explore and experiment on their own, undistracted.

A middle position is taken by Joshua Wolf Shenk (2014) in his book *Powers of Two*, in which he argues that creativity flourishes best when two people collaborate together or compete against one another. In both cases, each member of the pair feeds off the other's ideas, pushing his or her own creative work to new heights. Shenk's examples of creative pairs include Wilbur and Orville Wright, Vincent and Theo van Gogh, Simone de Beauvoir and Jean-Paul Sartre, Pablo Picasso and Henri Matisse, Susan B. Anthony and Elizabeth Cady Stanton, C. S. Lewis and J. R. R. Tolkien, John Lennon and Paul McCartney.

The Wright brothers pushed each other contentiously in a good-natured way. Theo van Gogh supported Vincent both financially and emotionally such that Vincent wrote that Theo was "as much the creator" of his paintings as he was. De Beauvoir and Sartre directed their intellectual gifts to a common philosophical purpose and often "thought as one." Picasso and Matisse were rivals, each trying to outdo the other in his creative work across artistic genres. Stanton said of Susan B. Anthony: "I forged the thunderbolts. She fired them." Lewis served as Tolkien's audience and sounding board, urging him on such that Tolkien attributed actually finishing the *Lord of the Rings* trilogy to his encouragement.

Lennon and McCartney, as Joshua Wolf Shenk notes, sparked each other through their opposite personalities and creative styles, Paul's persistence and attention to detail balancing John's anarchic, disorderly way of working. Apollonian rationality and control contested with Dionysian emotionality and disruption. McCartney's charm softened Lennon's brashness; McCartney's diplomat complemented Lennon's agitator. "The one's neatnik balanced the other's whirling dervish," as Shenk describes them.

Beyond musical partnerships, we might note the creative partnerships of comedy duos in television and film, exemplified by Laurel and Hardy, Abbott and Costello, Burns and Allen, Lucille Ball and Desi Arnez, Dean Martin and Jerry Lewis, Jackie Gleason and Art Carney, to cite a few notable ones.

And to push into another arena where competitive teamwork is at play we can look no further than professional sports—Roger Federer and Rafael Nadal, Chris Evert and Martina Navritolova in tennis, Larry Bird and Magic Johnson in basketball, Tiger Woods and his golf caddy Steve Williams, NFL quarterbacks Tom Brady and Peyton Manning, and boxers Muhammad Ali and Joe Frazier in the ring. In literature we have the fruitful creative pairings of Emerson and Thoreau, Dorothy and William Wordsworth, Nathaniel Hawthorne and Herman Melville, Thomas Wolfe and his editor Maxwell Perkins. Other artistic pairs include Christo and Jeanne Claude, George Balanchine and ballerina Suzanne Farrell, Pablo Picasso (again) with George Braque collaborating on new styles in modern art, cubism foremost among them.

Concepts as Cognitive Tools

The concepts of "cognitive tool" and "cognitive toolkit, of course, are metaphors. Normally, when you think of tools, you probably think of things like hammers and screwdrivers, among basic manual tools, and of computer software programs and applications, among electronic and digital tools. Cognitive tools, by analogy, are tools that enhance thinking rather than tools that enable doing various kinds of work (though thinking is certainly a kind of "work"). And a "cognitive toolkit," is simply a collection of such thinking tools, though with the sense that the toolkit keeps them accessible and ready for use.

A number of cognitive tools are identified in John Brockman's (2012) *This Will Make You Smarter*, a book of essays by different thinkers. Some examples include cognitive humility; the uselessness of certainty; the biases of technology; how each person is ordinary, yet one of a kind; how failure liberates success; how humans possess an "instinct to learn"; how creativity is provoked by constraints; how "wicked" problems differ from solvable ones; how you can "design" your mind—and many more.

John Brockman asked his contributors to focus on a question that leads to answers that can't be predicted, with the question about cognitive tools serving as a provocation. The question was also meant to stimulate thoughts the contributors might normally not have had—or at least to consider some of their most important ideas in new ways. The cognitive tools the contributors provided are meant to enhance creative and productive thinking.

One of the central themes that emerged from more than 150 contributors' essays is the questioning of basic assumptions. Another is the ways technology is altering culture and social interaction in both positive and negative ways. And still another is how it is necessary to move beyond deductive reasoning to include complementary kinds of holistic and emergent thinking. Collectively, the participants' suggestions for a cognitive toolkit involve thinking about thinking; they provide ways to think about the world and to engage with it more effectively.

Three cognitive tools

Among the cognitive tools worthy of consideration are these three: (1) The Pareto Principle; (2) Recursive Structure; and (3) Dualities.

The Pareto Principle is named after the Italian economist Vilfred Pareto, who discovered that the richest 20% of a country's population controlled 80% of its wealth. This principle has been applied to many kinds of situations and experiences. For example, 20% of users of an Internet site account for 80% of site activity; 20% of a company's employees account for 80% of its revenue; 20% of the people, papers, books, and other research we consult account for 80% of our work activity; 80% of a deli counter's activity centers on 20% of its products—think roast beef, boiled ham, and Swiss cheese.

The pattern replicates itself recursively, such that within the top 20% of a Pareto distribution, the top 20% of that distribution typically accounts for a disproportionate amount of whatever is being measured. One major effect of the Pareto distribution is to skew the average far from the commonly accepted notion of an average represented by a bell curve. Instead of an even distribution with the middle of the curve showing an average and a median (midpoint of the system) as the same, there is a strong imbalance reflected in the Pareto distribution percentages. The most volatile or most active element of what is being measured is twice as volatile or active as the second most active element and ten times as volatile or active as the tenth-most element. Such multiples are seen in the magnitude of earthquakes, the social connections of friends, and the habits of readers and book buyers, to cite just a few examples.

A second cognitive tool, "recursive structure," is one in which the shape of the whole is replicated in the shape of its parts. The tracery of Gothic architectural windows (the thin carved stone partitions that separate a window into small panes) is one example. Another is the way a country or state's coastline reveals the same pattern or shape in increasingly larger or smaller increments, such that its structure is similar at five yards or five miles.

Recursive structure helps identify and comprehend connections between art and technology. Aesthetic principles influence the thinking of engineers and technologists; the clarity and elegance reflected in those aesthetic principles undergird successful design. Recursive structure implies the need for a technology education that includes the aesthetics of design along with a study of the history of arts. One place where this conjunction can be seen is in the work done since the early 2000s at Apple with its popular products such as the iPhone and iPad. Apple's late CEO, Steve Jobs, emphasized the connections between the arts and technology; he saw himself as working at the crossroads of art and technology. His passion was to make products that were both flawlessly functional in their engineering aspects while also being elegantly beautiful.

A third example of a cognitive tool is the concept of dualities. In their respective essays entitled "Dualities" in Brockner's (2012) book, Stephon H. Alexander and Amanda Gefter each highlight a different aspect of this cognitive tool. Alexander focuses on physics, suggesting that some physical phenomena require an explanation from two different perspectives. The classic example is light, the nature of which cannot be fully explained apart from its particle-like and wave-like characteristics. To ask whether light is essentially particle or wave is to miss its underlying duality as both particle and wave. He suggests that dualities remind us and provoke us to use more than a single analytical lens in our attempts to understand anything.

Dualities transform the concept of "or" into one of "and." In emphasizing not "either/or," but instead "both/and" Amanda Gefter (2012) advances us beyond the conventional notion of duality as a dichotomy in which opposites clash. Instead of highlighting contradiction and conflict among dual terms such as east/west, male/female, light/dark, she encourages us to embrace the contraries and attempt to see how two very different things might be equally true. An appreciation for the power of dualities can serve as an antidote to the kind of adversarial thinking of "I'm Right, You're Wrong" that Edward de Bono advises against. Using the cognitive tool of dualities, along with those of recursive structure, and the Pareto principle can broaden your perception and enrich your understanding of yourself and of the world.

Applications

3-1. To what extent are you convinced by Guy Deutscher's arguments about language differences—how different languages shape our perceptions of reality? Perhaps you are more persuaded by McWhorter's view that culture shapes language. What other language(s) besides English do you know, or have you studied? How has your knowledge of another language influenced your perception of other people and their culture(s)?

3-2. Identify the following statements as reports, inferences, or judgments.

Explain your reason in each case.

1. She goes to the opera only to show off her jewelry.
2. Stock prices were up slightly today in light trading.
3. The Iraqi people do not want war.
4. Beauty is only skin deep.
5. An apple a day keeps the doctor away.
6. Mixing beer with wine or scotch leads to a terrible hangover.
7. America has never lost a war.
8. $a^2 + b^2 = c^2$
9. A credit score of 650 is good.
10. Eat blueberries and walnuts, as both foods are healthy for your heart.

3-3. Explain how you would verify two reports in the previous exercise.

Explain how you would provide supporting evidence for one inference and for one judgment you found in the exercise.

3-4. Read the first three or four paragraphs of a newspaper or magazine article you have access to, and identify the sentences in those paragraphs as reports, inferences, or judgments.

3-5. How would you characterize the differences in the journalistic philosophies or approaches taken by the *New York Times* and the *Herald Tribune*? Why do you think each newspaper approaches the story the way it does?

3-6. Add one example each for " Love is a physical force," and "Love is a patient."

For these additional ways of talking about love, provide two examples.

1. Love is war.
2. Love is magic.
3. Love is madness.

Provide one example for each of the following metaphors.

4. Ideas are plants.
5. Ideas are food.
6. Ideas are money
7. Time is money.
8. Time is a commodity.

3-7. Identify the metaphorical connections in the following examples. Explain what is being described in terms of what else—and what the effect of the comparison is. In thinking about the examples above, try to explain how the metaphorical connection helps you understand what's being said.

1. I wandered lonely as a cloud
   That floats on high o'er vales and hills. (William Wordsworth)
2. 'Tis with our judgment, as our watches, none
   Go just alike, yet each believes his own. (Alexander Pope)
3. O my Luve's like a red, red rose,
   That's newly sprung in June. (Robert Burns)

3-8. The following passage is densely packed with metaphors. Try to unpack the lines, identifying each metaphor and what it implies. What, for example, do you make of the candle? What does it represent? And what is the "tale" told by an "idiot"? By way of context: the lines come form Shake-speare's play *Macbeth*; they are spoken by Macbeth, who, goaded on by his wife, Lady Macbeth, has risen to power by murderous means. The passage comes at the point in the play when Macbeth has just discovered that his wife has killed herself.

> Out, out, brief candle!
> Life's but a walking shadow, a poor player
> That struts and frets his hour upon the stage
> And then is heard no more. It is a tale
> Told by an idiot, full of sound and fury,
> Signifying nothing.

3-9. Explain the differing implications of the following metaphors.
- Marriage as a legal and economic partnership
- Marriage as a form of friendship and companionship
- Marriage as an adventure and a journey

3-10. Select a term from column A to match up with a term from column B to forge a metaphorical link. Then explain the implications of the metaphor you create.

A	B
Writing	Praying
Reading	Working
Thinking	Traveling
Studying	Conversing
Singing	Swimming

3-11. Here is a list of nouns that suggest a range of metaphors about reading—ways of reading, we might say. Select two of them that interest, engage, or otherwise resonate for you. Write a few sentences about the implications of considering reading in each of those ways. What is the value and what are the benefits of reading in light of each of your chosen metaphors?

Conversation
Deliberation
Exploration
Inquiry

Perception

Play

Work

3-12. In *What We See When We Read,* Peter Mendelsund (2014) compares the reading experience to a wide range of things, including the following. Choose two and comment on what those images might suggest about the experience of reading.

Arch Arrow Bridge Candle Cloister Computer program Dream Eye Film Game of chess Knife Map Maze Microscope Sign Vision Walk

3-13. Consider the following metaphors of teaching. Like those earlier verbs that highlighted ways of reading, you have here a list of verbs that suggest ways of teaching. Pick two or three that strike you as especially interesting, important, necessary. Consider the implications of each of these verbal metaphors of teaching—what they require and what they yield for both teachers and students.

Teaching as:

Ministering

Subverting

Performing

Collaborating

Exploring

Guiding

Directing

Discovering

Transmitting

Provoking

3-14. Borrow, buy, or rent *Sister Act* and watch the scene described earlier. Identify two additional details that reflect critical and creative thinking and teaching.

3-15. Identify two simple tools for indoor or outdoor use that were most likely inspired by analogical thinking. Explain the concept that links the two aspects or parts of the analogy.

3-16. Choose one of Twyla Tharp's five strategies (Accident, Spine, Skills, Failure, The Long Run) for developing the creative habit. Explain how you could apply and adapt her suggestions to prepare yourself to be more creative, to develop your creative potential more fully.

3-17. Which approach to creative thinking are you most persuaded by: Sawyer's group innovation, Cain's solo creativity, or Shenk's collaborative and competitive pairs? Why?

3-18. To what extent are you intrigued, persuaded, or otherwise provoked to thinking, by Shenk's analysis of the creative partnership of John Lennon and Paul McCartney? Of other creative pairs?

3-19. To what extent are the following exemplary creative pairs in the manner Shenk describes? James Watson and Francis Crick, Marie Sklodowska (Curie) and Pierre Curie, Larry Page and Sergey Brin, Ralph Abernathy and Martin Luther King, Jr., Mel Brooks and Carl Reiner, Sigmund Freud and Carl Gustav Jung? What other creative/competitive pairs can you identify?

3-20. How do you respond to the observations about multi-tasking by Daniel Levitin? Do you agree that multi-tasking limits your and others' effectiveness? Or do you think that you are a successful multi-tasker?

3-21. Identify a simple focus for each of the following situations.
   1. Being in a long line at an airport for a security check.
   2. Putting stamps on 500 envelopes you are mailing.
   3. Sitting in a meeting where everyone's head is down on a Blackberry.
   4. Waiting for a slow elevator in a tall building.

3-22. Think of a general area focus and a more purpose directed focus for the following:
   1. Hotels
   2. Shopping malls
   3. Movie theaters
   4. Supermarkets
   5. Underground trains

3-23. To what extent do you find the concepts of "cognitive tools" and "cognitive toolkit" helpful? Do you agree with the values ascribed to them?

3-24. Which of the kinds of cognitive tools—those about humility, failure, certainty, technology, constraints, ordinariness, wicked problems—catches your interest most. Why?

3-25. Which of the three cognitive tools explained above do you find most promising and attractive? What interests you about this cognitive tool, and how do you think your thinking might benefit from it?

References

Alexander, Stephon H. 2012. "Dualities." In *This Will Make You Smarter*. Ed. John Brockman. New York: Harper Collins.

Bergen, Benjamin K. 2013. "Metaphors Are in the Mind." In *This Explains Everything*. Ed. John Brockman. New York: Harper.

Brockman, John, ed. 2012. *This Will Make You Smarter*. New York: Harper Collins.

Brockman, John, ed. 2013. *This Explains Everything*. New York: Harper Perennial.

Cain, Susan. 2012. *Quiet*. New York: Crown, Broadway.

de Bono, Edward. 1993. *Serious Creativity*. New York: HarperBusiness.

Deutscher, Guy. 2011. *Through the Language Glass*. New York: Picador.

Donoghue, Denis. 2014. *Metaphor*. Cambridge, MA: Harvard University Press.

Gefter, Amanda. 2012. "Dualities." In *This Will Make You Smarter*. 2012. John Brockman. New York: Harper Collins.

Hayakawa, S. I. 1991. *Language in Thought and Action*, 5th edn. Boston: Harvest.

Lakoff, George and Mark Johnson. 2005. *Metaphors We Live By*, 2nd edn. Chicago: University of Chicago Press.

Levitin, Daniel. 2014. *The Organized Mind*. Toronto: Penguin Canada.

McWhorter, John. 2014. *The Language Hoax*. New York: Oxford University Press.

Mendelsund, Peter. 2014. *What We See When We Read*. New York: Random House Vintage.

Paul, Richard and Linda Elder. 2009. *Miniature Guide to Critical Thinking: Concepts and Tools*. Berkeley: Foundation for Critical Thinking.

Pollack, John. 11/8-9/2014. "See the Analogies, Change the World." *Wall Street Journal*.

Sawyer, Keith. 2007. *Group Genius*. New York: Basic Books.

Searle, John. 1999. *Mind, Language, and Society*. New York: Basic Books.

Shenk, Joshua Wolf. 2014. *Powers of Two*. New York: Houghton Mifflin Harcourt.

Tharp, Twyla. 2003. *The Creative Habit*. New York: Simon and Schuster.

Interchapter 3

Embodying Experience

Embodied experience is knowledge felt in the body. When you hear a catchy tune and sway to its rhythm or tap your foot to its beat, you are "embodying" your experience of the song. You embody knowledge experientially when you wince at your own or someone else's pain, feeling the pain literally and physically, or feeling something that connects you empathically with another.

You experience the world through your body—seeing, hearing, touching, tasting, smelling, balancing. You embody a poem by saying (and hearing) it aloud. You embody a story or play by reading its dialogue aloud, perhaps with a partner. Those forms of embodying a text bring it to life through the physical action of reciting the words. In the process you may find yourself not simply reading and hearing the words aloud, but using your physical self to emphasize particular sounds or details. Consider this couplet by Robert Frost:

> The Span of Life
> The old dog barked backward without getting up.
> I can remember when he was a pup.

In reading the lines out loud, try to feel the words in your mouth and on your tongue. The first line reads slowly, as if overcoming obstacles as you negotiate stacked consonants—"d" and "g" and "k" and "d" and "b" and "t" and "p." The first half of the first line

Critical and Creative Thinking: A Brief Guide for Teachers, First Edition. Robert DiYanni.
© 2016 John Wiley & Sons, Inc. Published 2016 by John Wiley & Sons, Inc.

is particularly heavy with hard consonants. It reads more slowly than the second half. Say it aloud slowly and feel how the second half of the line picks up speed.

Now read the second line aloud. What do you feel in your mouth and on your tongue? It skips right along, doesn't it? Partly, this is an effect of rhythm. It moves like this: ONE two three ONE two three ONE two three ONE. Like a waltz.

I can re MEM ber when HE was a PUP.

Why, you might ask, does this matter? One reason certainly is that the slowness of the first line and the speed of the second line echo what is described in each—and OLD DOG and a YOUNG PUP.

Let's consider some other ways the physical is related to knowledge. Leonardo da Vinci valued all things physical, especially the human body. His anatomical studies (see Figure 3.2) are but one indication of this special regard.

He was curious about the structure of things and how structure informed their function—in short, how things worked. This was as true for Leonardo's observation of the body's bones and muscles as it was for his study of the energies of nature. Himself an example of fitness, balance, and poise, Leonardo enjoyed good food and valued good health. He could be claimed as an early advocate of healthy living.

Leonardo possessed extraordinary physical gifts. Renaissance art historian Giorgio Vasari (1988) writes that "he could bend the iron ring of a doorknocker or a horseshoe as if it were made of lead." He notes that Leonardo was physically graceful, exhibiting poise, dexterity, and strength.

When we sing and dance, play music, engage in sports, we "think" with our bodies. The ballet impresario, Lincoln Kirstein once remarked that ballerinas think with their feet. And in D. H. Lawrence's short story, "The Blind Man," the story's sightless protagonist is described as having "intelligent" hands.

Research has shown that your stomach and heart contain the kind of neurons found in your brain. You have a knowing gut and a smart heart. Each aspect of body and mind complements and completes the other. This embodiment of thinking suggests that we are integrated beings rather than divided ones.

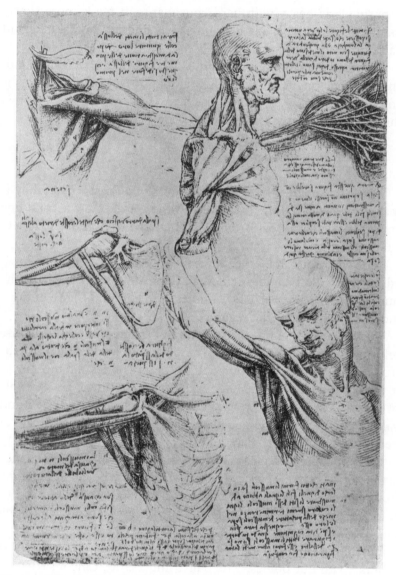

Figure 3.2 Study of shoulder joints, Leonardo da Vinci. © The Print Collection Heritage-Images

In "Life Is the Way the Animal Is in the World," Alva Noe (2013) refers to the bodily aspect of consciousness as "practical bodily understanding." He is concerned with how consciousness looks outward toward the world rather than inward toward the self, how it involves our bodily connection with the environment.

Another illustration of our bodies helping us communicate with each other comes from Nicholas Epley (2014) in *Mindwise*, where he suggests that your body knows what another person feels and that "you feel what your body shows." When you see your child in pain, your body mimics that pain. When you hear another laugh, you laugh in response. Your understanding of another person is reflected in your bodily response to that person's thinking and feeling. Something called "mirror neurons" stimulate such mimicry responses.

In a *New York Times* article, Richard Kearney (2014) explains his fear that we are losing touch with our senses, that we are "losing our touch." He attributes this loss to an increasing reliance on virtual experience through the use of digital technology. Your physical senses are an integral part of how you know, learn, and express yourself. Re-connecting with your tactile sensing self can enhance your ability to understand and connect with others.

Kearney's concerns are echoed by Nicholas Carr (2014), who in *The Glass Cage*, explains how developments in computer technology have contributed to a degrading of your navigation skills, your sense of being physically in a place, even your sense of yourself as a physical being. Carr suggests that an increasing reliance on navigation technology erodes not just your ability to find where you are going, but to know where you have been, in the process diminishing memory and diluting the experience of places.

He claims, further, that these diminishments are more seriously at work in fields like medicine and architecture, which once relied on careful attention to the body as an object and as an instrument of creation and discovery. Doctors' increased reliance on Computer-fed data distracts them from the full attention to their patients' physical presence. Analogoulsy, the increased use of computer-assisted design (CAD) by architects erodes their drawing skills, inhibits their memory of the process of creating plans, and limits their creativity.

Applications

1. Where might you go to look into the claims made for an intelligent gut and a smart heart? How might you evaluate those claims?

2. What do you think you might do to improve your own physical abilities? How might you improve your balance and your posture? What can you do to increase your strength and stamina? To what extent do you think these improvements might contribute to improved thinking?

3. Read the following lines of poetry aloud. What do you notice, physically in your mouth and tongue, as you speak the lines?

> When Ajax strives, some rock's vast weight to throw,
> The line too labors, and the words move slow;
> Not so, when swift Camilla scours the plain,
> Flies o'er th' unbending corn, and skims along the main.
> (Alexander Pope, from "An Essay on Criticism")

4. Think of a time when you "felt another's pain" in your own body. Or identify a situation when your body moved in synch with the bodily movement of another. What was at stake or in play in that situation? To what extent was your physical movement or gesture a manifestation of your thought and feeling? Why?

5. To what extent have you experienced a deterioration of your physical skills—your sense of being able to find your way— for example, due to increased use of navigation apps? How do you respond to the situations Carr describes in the realm of medicine and architecture?

References

Carr, Nicholas. 2014. *The Glass Cage*. New York: Norton.
Epley, Nicholas. 2014. *Mindwise*. New York: Knopf.
Kearney, Richard. 9/7/2014. "Losing Our Touch." *The New York Times*.
Noe, Alva. 2013. "Life Is the Way the Animal Is In the World." In *Thinking*. Ed. Brockman. New York: Harper Perennial.
Vasari, Giorgio. 1988. *Lives of the Artists*. New York: Penguin.

4

Critical Thinking Strategies and Applications

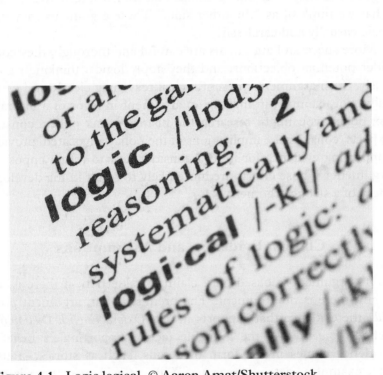

Figure 4.1   Logic logical. © Aaron Amat/Shutterstock

An educated mind is able to entertain a thought without accepting it.
—Aristotle

The eye sees only what the mind is prepared to comprehend.
—Henri Bergson

Critical and Creative Thinking: A Brief Guide for Teachers, First Edition. Robert DiYanni.
© 2016 John Wiley & Sons, Inc. Published 2016 by John Wiley & Sons, Inc.

The Nature of Argument

The primary goal of argument is to persuade, to convince someone or some group of people to consider a claim, a perspective, an idea one way rather than another way. Arguments at their best are grounded in thoughtful reasoning, in logical thinking.

Sometimes an argument may present a position or claim while offering only a small amount of supporting evidence for it. Such arguments may overlook possible objections, alternative views, what we think of as "the other side." These arguments may use logic casually and carelessly.

More successful arguments are careful and thorough; they consider potential objections, and they apply logical thinking rigorously. Such arguments present logical reasoning clearly and carefully. For example, in making an argument in favor of a flat rate tax policy, you might research the history of tax policy, consult experts, consider the implications of the policy advocated, provide supporting evidence for it, and consider how to refute opposing arguments. Those efforts are more likely to result in the development of a strong argument.

Claims, Evidence, and Assumptions

Every argument is based on a claim, or assertion; if there is no claim, there is no argument. The premises of an argument provide the evidence that supports it. *The Oxford English Dictionary* defines *evidence* as "the available facts...supporting...a belief." Evidence comes in the form of details, such as stories, statistics, examples, data, or reasons. Without evidence, there is no argument—only a claim, which may be stated as an opinion. An argument requires both a claim and the evidence to support it.

Arguments often involve assumptions about what people believe and what values they hold. An assumption is what is being taken for granted—something the speaker or writer believes does not need proof or evidence in its support. Although an argument's claim and its evidence are always explicitly stated, its assumptions remain implicit, unstated. A writer's or speaker's assumptions need to be discovered and made explicit if an argument is to be fully understood, and more importantly, if it is to be contested and perhaps refuted.

For any argument to be convincing, the premises must be true. Consider the assumptions behind the following two arguments:

A. Ms. Jones will bring a new perspective to the state government. As the outsider candidate, she is the choice we need.
B. Mr. Johnson has served the city for more than a decade. He knows the system and has the experience to get things accomplished.

The first premise in argument A assumes that outsiders make better political representatives than people who are currently holding a political position. It relies on the belief that fresh ideas are better than current ones, and that the time for new ideas has arrived. The second argument assumes that experience is more important than a new perspective, with the further implication that a new and inexperienced representative will not be able to get things done. In both cases the assumptions are unstated; once these assumptions are identified, it is much easier to decide whether or not to agree with either point of view.

Arguments stand or fall based on the evidence that supports the claims they make. What counts as evidence? Examples provide one important type of evidence; other types of evidence include illustrations that clarify; comparisons or analogies that illuminate; facts, details, and statistics that inform; stories that convey experiential truth; logical connections among accurate and factual premises—these and more provide evidence for an argument's claim.

Argument and implication

Implication refers to the ways in which an argument's claim or conclusion might affect other areas beyond the limits of the argument itself. In *Good Arguments*, Connie Missimer (2008) describes implications as "possible outcomes that follow from an argument." An outcome of an argument is a kind of practical upshot or consequence resulting from it. Implications extend an argument's reach and enlarge its practical consequences.

Consider, for example, the following argument. Because of the increasing age at which people in the United States marry (premise 1); and the fact that women are remaining in the workforce longer (premise 2); average family size will decrease (claim).

That's the argument. What are its implications? One implication is that there will be fewer people in the workforce to support an aging population—and thus, the further implication that the next generation of workers will bear a higher tax burden. Another implication is that generational conflict might result from the difficulties the working population confronts in sustaining entitlements for the aged. And a further implication of this consequence is that the conflict might lead to social unrest, which could, possibly, result in violent demonstrations. As you can see, one implication can lead to another, and then another and another.

The notion of implication is important not only for argument, but also for analysis and interpretation. Whenever you interpret, you are, essentially, explaining implications—what is implied by a text, an image, an object, an event, an argument. Texts, images, objects, events, and arguments bear unstated meanings or significances; you "read" into and out of them, meanings, which are, simply, a sum of the implications they possess.

Implications, in the sense just described, offer interpretive possibilities—potential outcomes of meaning. Implications, of course, might also involve outcomes of action. Consider that aging population once again. To what extent might advertising change to address the needs of the aged? To what extent might more doctors specialize in geriatric medicine to accommodate them? And how many and what kinds of facilities for assisted living might be constructed for the increasing population of the elderly? The key terms of argument are given in Table 4.1.

Table 4.1 Key terms of argument

Claim
Evidence
Assumptions
Implications

Evidence: Claims and Warrants

In *The Uses of Argument,* Stephen Toulmin (1969) provides some additional terms and refinements on the basic terms of claim, support, and evidence, in considering evidence and its relationship to an argument's central claim. He identifies three elements common to most arguments: a claim, support, and a warrant. A **claim** is simply a thesis or central idea of an argument that is being proposed or defended. It's an assertion, a declarative statement. He suggests that a claim should be a conclusion whose merits you attempt to establish after having tested the evidence.

Support is the evidence—details, examples, facts, statistics, and the like. Support provides the grounds for the claim. Grounds may also include proof of expertise.

A **warrant is** the "bridge" that connects the claim and its various types of supporting evidence. The warrant links the claim to the support by showing the grounds or data and reasoning to be relevant.

A fourth term is "backing," which consists of additional data and other assurances that strengthen the authority of the warrant.

A **warrant** can be either implicit or explicit. An implicit warrant is similar to an enthymeme—a syllogism with one of its parts implied rather than explicitly stated. A warrant is a type of assumption. For example, if you wish to claim that the *Harry Potter* movies are the greatest fantasy films ever made, you need to consider the assumptions, or warrants, the audience might have about the film genre that the *Harry Potter* movies exemplify. You need to consider other fine films of the fantasy genre, such as the *Lord of the Rings* trilogy or the *Star Wars* trilogy, and provide comparative and contrastive analysis of the strengths and weaknesses of one group of films against the others.

What assumptions do people make about why such movies become successful? One assumption involves plot—a movie's convolutions and complications of action, keeping the story interesting with plot twists and turns. Another assumption involves characters with their human interest, their complexity, and their relationships. And a third involves the setting and visual effects used to create a complex and believable alien world or alternate reality. If you think that one of these, the last, for example, is the most important indicator for a great fantasy film, that warrant or

Table 4.2   Toulmin's types of claims and arguments

Claims of fact—Arguments about facts
Claims of value—Arguments about values
Claims of policy—Arguments about policies

assumption needs to be accepted by your audience for the argument to be persuasive. A warrant such as this can itself become an argument claim, in which case you would need to explain why this claim merits attention and ultimately conviction.

An additional set of terms Toulmin uses are "qualifier," "reservation," and "rebuttal." A **qualifier** limits and restricts the range of a claim. A **reservation** explains the terms and conditions the qualifier necessitates. And a **rebuttal** identifies objections to the warranted claim. Rebuttals suggest conditions that might refute the claim. A rebuttal is itself an argument and may include a claim, warrant, and backing.

Toulmin also identifies three types of claims: claims of **fact**, claims of **value**, and claims of **policy**. **Claims of fact** refer to a truth that requires significant research to be substantiated. **Claims of value** express acceptance or denial of a standard of taste or of morality. **Claims of policy** assert that a particular policy or way of doing business should be adopted. Claims of policy require evidence that strongly suggest their likelihood of success. Perhaps the policy has worked somewhere else, somewhere similar to the community where a particular policy being proposed is claimed to work.

Arguments based on these types of claims are, essentially, arguments about facts, values, and policies, respectively (see Table 4.2).

Inductive and Deductive Reasoning

Argument involves careful reasoning. Two different but interrelated kinds of reasoning—*inductive reasoning* (inductive thinking) and *deductive reasoning* (deductive thinking)—are important. Inductive reasoning often (but not always) begins with a limited number of observations. In such cases it continues with additional observations until arriving at a general claim or conclusion based on them. Inductive reasoning involves making inferences, reasoning from past occurrences and regularities to future ones. It offers probability rather than certainty.

Deductive reasoning works the opposite way—from the general to the particular. In reasoning deductively, you begin with a general principle or theory and then apply that theory to one or more specific, particular instances to see if it holds true.

The difference between deductive and inductive argument derives from the relation that exists between the premises and the conclusion of each type of argument. If the truth of the premises *definitely* establishes the truth of the conclusion, then the argument is deductive. If the truth of the premises *possibly or probably* establishes the truth of the conclusion, then the argument is inductive. Inductive arguments are assessed in terms of reliability, in terms of their likelihood as being sound and believable. Deductive arguments are assessed in terms of validity, the extent to which the relationship between their premises and conclusion is logically valid.

The following is a deductive argument:

Oslo is either in Norway or Sweden. If Oslo is in Norway, then Oslo is in Scandinavia. If Oslo is in Sweden, then Oslo is in Scandinavia. Therefore, Oslo is in Scandinavia.

Although this argument begins with a statement about a specific place, it is deductive because its structure requires that if the premises are true (and they are) there is no way the conclusion can be false.

Inductive arguments can deal with statistical data, generalizations from past experience, appeals to signs, evidence, authority, analogy, and causal relationships. Here is an example:

My cat sleeps a lot during the day. Other cats I have had slept a great deal during the day. Cats must be nocturnally active, as our new kitten coming next week will be, too.

The following arguments, even though they reason from the general to specific, are inductive; their conclusions are at best highly likely rather than certain.

> The members of the Williams family are Susan, Nathan, Alexander, and the baby, Jill. Susan, Nathan, and Alexander wear glasses. Jill will also wear glasses.

There is no way to know for certain whether the baby, Jill, will wear glasses like her siblings. It is certainly possible, and probably likely that she will. But there is a chance that her genetic inheritance for vision will be better than the vision capability inherited by her brothers and sister.

Here is yet another inductive argument:

> It has snowed in Boston *every* December in recorded history. Therefore, it will snow in Boston this coming December.

Once again, given the history of Boston's weather patterns, there is a strong probability that it will snow there this coming December. But there is no guarantee that it will. The conclusion of this inductive argument is at best highly likely.

Inductive reasoning typically works by looking at a series of examples, not just a single instance—though it can certainly begin with a single one. From a group of disparate details, examples, instances, you reason inductively by seeing a pattern of connections, and thereby deriving a general principle, which serves as a conclusion or interpretation of the evidence. Reading a poem or short story is a typical example of inductive reasoning, as the details of the story's or poem's language, structure, characters, setting, plot, and so on, provide the concrete particulars upon which to base an interpretation, your understanding of the work's general idea or larger meaning.

In their book *Philosopher's Toolkit* Julian Baggini and Peter S. Fosl (2010) note that inductive reasoning does not always involve reasoning from the specific to the general. Nor does it necessarily involve reasoning about the future based on observations about the past. Inductive reasoning may reason, for example, from a more general past conclusion, as for example, that no athlete has run 100 yards in under 8 seconds to a more specific past claim that a friend who claims he accomplished this in high school is probably not true.

The process of scientific investigation provides an interesting case of inductive thinking, as scientific experiments begin with empirical observations, with what you notice by means of your senses. Inductive reasoning in the sciences—both the natural sciences and the social sciences—is formalized in a set of processes known as the scientific method. The basis of the scientific method is the gathering, testing, and analysis of data by means of experiment. This experimental data serves as the set of specific observations, the set of instances and examples that form the evidence from which inferences are made, and hypotheses, principles, and theories derived.

Historical investigation follows an analogous process, mostly using primary and secondary source documents rather than experiments as evidence upon which to develop conclusions through reasoning inductively about particular instances and arriving at general principles. The particular details of history—historical facts, data, and other forms of information—provide the evidence for the development of inferences and theories of historical explanation.

Both scientific experimentation and historical analysis, however, may also begin with a theory or an idea—that is, with a generalization the investigator sets out to test, either by finding evidence that supports it or evidence that falsifies it. In such cases, the process of thought moves from a general idea or concept to the search for support in the form of specific types of evidence.

Thinking typically involves interplay between inductive and deductive reasoning, moving back and forth between them repeatedly. This process of alternation between the concrete and the abstract, the specific and the general—and the logical connections between them—informs sound thinking.

Sherlock Holmes as a Logical Thinker

Sherlock Holmes is the quintessential detective, a problem solver who uses logical reasoning and thoughtful reflection while analyzing carefully observed details to solve crimes. But just what thinking processes does Holmes use? What kind of mindset and what habits of mind does this epitome of sleuthing employ? Maria Konnikova (2013) in *Mastermind*, identifies four essential components: (1) careful observation; (2) patient inference; (3) a blend of inductive and deductive thinking; (4) a combination of intuition and rigorous logical thinking. For Holmes, everything begins with observation. He notices the way mud clings to someone's boots, the way an individual's fingertips are calloused, how a person's shirt cuffs are frayed.

Holmes decides which facts are incidental and which are vital. He focuses on significant details while ignoring irrelevant ones. (How he knows which are important and which not is largely dependent on experience and knowledge.) He eschews details that distract him from plausible explanations, shunning explanations that cannot be supported by factual evidence.

Holmes makes inferences based on his observations slowly and deliberately. He does not jump to quick conclusions, but rather considers multiple possibilities for the significance of any such detail. He puts the observed details into a context, a broader framework of thinking that enables him to formulate a series of potentially useful hypotheses about their significance.

Holmes's ability to do these things is attributable to his broad general knowledge and his deep knowledge of past crimes and cases. His ability to solve crimes is ultimately attributable to his balancing of probabilities, choosing the most likely in what he calls "the scientific use of the imagination." Yet here, too, his deep reservoir of experience figures.

Holmes's thinking oscillates between inductive and deductive reasoning. His observations and inferences exemplify his inductive approach. Once he formulates a hypothesis about the crime based on a series of observations and inferences, he shifts to a deductive mode of thinking. In reasoning deductively, Holmes works much like a scientist. He tests multiple hypotheses, considering each in turn. He looks for counter-evidence, for ways each hypothesis might be falsified. Eventually he arrives at a hypothesis he cannot disprove. At this point, then, he has his solution to the crime, an interpretation that fits all the relevant evidence.

It is important to stress the imaginative work that Holmes does in the process of solving crimes. In considering various possibilities, he imagines alternative explanations. He does this to avoid being driven to the most conventional or most likely explanation— the explanation that the local police inspector typically offers, and one that is always, in the Sherlock Holmes stories, incomplete, inadequate, and ultimately incorrect.

Holmes supports this thinking protocol with a natural skepticism and a habit of continuous questioning. He takes nothing at face value, for he knows that things are rarely what they first appear to be. In short, Holmes's thinking can be described as both mindful and purposeful. His thinking challenges conventional explanations; it avoids easy answers; it questions everything.

Sherlock Holmes has been described as "an artist of reason," which suggests the combination of art and science, intuition and logic his thinking embodies. Not to be overlooked is his passion for getting at the truth, which allies him with the Socratic philosophical tradition.

Sherlock Holmes is one of the first professionals to demonstrate the value of listening. His typical first act is to have the client tell his or her story—and in great detail. His sidekick and partner, Dr. Watson, usually expresses impatience with these detailed case histories. But, as Holmes insists, it is the small details, the little things that often lead to the solution of the crime.

An additional attribute of Holmes's method is one of focus and concentration. His concentration is intense, his focus absolute. He allows nothing to distract him from thinking about the problem that confronts him. He does this rigorously until he gets stuck, at which point he takes a break, shifts gears, clears his mind by doing something different; he goes for a walk, for example, or turns to one of his hobbies, which include playing the violin.

As David Baggett and Philip Tallon (2014) remind us in *The Philosophy of Sherlock Holmes*, the famous sleuth is a "consulting" detective. He comes in at the request of a client, either a private client or a public one, such as Scotland Yard, the official investigative arm of the London police. In each situation, Holmes follows his habitual practice of listening intently and questioning vigorously to acquire as much information and as many details as possible before conducting his physical investigation.

As a professional problem solver, Holmes is aware of the potential arrogance at his own superiority and modesty, and so he is careful not to claim too much for himself. Yet he is confident that with enough information, he will be successful and solve the crimes and mysteries presented to him.

This array of Holmesian qualities—from focus and concentration, through modesty and confidence, to the ability to listen carefully and draw information out of people—constitute a set of dispositions and habits that can be emulated and improved through practice. While you won't necessarily develop the superior degree of skill of a Sherlock Holmes, he nonetheless provides a high standard of investigative excellence and problem-solving competence.

Syllogisms, Enthymemes, and Argument

One important and familiar type of deductive reasoning is represented by the syllogism. A syllogism is a type of argument arranged in three parts: a major premise, a minor premise, and a conclusion. The classic example is this:

> *Major premise:* All men are mortal.
> *Minor premise:* Shakespeare is a man.
> *Conclusion:* Shakespeare is mortal.

As you can see, the major premise is the more general of the two. If you accept the major premise or statement as true, and the minor premise also as a true statement, then the conclusion follows logically, even necessarily, from it. There is no escaping it; if Shakespeare is a man, and all men (humans) are mortal, then he, too, will surely die, (which, of course, he did, having lived from 1564 to 1616).

Enthymemes

Most everyday arguments do not follow a strict and complete syllogistic pattern. A newspaper editorial that supports the closing of military bases, or a magazine column that argues for a student loan program run by the federal government would very likely be presented with its major premise implied rather than explicitly stated.

Syllogisms are often truncated in everyday arguments. You might hear someone argue, for example, that it's time for new technologies to be introduced to college instruction because they can save money and because today's students are technology savvy. This kind of everyday argument leaves out a major premise: that technology provides the best and most successful means of instruction as measured by student learning.

An argument in which the major premise, minor premise, or conclusion is not explicitly stated is called an enthymeme. Here is an example:

More than half of all varsity football players at State University do not receive a diploma after six years at the university. We have to do something to improve that figure, or we should eliminate the football program at State.

In syllogistic form, the argument looks like this:

Major premise: (*Unstated*) Students, including varsity football players, should earn a diploma within six years.
Minor premise: More than half of all varsity football players at State University do not receive their diplomas within six years.
Conclusion: Therefore, we have to improve that figure or eliminate the football program at State.

You might agree or disagree about the reliability of the enthymeme's unstated premise, which, in this case, is an assumption. But the argument is easier to evaluate with that premise explicitly stated. You should be alert for arguments containing unstated premises. Supplying unstated premises enables us to more easily assess their accuracy or reliability. An argument is only as strong as its premises. If an argument's premises are faulty, or if an argument includes unsupported assumptions, it can be easily refuted.

Argument and Authority

The persuasiveness of an argument depends on the validity of its structure and the truth of its premises. Yet another aspect of arguments is the extent to which the people who make them are credible and authoritative. Writers gain credibility with readers by demonstrating knowledge, providing clear and cogent reasoning, and being fair and reasonable.

An authority can lend credibility to an assertion or claim. Typical authorities are individuals and institutions with demonstrated knowledge, experience, rank, position, or accomplishments. Appeals to authority can be persuasive, but they are not always effective. In political advertising, for example, authorities often provide inadequate support for candidates.

In addition, any authority may be wrong in a particular instance. Authorities are fallible, and they often disagree. Equally reputable authorities can arrive at conflicting or incompatible conclusions about complex matters. In addition, authorities have their biases as

Table 4.3   Questions for analyzing authorities

---

1 What are the authority's credentials and qualifications?
2 Is the authority presenting evidence, information, or judgments within his or her area of expertise?
3 What kinds and amount of evidence does the authoritative expert provide to support a position or judgment being advanced.
4 How sound are the authority's arguments?

---

well as their expertise. Medical experts testifying to the safety of a new drug, for example, may be biased, especially if they have been paid by the pharmaceutical company that developed the drug.

Moreover, authorities may simply be wrong. Because arguments based on authority are inductive, they are, at best, highly likely. A doctor's recommendation of a particular medication is just that, even though the recommendation is based on previous research and experience. There is no guarantee, however, that it will be effective. Use the questions in Table 4.3 to evaluate the use of authorities.

Similar to authority is testimony—a statement made in support of a fact or a claim. Testimony can be offered by experts or by individuals with specialized knowledge, but it can also be provided by ordinary people. Law courts, for example, typically rely on the testimony of both experts and witnesses to ascertain the facts of a case.

Testimonials rely on non-logical attempts to influence decisions. Because athletes and celebrities who appear in advertisements typically receive large sums of money for their endorsements, their testimonials are typically viewed with skepticism. This does not mean, however, that the claims made in testimonials are necessarily false. In fact, testimonials are often valuable when used to support arguments—as long as the testimony is credible. To be credible, the person providing the testimony must be operating within his or her area of competence or expertise. The testimony must also be accurate, current, and representative.

Argument and Analogy

Analogical argument is a type of inductive reasoning. Thinking analogically, you reason that if two things are similar in some features, then it is possible, or even likely, that they will be similar in other ways. For example, those opposed to the war in Afghanistan saw similarities to the US war in Vietnam three decades earlier. Both wars were fought on foreign territory against enemies that knew their homeland terrain and fought in unconventional ways. On the basis of these known similarities, those against the war in Afghanistan argued that other similarities would emerge—as for example, that the war would be protracted, that it would be costly in money and in lives, that it would create anti-American feeling around the world, and that it might very well be unwinnable.

The further an analogy can be taken—that is, the more the two things being compared are truly alike—the better the analogy and the more persuasive the argument made with it. On the other hand, the quicker the analogy breaks down—the more readily it appears that major differences exist between the things compared—the weaker the argument. An analogical argument's persuasiveness depends not only on the number of similarities, but also on the strength of the similarities. The problem, however, is that what one person accepts as a strong similarity, another may see as weak and unconvincing.

Sometimes, writers argue by means of analogy, in which one state of affairs is compared with another, said to be like another. Analogies help readers understand what writers mean. They also help writers clarify their thinking. They provide alternative ways of seeing or saying things. However, you can take an analogy only so far before the similarities between the two things compared end and important differences emerge. A baseball double play, in some ways, is like a dance. In other ways it is not. A heart is like a pump, but only to a degree. Polar bears and hippos have some things in common, but they differ in other ways. If they have features common with other animals threatened with extinction, we might argue that the same could happen to them.

Consider the following argument by analogy made by George Orwell in his essay "Politics and the English Language."

It is clear that the decline of a language must ultimately have political and economic causes: it is not due simply to the bad influence of this or that individual writer. But an effect can become a cause, reinforcing the original cause and producing the same effect in an intensified form, and so on indefinitely. A man may take to drink because he feels himself to be a failure, and then fail all the more completely because he drinks. It is rather the same thing that is happening to the English language. It becomes ugly and inaccurate because our thoughts are foolish, but the slovenliness of our language makes it easier for us to have foolish thoughts. (George Orwell, "Politics and the English Language")

To what extent does this analogical argument meet the four criteria outlined above?

Commentary

In arguing that the English language is in decline, George Orwell suggests but does not identify a group of "political and economic causes." He proposes that an effect (the decline of English) can become a cause furthering that decline. He then introduces an analogy with drinking as a way of supporting his argument about effects becoming causes that further intensify the original problem. You need to be clear about the idea expressed in the analogy and second and about how well the analogy supports his claim.

Just what does his analogy say? It says, essentially, that drinking intensifies a person's decline so that the person, as a result, drinks even more—which leads to even greater failure. The analogy explains how the effect of a failure can become a cause of further failures. In applying his analogy about drinking as cause and effect, George Orwell argues that the English language has declined because some people are sloppy in their thinking and writing.

Argument and Causality

Causality refers to a relationship between or among events in which one event appears responsible for the occurrence of another. Smoking cigars causes cancer, for example. Taking aspirin reduces pain. Single-cause explanations of complex events, however, often oversimplify, and are almost always unsatisfactory. To reduce the causes of World War I to the assassination of Archduke Ferdinand of Austria, and to explain the poor record of a professional football team by isolating its quarterback's weak performance are oversimplifications. So, too, is explaining the cause of the depressed job market as a result of insufficient government spending. Other contributing factors include tight credit, business failures, bank and trading scandals, the housing bubble, an escalating national debt, a sliding trade deficit, an increase in consumer debt—and more.

Just as there can be multiple conditions for an event to occur, so too, in other words, can there be multiple causes for something to happen. Those multiple causes can overlap in what we call a "causal chain," in which A causes event B, which causes outcome C, which causes D, and so on. You may have seen one or more of a set of comical television commercials for satellite TV in which a series of preposterous events affect a viewer who subscribes to cable TV. The sequence of interlinked negative outcomes causes him to cancel his cable subscription and subscribe instead to satellite television.

Causal claims can be made as both particular statements and as generalizations. Human Immunodeficiency Virus (HIV) causes Acquired Immunodeficiency Deficiency Syndrome (AIDS) is a particular causal claim. A general claim would be that possessing the genome of a dog causes the puppy, "Belle," to grow up as a dog. It is important to note that in the case of HIV causing AIDS, HIV functions as a necessary cause. That is, HIV is required for AIDS to develop. Without HIV present, AIDS will not develop. But HIV is not sufficient by itself to cause AIDS; other factors are also involved.

In the example of a dog genome causing the development of the puppy into an adult dog, we have both a **necessary condition** and a **sufficient condition**. That is, the genome of a dog is all that is needed to achieve the result of an adult dog. It is necessary because without the genome of a dog, a dog will not develop. And it is sufficient because nothing else except the genome of a dog is required. A necessary condition is *required* for something to occur. A sufficient condition is *enough* for something to occur.

In logical terms, a cause C of an effect E is sufficient "if and only if" C always produces E. A cause is necessary "if and only if" the effect E (e.g. AIDS) cannot occur in the absence of the cause C (e.g. HIV). And a cause is both necessary and sufficient "if and only if" C (a dog genome) is the only cause of E (an adult dog).

The criteria for what is considered adequate evidence for causal explanations are not easy to apply. Causality does not usually involve ironclad proof, but rather likelihood or possibility, instead. That's what makes causal arguments inductive rather than deductive.

Causality is rarely easy to establish. Since complex events have multiple causes, identifying those causes and deciding which are most influential often leads to disagreement. Scientists disagree, for example, about the causes of dinosaur extinction. Educators disagree about the causes for the decline in SAT scores. Economists disagree about the causes of slow job growth and what to do about it.

One of the reasons for the difficulty in assigning clear causes to an event, action, or outcome is that complex systems are affected by a web of causation, a network or nexus of causes, which do not operate in a single linear direction. Systems as diverse yet complex as weather patterns and financial markets involve such causal webs. The evolution of life on earth, the continuing evolution of species, including their extinction, involve multiple networks of causes. One of the dangers of causal explanations is that those explanations can be made to appear certain and clear, definite and definitive, when that is anything but the case.

Consider, for example what caused the Roman Empire to fall. In his book *Collapse*, Jared Diamond (2011) summarizes two competing explanations offered by historians. The first chain of causes attributes Rome's fall to the barbarian invasions, with the empire's demise occurring around 476 CE. Yet the Romans had held off barbarian invaders for more than a thousand years. What changed such that the barbarians finally overcame the Romans? Did the barbarians evolve a greatly enlarged force? Did they become better organized, acquire more sophisticated and powerful weapons, breed faster and better horses and more of them? Perhaps they benefited from climate change in their central Asian environment that led them to become physically stronger and more powerful. Perhaps they had better leaders in the fifth century CE than previously.

That's one set of related possibilities, all of which put the responsibility for Rome's fall on the barbarians. Another set of possible causal explanations turns on Rome as being the cause of its own destruction. Destruction from within, due perhaps to a society gone soft, an empire poisoned by corruption, given over to idleness, lacking in vigor, valor, and virtue. Perhaps Rome was weakened less by a kind of moral malaise than by some combination of political, economic, and environmental problems. Perhaps its military leaders at the time of the successful barbarian invasion were not as capable as they had been in the past. In this causal analysis, the barbarians provided the finishing touches on what was already a declining empire, one ready and ripe for collapse.

The flip side of causal explanation emphasizes effects or consequences. For example, although today considerable emphasis is placed on the harmful effects smoking has on a person's health, in the seventeenth century, tobacco use highlighted very different effects. These included the use of tobacco by Native Americans to induce trances that enabled shamans to mediate between the natural and supernatural worlds. In *Vermeer's Hat*, Timothy Brook (2008) explains how the burning of tobacco was thought to attract the attention of spirits and to enable the shamans to peer into the spirit world and see the future. In addition, tobacco was used for its medicinal properties. Smoking was used as a treatment for toothache, hunger, asthma, and snakebite. Other non-medicinal effects included its use as a means of social glue, a medium for enhancing sociability.

To take another historical example, consider the many and varied consequences that resulted from World War I, or The Great War, as it was first called. The war shaped the modern world, destroying kings, kaisers, czars and sultans, as Steven Erlanger (2014) notes in a *New York Times* article, "The GREAT WAR: A Conflict That Shaped the Modern World." The war ended empires; it introduced new forms of devastating weaponry, including chemical weapons; it brought millions of women into the workforce across Europe and the United States, helping prepare the way for women's suffrage. It made a number of countries independent, including Poland, Ukraine, Latvia, Lithuania, and Estonia; and it created a number of Middle East nations, including Iraq. In addition, it introduced postwar psychological concepts and afflictions, such as shellshock and post-traumatic stress. And beyond this array of consequences, the war provided the opportunity for the United States to begin its ascent to global power.

A related concept is the law of unintended consequences, which operates in complex systems. One example involves the rats that bore fleas that conveyed plague to inhabitants of Sydney, Australia, in 1900. To curtail the spread of disease, authorities offered people a bounty to encourage the killing of rats. They did that. But they also bred rats to be killed—an unintended consequence that had, of course, no effect on reducing the incidence of the disease. Similarly, again in Australia, rabbits were released into the wild where they proliferated uncontrollably, causing significant ecological destruction. To control the rabbits, authorities built a long fence, which had the positive unintended consequence of guiding three young girls home in the 1930s, the story of which was told in the 2002 film *Rabbit-Proof Fence*.

Causality, Coincidence, and Correlation

Causality is closely linked with two related concepts, *coincidence* and *correlation*. Let's distinguish among these terms by means of examples. In attending a baseball game, you may wear your "lucky hat," perhaps with the brim facing backwards or sideways. If your favorite team, wins the game each time you do this, you may think that there is a causal relationship—that is, that wearing your lucky cap that way is related to your team's winning. This is nonsense, of course. There is no logical relationship—no causal relationship between those two events. It is mere coincidence that your team won its games on your hat-wearing days. Those two facts—your wearing of the cap and your team winning games—simply occur together; they are co-incident(al). Coincidence is a particular type of correlation.

A correlation occurs when there is no actual cause-and-effect relationship, but rather a relationship between events that is more tenuous or limited. For example, there is a high correlation between being tall and being a professional basketball player. It's not that every pro basketball player is tall, nor is every tall person a candidate for the National Basketball Association. Rather, there is an exceptionally high percentage of tall basketball players in the professional ranks, making the correlation between height and being a pro in the NBA a significant one. A similar kind of high correlation obtains between weight and being a professional football player, especially when restricting that correlation to the weight of linemen who play in the National Football League.

In *The Why Axis*, Uri Gneezy and John A. List (2013) offer the following illustration of how correlations can confuse our understanding of causality. During a consulting project for a business, they were shown a sales chart that illustrated a very strong link between the number of advertisements a company ran and the dollar volume generated. The positive relationship between ads and sales—1,000 ads generated $35 million while 100 ads generated $20 million—suggested that the company should run more ads (since their cost was far below the $15 million the ads generated).

The authors, however, produced a similar chart—one that showed a strong link between ice cream sales and drownings. As more ice cream cones are consumed, the graph for drownings goes up sharply. What each of their charts demonstrates is a correlation not a causal relationship. Ice cream cone sales correlate with drownings, and increased advertising correlates with increased revenue. But ice cream cone sales do not "cause" drownings; nor do advertisements "cause" the increased revenue. In both cases, there is a hidden variable; that is, something else is involved that influences the increase in drownings and the rise of revenues. A moment's reflection allows for the realization that ice cream cone sales increase in the summer months, when people swim more. And more people swimming results in more people drowning. Something similar affects the connection between increased advertising and higher revenues. The company placed more ads in the months of November and December, the holiday shopping season during which businesses typically generate the lion's share of their annual revenue. The causal relationship between ads and sales was an illusion, as was the apparent causal relationship between ice cream cone sales and drownings.

Additional challenges in establishing causation include what has been called "reverse causality" and "omitted variable bias." In *Naked Statistics*, Charles Wheelan (2013) explains that just because a statistical association exists between two events or variables, (let's designate them A and B), that does not necessarily mean that A causes B. It's possible that the reverse is true—that B is causing A. States that spend more money on K-12 education experience greater economic growth than states that spend less money on this educational sector. What's not certain is whether investing in K-12 education in some way causes economic growth; or, whether states that have more money to invest because their economies are in better shape cause the investment in education. Another possibility is that there could be a reciprocal causal effect, with increased spending on education boosting economic growth (or at least contributing to that growth), with that economic growth then providing additional dollars that can be invested in higher levels of educational investment.

"Omitted variable bias" is evident in headlines such as "Golfers More Likely to Develop Cancer and Arthritis," which seems counterintuitive since exercise and socialization generally improve people's health. What's missing in this instance is the fact that golf is typically played as people get older; those who play golf increase their golfing outings when they retire and have more time to play. So a headline that appears to suggest that playing golf causes physical deterioration and even a deadly disease, omits the variable of age. If you control for the variable of age and say "among people near the same age," you will very likely say something very different—perhaps that golfers may enjoy slightly better health, as measured by increased longevity, greater physical abilities, and a slightly lower incidence of serious illness.

Further Causal Consequences

In *How We Got to Now*, Steven Johnson (2014) describes how biological and technological developments initiate a complex chain of consequences far beyond what might have been imagined based on the original event or breakthrough. One biological example Johnson offers is the coevolving symbiosis between flowering plants and insects that favored the continued development of both. The plant/insect symbiosis provided an opportunity for the evolution of hummingbirds, which extract the nectar from plants through an extraordinary form of aerodynamics that allow the jeweled miniature flyers to hover over flowers in a distinctive manner. As Johnson puts it: "the sexual reproduction strategies of plants end up shaping the design of a hummingbird's wings."

In the technological realm, his example is about an often overlooked consequence of the invention of the printing press: the surge in demand for spectacles. The reason? That Europeans realized once books were being printed that they were farsighted and thus needed spectacles, which began to be produced in increasing numbers. The demand for spectacles stimulated experiments with lenses, which led soon after to the invention of both the microscope and the telescope. Each of these inventions had far-reaching implications, the microscope for the discovery of cells, which began a cascading set of further discoveries of ever smaller biological organisms, the telescope for the discovery of astronomical facts that turned religious belief inside out once it was discovered that the earth was not the center of the universe.

Johnson's larger point about many technological inventions is that they lead to discoveries and to changes far removed from their origin. One final example he provides near the end of his book is how the invention of refrigeration, first through blocks of ice and later through air-conditioning has changed the demographics of cities. Before the twentieth century the world's largest cities all lay in the temperate zone; New York, London, Paris, Tokyo. In the twenty-first century, the largest megacities are in zones with much higher and hotter temperatures—Bangkok, Manila, Karachi, Lagos, Dubai, Rio de Janeiro.

Applications

4-1. Analyze the following arguments by identifying the conclusion, evidence, and assumptions(s).
1. Since Michael earned a high score on his college entrance exam, he will certainly be successful in his academic work in college.
2. South Korea is the most technologically advanced country in the world. More South Koreans own computers and smartphones than any other country in the world.
3. I shop at ShopRite rather than A&P because prices are 5% lower there.
4. We should reduce our prison population because imprisoning people doesn't solve the problem of crime.
5. We should celebrate art that shocks since it brings change and new approaches.

4-2. Identify possible outcomes, good and bad, of the following truncated arguments.
1. Banning fraternities and sororities from college campuses because they are exclusionary.
2. Moving to a state with a low or nonexistent state income tax to keep a larger portion of earned income.

3. Delaying marriage and a family until to one's later thirties or even forties because of lucrative and highly competitive employment.

4. Borrowing heavily for a new social media business venture to capitalize on the heightened interest in and use of social media.

5. Taking a year off from work to travel or earn a graduate degree.

4-3. Identify each of the following as a claim of fact, a claim of value, or a claim of policy. Explain what kinds of evidence are necessary to support or refute each claim. What assumptions and implications would you associate with each claim? What warrants?

1. The popularity of reality television has decreased the willingness of media executives to develop, fund, and support more imaginative television shows.

2. Rather than sending men and women into outer space, we should be using those resources to fix the problems with public schools.

3. Global warming is a misnomer; what is happening is less a result of human energy use and more a simple experience of long-term climatic change.

4. Social harmony is more important than personal freedom.

5. It is necessary that people be allowed to curse and use foul language on occasion; such uses of language lets off steam that might otherwise result in violence.

4-4. On a topic of your choice, create one example each of a claim of fact, a claim of value, and a claim of policy. Then explain how you would provide evidence in the support of each of those claims.

4-5. Read the following excerpt from Arthur Conan Doyle's *The Sign of Four*. The description is provided by Dr. Watson, Holmes' friend and sidekick. As you read, consider a few different ways the details might be put together in a set of inferences about Miss Morstan.

Miss Morstan entered the room with a firm step and an outward composure of manner. She was a blonde young lady, small, dainty, well gloved, and dressed in the most perfect taste. There was, however, a plainness and simplicity about her costume which bore with it a suggestion of limited means. The dress was a somber grayish beige, untrimmed and unbraided, and she wore a small turban of the same dull hue, relieved only by a suspicion of white feather in the side. Her face had neither regularity of feature nor beauty of complexion, but her expression was sweet and amiable, and her large blue eyes were singularly spiritual and sympathetic. In an experience of women which extends over many nations and three separate continents, I have never looked upon a face which gave a clearer promise of a refined and sensitive nature. I could not but observe that as she took the seat which Sherlock Holmes placed for her, her lip trembled, her hand quivered, and she showed every sign of intense inward agitation.

4-6. Read each of the following scenarios and provide two or three prospective solutions to the problem or challenge each scenario presents.

1. "This should prove a gentle warm-up. There is something you own that is yours, and always has been. Despite this, all your friends use it, whilst you yourself rarely get to make use of it at all. What am I talking about?"

2. "A couple were found dead in a quiet valley in the Highlands," Holmes said to me one morning, apropos of nothing. "They were murdered," I assume?" It was rather rare for Holmes to take an interest in cases where foul play was not involved.

   "It seems not," was his surprising reply. "They were found lying next to each other, hand in hand, in a pleasant field carpeted with new spring flowers. There was no sign of whatever it was that killed them. They were less than a mile to the nearest village. There was no evidence of any sort of murderous assault, no broken limbs, nor any of the tell-tale signs that suicide might have left. Lightning would have left char marks, rocks would have caused clearly visible wounds, and the physicians found no evidence of poisons or disease. They did not appear to have been robbed, either. I have an idea, of course. But what do you make of it?"

4-7. Construct a valid syllogism for each of the following premises.

1. Cigarette smoke is dangerous to the health of nonsmokers who may breathe it.
2. Walking vigorously for thirty minutes a day provides excellent cardiovascular exercise.
3. Macy's reported substantial losses in revenue for the last two years.
4. Speaking a foreign language can enhance one's pleasure when traveling.
5. Interest rates have declined consistently in the past two years.
6. Spanish banks are in crisis.
7. Newspapers and magazines are scaling back print publication and moving to the Internet.
8. The New York Mets have had late season collapses three times in the past five years.
9. When in Rome, do as the Romans do.
10. Laughter is the best medicine.

4-8. Analyze the following arguments. When necessary, supply the missing premises.

1. To improve the economy, the president and Congress should create public works projects and increase the number of available jobs.
2. I'm doing twice as much work today as I did a year ago. I should be paid double what I earned last year.
3. People should be penalized by tax or other means for not looking after their own health.
4. Harriet is a superb student. She's been on the Dean's List three straight terms.
5. Guns should be outlawed for civilians. The world has changed radically since the framers of the Bill of Rights included the right to bear arms.
6. Josh attends the local community college, so he probably didn't get in anywhere else.
7. Pitching horseshoes should be an Olympic sport since it involves strength, skill, and concentration.
8. Vegetarians don't eat pork; Gandhi didn't eat pork; therefore, Gandhi was a vegetarian.

4-9. Find an advertisement that uses an authority to advance its claims. Evaluate the claims of the ad and consider the extent to which the authority enhances the ad's persuasiveness.

Find another advertisement that uses one or more ordinary people to provide a testimonial. Evaluate the claims of the ad and consider the extent to which the testimonial enhances the ad's effectiveness.

4-10. To what extent is George Orwell's analogy a persuasive part of his overall argument? Does the fact that an effect can become a cause, as the analogy demonstrates, apply to the decline of the English language in the way he suggests? How strong is his analogy? How relevant is it to his claim about the decline of English? Does it help convince us that a decline was occurring among some users of English? Or does it, instead, simply clarify his idea, enabling us to better understand his claim?

4-11. Explain how the analogy in the following passages work— either to clarify an explanation or to develop an argument, or both.

A. "History is to the nation rather as memory is to the individual. As an individual deprived of memory becomes disoriented and lost, not knowing where he has been or where he is going, so a nation denied a conception of its past will be disabled in dealing with its present and its future." (Arthur Schlesinger, Jr., *The Disuniting of America*)

B. "By far the most exciting of our future technologies are those that enter into a symbiotic relationship with us: machine + person. Is the car + driver a symbiosis of human and machine in much the same way as the horse + rider might be? After all, the car + driver splits the processing levels, with the car taking over the visceral level and the driver the reflective level, both sharing the behavior level in analogous fashion to the horse + rider. Just as the horse is intelligent enough to take care of the visceral aspects of riding (avoiding dangerous terrain, adjusting its pace to the quality of the terrain, avoiding obstacles), so too is the modern automobile able to sense danger, controlling the car's stability, braking, and speed. Similarly, horses learn behaviorally complex routines for navigating difficult terrain or jumping obstacles, for changing canter when required and maintaining distance and coordination with other horses or people. So, too, does the modern car behaviorally modify its speed, keep to its own lane, brake when it senses

danger, and control other aspects of the driving experience." (Donald Norman, *The Design of Future Things*)

4-12. Explain the kind of causal reasoning at play in each of the
following examples. Decide if the reasoning is valid or not.

1. Professional cyclists typically have between 5 and 10%
   body fat. If you decrease your body fat percentage to that
   low level, you could become a world-class cyclist.

2. Average SAT scores at highly competitive universities
   have consistently risen over the past decade. This suggests that high school students taking the SATs have
   been improving their math, reading, and writing skills.

3. This newspaper headline has been a familiar one: "Obesity Linked with Depression." In which direction would
   you draw the arrow between obesity and depression?
   Why? Is the linkage a correlation or a true cause and
   effect relationship?

4. Student cheating on tests has been uncovered in Atlanta,
   Washington, DC, New York, and Boston. This is
   because moral standards have eroded in the past decade.

5. SAT scores are positively correlated with how many cars
   a family owns. Does the number of cars a family possesses "cause" or contribute to higher SAT scores of children in those families?

4-13. Identify some possible intended *and* unintended consequences of the following interventions.

1. Banning alcoholic beverages from professional sports
   events.

2. Banning smoking from bars and restaurants.

3. Banning the sale of kidneys.

4. Doubling the taxes on cigarettes and other tobacco
   products.

5. Introducing bicycles, bike racks, bike lanes, and a system
   for renting bicycles in all major American cities.

4-14. Identify the causes and effects of two of the following:

1. The American Civil War

2. The United States involvement in Afghanistan

3. The collapse of the Berlin Wall

4. The rise in salaries of professional athletes

5. The demise of the independent bookstore

6. The popularity of Facebook

7. The success of Starbucks
8. The spread of wildfires
9. The success of Twitter
10. The popularity of reality television shows

4-15. What does Steven Johnson's explanation about the range and breadth of the consequences of evolutionary and technological changes suggest?

References

Baggett, David and Philip Tallon, eds. 2013. *The Philosophy of Sherlock Holmes*. Lexington: University of Kentucky Press.

Baggini, Julian and Peter S. Fosl. 2010. *The Philosopher's Toolkit*. Hoboken: Wiley-Blackwell.

Brook, Timothy. 2008. *Vermeer's Hat*. London: Bloomsbury.

Diamond, Jared. 2011. *Collapse*. New York: Penguin.

Erlanger, Steven. 2014. "THE GREAT WAR: A Conflict that Shaped the Modern World." *The New York Times*.

Gneezy, Uri and John A. List. 2013. *The Why Axis*. New York: Public Affairs.

Johnson, Steven. 2014. *How We Got to Now*. New York: Riverhead.

Konnikova, Maria. 2013. *Mastermind: How to Think Like Sherlock Holmes*. New York: Viking.

Lunsford, Andrea, John Ruszkiewicz, and Keith Walter. 2009. *Everything's an Argument*. Boston: Bedford/St. Martins.

Missimer, Connie. 2008. *Good Arguments*, 4th edn. Upper Saddle River: Prentice Hall.

Toulmin, Stephen. 1969. *The Uses of Argument*. Cambridge: Cambridge University Press.

Wheelan, Charles. 2013. *Naked Statistics*. New York: Norton.

Interchapter 4

Blending Art and Science

In his *Creating Innovators*, Tony Wagner (2012) posits a set of six criteria essential for developing innovative thinkers. He highlights the significance of these criteria by contrasting them with six opposite characteristics. The first term of each pair fosters innovation; the second term inhibits it.

1. Collaboration vs. Individual Achievement
2. Multidisciplinary Learning vs. Specialization
3. Trial and Error vs. Risk Avoidance
4. Creating vs. Consuming
5. Intrinsic Motivation vs. Extrinsic Motivation
6. STEM subjects (Science, Technology, Engineering, Math) vs. Liberal Arts

One important qualification must be made regarding the last item. Wagner values *both* science-related thinking and subjects *and* humanities subjects and thinking. He argues that innovation occurs when individuals combine approaches and ways of thinking across the sciences/humanities divide.

Consider the science of engineering, for which you need to have a strong foundation in mathematics and physics. Engineers can't

Critical and Creative Thinking: A Brief Guide for Teachers, First Edition. Robert DiYanni.
© 2016 John Wiley & Sons, Inc. Published 2016 by John Wiley & Sons, Inc.

function without a deep knowledge of these subjects. But they also need to know and appreciate something about arts and psychology. The buildings and bridges they construct will be more meaningful and more valuable if they are beautiful as well as functional. The same might be said for architects, for whom a similar kind of combination of different kinds of knowledge is also needed—though architects would need less science and math than engineers, and engineers less of arts and psychology.

There is also a way of seeing the arts and human behavior from a scientific perspective and the sciences from an aesthetic one. We find beauty in mathematics and in scientific ideas, just as we see beauty in paintings and sculptures, poems and plays and stories. The operative connecting word is "and." Science *and* Arts. Science *and* Humanities.

There is some debate about whether Leonardo da Vinci was primarily an artist or a scientist. As one of his biographers, Sherwin Nuland (2005), has noted, Leonardo saw "science from the viewpoint of art and he saw art from the viewpoint of science." What matters more, however, is how Leonardo's scientific studies enriched his art and how his works of art fueled his fascination with nature.

British art historian Sir Kenneth Clark (1989) suggests that not only did Leonardo draw so well because he knew about things, but he also "knew about things because he drew so well." Drawing things helped Leonardo see them better; drawing increased his knowledge and sharpened his perceptual powers. Leonardo was both a scientist who studied art and an artist who studied science.

For Leonardo, art and science were inseparable, indivisible. He admonishes us with this advice: "study the art of science and the science of art." Moreover, Leonardo's emphasis on close observation of the natural world in all its aspects bears out the later saying of William Blake: "For Art and Science cannot exist but in minutely organized [and observed] Particulars."

You can use deliberate strategies to develop a more whole-minded approach to thinking that includes analysis and synthesis, science and art, logic and imagination. Don't stay on one side of the science/art divide.

Applications

1. Describe a situation that you experienced directly yourself or one that you saw, heard, or read about that involved both science and art, a STEM subject approach *and* an arts or humanities aspect.
2. Select a product or device you use regularly that was created with knowledge of both arts and sciences. What appeals to you about this product or device? To what extent does its appeal derive from its beauty—from aesthetic pleasure—as well as its functionality?

References

Clark, Sir Kenneth. 1989. *Leonardo da Vinci*. New York: Penguin.
Nuland, Sherman. 2005. *Leonardo da Vinci*. New York: Penguin.
Wagner, Tony. 2012. *Creating Innovators*. New York: Scribner.

5

Creative Thinking Strategies and Applications

Figure 5.1 Vision, Imagination, Creativity, Innovation. ©
Madartists/Dreamstime

The essential part of creativity is not being afraid to fail.
—Edwin H. Land

Creativity requires the courage to let go of certainties.
—Erich Fromm

Creativity is the ability to introduce order into the randomness of nature.
—Eric Hoffer

Imagination First

Imagination is something we are born with. It's an unalienable right each of us possesses. And yet it's a capacity that we let wither, that we too often allow to languish. Why? The answer, in part, is that as we go through school and "grow up," we receive messages that imagination is not so important, that cultivating imagination needs to give way to developing a hard-nosed, realistic under-standing of the world. As Ursula K. LeGuin (2014) has noted, "many Americans have been taught to repress their imagination, to reject it as something childish." Imagination becomes replaced with analysis. The playful and imaginative frame of mind gives way to the factual and the serious. This is a grave mistake, one that lim-its the potential transfiguring power that imagination has on our experience.

In *A New Culture of Learning: Cultivating the Imagination for a World of Constant Change*, Douglas Thomas and John Seely Brown (2011) suggest that our ability to participate successfully in the world is governed by the play of imagination. They claim that play and imagination are critical for successful living in a world of accel-erating change. Being "open to the imagination" and allowing for places where the imagination can be at play are essential conditions for fully developing our mental potential.

Why imagination?

Why is it important to develop our imaginative capacities? Without imagination, creative thinking and creative discovery are impeded. That's the practical answer. But there is another explanation: imagination is a splendid and amazing human capacity. Like our ability to analyze and reason, our capacity to imagine is a big part of what makes us human. Imagining is also one of life's pleasures; it's a joy to imagine "alternative realities," to conjure up prospective possibilities, to conceive of images, patterns, and ideas. Imagina-tion is also necessary to perceive, understand, and appreciate the creations, ideas, and productions of others.

Find on the Internet the following painting, *Les Valeurs Person-nelles (Personal Values)*, by René Magritte. Consider how it reveals an imaginative cast of mind.

What has the artist done to transform everyday reality? What surprises and shocks does the work provoke? What might be the purpose of such uses of the imagination? These are the kinds of questions we can ask ourselves when we engage with provocative works of the imagination, like this Magritte painting.

Magritte himself has noted that through a sense of "dis"-proportion, he establishes a "sense of disorientation and incongruity." By inverting inside and outside, Magritte creates a "paradoxical world that defies common sense." He wrote: "I describe objects and the mutual relationships of objects in such a way that more of our habitual concepts or feelings are linked with these."

Imagination, Creativity, and Innovation

The twentieth-century American philosopher John Dewey described imagination as being able "to look at things as if they could be otherwise." Another way of saying this is "to conceive of what is not," in the words of Eric Liu and Scott Noppe-Brandon, authors of *Imagination First*! These writers go further by distinguishing among imagination, creativity, and innovation, terms often used interchangeably, even synonymously. They suggest, instead, that we think of creativity as applied imagination, the doing or making of something, sparked by an initial imaginative conception. We can diagram the relationship among these terms and concepts as shown in Table 5.1.

Here are some examples: A writer imagines a world where a human being can become a man during one part of the year and a woman in another. The writer creates this world in an innovative book that describes an alternate universe something like our own, yet distinctively different. The book's people are somewhat like us, but with this unusual gender-switching difference, including the

Table 5.1 From imagination to innovation

Imagination	→	Creativity	→	Innovation
		(Applied imagination)		(New creation)

stunning possibility of being physically both father and mother to a child. This imaginative work is Ursula Le Guin's award-winning 1969 science fiction novel, *The Left Hand of Darkness*.

Or take a more recent example: the film *Avatar*, directed by James Cameron, who also directed *Titanic*. Before Cameron could develop the innovations for either of these amazing films, he had to imagine what the very different worlds portrayed might be like. These acts of imagining led him to explore a series of creative possibilities. In turning his imaginings into creative realities, Cameron actualized imaginative potential, and he collaborated with others to develop innovative techniques to bring his conceptions to life on the screen. (As this book goes to press, James Cameron is preparing a series of sequels to *Avatar*, to be released one per year from 2015 to 2017.)

The Limits of Imagination

In an essay, "Imagination: Powers & Perils," in the journal *Raritan*, Mark Edmundson (2012) explores the virtues and dangers of imagination. He identifies a number of ways in which imagination can run amok—through excessive worry and fear, through fantasies that lack all connection with plausibility, and through jealousy and ambition that can result in destructive acts.

Remedies for the abuses of imagination can be found in psychological counseling, in friendship, and in literature, each of which provides a potential antidote. Counselors and friends can ground and center us, redirect our imagination in more useful and productive directions. Great novels such as George Eliot's *Middlemarch* or Charles Dickens' *Bleak House* can provide alternative visions of the world we can share imaginatively.

Yet even with the dangers of letting loose the imagination, stifling the imagination can be much worse. A dead imagination is far worse than an overactive imagination. Abuses of imagination can be checked with judgment, with questioning, with cautions, with course corrections. In these and in most cases imaginative prowess requires the pushback of critical judgment. Authentic imagination balances and blends vision with judgment. We need to discipline our imagination to use it effectively.

As Nicholas Alchin and Carolyn P. Henly (2014) point out in their *Theory of Knowledge*, we need to use our imagination across academic disciplines—in reading literature, making and appreciating art, understanding history, conducting scientific experiments, and more. Any time we hypothesize, we imagine. Any time we attempt to discern and understand the past, we use our imagination. Whenever we conjure possibilities, we are imagining future outcomes.

We use imagination to envision images of past experiences and to create mental pictures of future events—how a sporting event or a social experience might turn out, for example, or how a job interview or midterm exam might go. This use of the imagination to entertain possible outcomes or consequences, to consider possibilities, Nicholas Alchin and Carolyn Henly call "cognitive imagination" to distinguish it from "sensory imagination," which refers to forming mental images. It is cognitive imagination that enables us to solve problems through imaginative alternative solutions. It is cognitive imagination that we use over and over in the process of learning in school and out, and in negotiating our way through the challenges with which life confronts us.

Capacities for Imaginative Thinking

What are the elements and aspects, the components and characteristics of imaginative thinking? What can we do to develop our capacity for imagination, for strengthening this creative mental muscle? Lincoln Center Education highlights the following capacities for imaginative thinking and learning:

- **Noticing deeply**: perceiving layers of detail through patient observation
- **Questioning**: asking the many kinds of thoughtful questions, including "Why," and "Why not"; "How," and "What if?"
- **Embodying**: experiencing things through our senses and emotions, through physical and psychological engagement
- **Identifying patterns**: identifying relationships among details that we notice; linking them together and grouping them into patterns

- **Making connections**: linking the patterns you notice with prior knowledge and experience
- **Exhibiting empathy**: understanding, appreciating, and respecting the experience and perspectives of others
- **Creating meaning**: developing viable interpretations based on our observations, patterns, connections, questions, and expressing this meaning in our own individual spoken and/or written voice
- **Reflecting and assessing**: looking back on our actions, learning, and thinking to identify additional challenges and questions
- **Taking action**: acting on what we have learned and interpreted; doing something to further our thinking and learning
- **Living with ambiguity**: accepting uncertainty, complexity, and the volatility of experience both literal and virtual

These Lincoln Center Education capacities for imaginative thinking and learning were originally designed for education in the arts, but they are clearly relevant for all aspects of education—and for thinking and learning beyond the classroom, in every aspect of our lives. Developing these capacities so they become habits of mind can deepen our understanding, strengthen our thinking, and enrich our experience.

Let's briefly consider just the first one, noticing deeply, and how it can lead to insights and innovations. In their book *The Innovator's DNA*, Jeff Dyer, Hal Gregersen, and Clayton M. Christensen (2011) tell the story of Ratan Tata, chairman of India's Tata group of businesses, who one day noticed something he had seen before but which had never really registered to any effect. What he noticed was a family of four riding a scooter through the rain in an Indian village. He asked himself why that family couldn't afford a small cheaply made car in which they could ride more comfortably without getting soaked. He knew that there was a large market for scooters in rural Indian villages. He wondered how he might make a car cheaply enough that scooter buyers would be able and willing to buy his cars. After experimenting with scooter parts for a while he built a prototype, which failed to capture people's imagination. After additional prototyping and investigating materials and production costs, he developed the Tata Nano, a small car that sold for $2,200.

Table 5.2 Capacities for imaginative thinking and learning

Noticing deeply	Making connections	Creating meaning
Questioning	Exhibiting empathy	Taking action
Embodying knowledge	Reflecting and assessing	Living with ambiguity
Identifying patterns		

Tata and his team discovered that scooters were not sold in special shops, but were brought, instead, on a truck in the village market and lined up at a stall in the way other goods were displayed and sold. Tata decided he would sell his cars the same way.

After asking many questions and the essential question, "what will it take for rural villagers to be able to drive off a new Tata Nano from their village marketplace," he realized that people couldn't afford to buy his cars without obtaining credit. So he arranged for credit on the spot. He learned further that they would need insurance, which he also decided to provide. And they would need a driver's license and a few lessons in how to drive a car. These services, too, Tata offered, as part of a complete suite of products and services at the village market. It all began with the act of noticing (see Table 5.2).

Why Ideas Are Important

People in many kinds of work are responsible for generating, developing, and presenting ideas. They might be charged with writing advertising copy or commercials. Perhaps they run companies or departments within companies. They might be engineers or account executives; perhaps one of them is a fifth-grade teacher needing to plan a grade-wide project; perhaps another is a volunteer for the annual church carnival, a hospital worker who sees how to improve an everyday process, a mother planning a baby shower for her daughter or a birthday party for her granddaughter, or a school administrator organizing a global conversation on innovation in developing countries. Like these people, the rest of us need to know how to get ideas, as well. Why, you might ask?

One answer is that ideas drive progress and innovation. Without ideas there is no movement; without movement, there is no progress. Finding ideas is critical to our success, whatever work we do, whatever our walk in life.

Ideas are also important because we are increasingly being inundated with an overflow of information. That information needs to be sifted and filtered, combined and synthesized to form ideas that can help solve problems and improve processes and products, ideas that can inspire as well as enrich, enlighten as well as entertain.

Ideas drive creativity and innovation. Learning to get ideas is at the heart of creative thinking. Acquiring ideas, then, is a priority. Figuring out some ways to do that is our next goal.

How to Get Ideas

So now that we have a sense of what ideas are and why they're important, how do we go about getting them? We have already explored a number of strategies and tried various tools for generating ideas in earlier chapters. Here, we will introduce some strategies developed by Jack Foster, who enjoyed a 35-year career as an advertising writer and director in Los Angeles.

Foster presents a process for getting an idea that includes five steps:

1. Define the problem.
2. Gather information.
3. Search for the idea.
4. Forget about it.
5. Enact the idea.

We might notice that the idea should appear somewhere between steps 4 and 5—so we'll add step $(4\frac{1}{2})$–Collect the idea as it "comes to you." We might notice, too, that Foster requires that the idea be used or applied. This echoes Eric Liu and Scott Noppe-Brandon, who emphasize "innovation," the application of creativity as stimulated by imagination.

What is more important, perhaps, about Foster's thinking about creativity is that we can't use his approach—or any approach to gathering or generating ideas—unless we prepare ourselves for ideas. The Lincoln Center strategies for imaginative help us do just that. So too do the ten strategies Foster presents in *How to Get Ideas*:

1. Have fun.
2. Be more like a child.
3. Become idea-prone.
4. Visualize success.
5. Rejoice in failure.
6. Get more inputs.
7. Screw up your courage.
8. Team up with energy.
9. Rethink your thinking.
10. Learn how to combine.

We focus here on four of Foster's strategies.

Have fun

Foster makes having fun his first idea-getting strategy and his most important one. He makes this claim because his experience in the advertising world confirmed that teams having the most fun produced the best results—the best ads, the best billboards, the best television commercials. Having fun led those teams to generate effective ideas. We may have had similar experiences ourselves. After all, isn't it the case that when people enjoy what they're doing, they tend to do it better?

Having fun is both a result and a form of play, and play is an essential aspect of human culture. In his classic book *Homo Ludens*, John Huizinga (1971) charts the importance of play throughout history. He claims that play is a fundamental attribute of our humanity, antedating recorded history. Play is a form of activity, a way of doing things, even of making things. And so *homo ludens*, is akin to *homo faber*, man the maker, the creator, the inventor. It is believed that the earliest human tools, for example, resulted from a form of play—initially with sticks and stones. Play is an important stimulus to creative activity. Someone once defined creativity, in fact, as "intelligence at play."

French poet Paul Valéry remarked: "People with ideas are never serious." And science fiction writer and biochemist Isaac Asimov noted that new discoveries are often heralded with the remark "that's funny."

Humor is a key element in creative thinking, largely because humor relies on combining things not normally put together. The incongruity makes us laugh. The notion of incongruity, however, results in more than humor; it also leads to inventions. And even though it might not have taken a joke to arrive at the following inventions, they share with humor the baseline of surprising combinations, putting things together that are not normally considered related. The juxtaposition of two different things is a powerful strategy for invention. Here are just a few:

- Putting fire and food together yielded cooking
- An alarm + a clock = an alarm clock
- A rag and a stick make a mop
- A coin punch and a wine press = the printing press
- Dreams and art conspired to form Surrealism

Shelly Carson (2012) in *Your Creative Brain* notes that recent research has shown the value of play and games in stimulating areas of the brain associated with creativity. Developing a playful frame of mind also increases motivation to engage in problem solving. The fun we have in the process of working creatively on a project helps us persevere with it. Our rewards for working on a project with play and game aspects are intrinsic and self-motivating.

In *Creative Intelligence,* Bruce Nussbaum (2013) notes how important play was in the lives and education of the founders of many new companies, including Android, Flickr, Instagram, Kickstarter, Tumblr, and YouTube. Google founders Larry Page and Sergey Brin, Amazon founder Jeff Bezos, and Wikipedia founder Jimmy Wales all attended Montessori schools, which use games to stimulate imaginative thinking, inquiry, and discovery. The habit of "playing around," sometimes called "messing around," is central to the concept of play, which differs significantly from the notion of "problem solving." Unlike problem solving, in which we know the problem for which we are seeking a solution, play is experimental and exploratory—as much for the questions and problems that need to be identified as for the answers that lead to innovative solutions.

Be more like a child

What is it about children that nourishes and incites creativity? Jack Foster writes: "The child is innocent and free and does not know what he cannot or should not do. He sees the world as it actually is, not the way we adults have been taught to believe that it is."

Foster references Gary Zukav (2001) in his book *The Dancing Wu-Li Masters* to the effect that adults are full of opinions and knowledge of the obvious, with common sense and self-evident truths that sabotage the freedom necessary for creativity. Foster also quotes the French psychologist Jean Piaget, who recommends that we "stay in part a child, with the creativity and invention that characterizes children before they are deformed by adult society."

Children are curious. Their questions keep coming—until they get older. And the older they get the fewer their questions. Neil Postman, the educator, writes: "Children enter school as question marks and leave as periods." The trick for each of us is to keep learning, without losing our enthusiasm for learning and especially for asking questions. Asking the right kinds of questions— open questions, probing questions, provocative questions, authentic questions, questions based on innate curiosity and a passion to know are essential for creative thought.

Amanda Lang (2012), in *The Power of Why*, claims that thinking like a child involves a few other things as well. She suggests that a child listens without bias and preconceived notions, and accepts mistakes as part of the learning process, as partial successes rather than as abysmal failures. Children don't blame themselves for failure; they just carry on. And they tend to engage themselves fully, completely, in whatever they are doing. Play is the name of the game for them, play engaged in with unabashed enthusiasm and joy.

And Steven D. Levitt and Stephen J. Dubner (2014), in *Think Like a Freak*, note that children are devoid of preconceptions that prevent adults from seeing things as they really are. These authors write: "Kids are in love with their own audacity, mesmerized by the word around them, and unstoppable in their pursuit of fun." Those characteristics of boldness, astonished curiosity about the world, and always seeking enjoyment drive children and can drive adults in thinking more creatively. It is important to have fun because when we are enjoying our work and pursue challenges, we are more willing to persist, to keep at it. To remain curious suggests an authentic interest in all aspects of life.

Children are also much less readily fooled than adults by magic tricks. Why? In large part because adults follow the cues the magician wants them to see. They pay scrupulous attention to what the magician seems to be doing only to be fooled by what he is actually doing, largely because they have preconceptions about what is happening. Kids, on the other hand, don't have those preconceptions. They are genuinely curious about what is going on, trying to figure out the magician's tricks by observing carefully, without the baggage adults bring. Kids also see things from a different perspective. They are smaller than adults, a seeming height dis-advantage that actually enables them to see things that adults literally can't. A child's perspective sometimes has advantages over the perspective of an adult.

If we could recapture the sense of wonder and curiosity of our younger child-selves, we would be more willing and able to embrace change, to accept surprise, to anticipate the new with joyous expectation. Somewhere along the way too many of us lose our wide-eyed openness to the unfamiliar and the unexpected; like most people, we have matured into adults for whom surprises and changes are unwelcome as we seek to control our lives as much as possible. When we resist what Ed Catmull calls "the beginner's mind," we tend to be less open to possibilities and potentialities, less accepting of change and of failure, and more likely to stick with what we know, remaining in our comfort zone. Such an attitude hinders creative thinking.

Rethink your thinking

There are no rules for thinking. There are guidelines, suggestions, and strategies. There are tools and tactics and techniques.

To "rethink" your thinking means to come at thinking in some different ways. The first of these alternative routes to creative thinking is to think visually. Visual thinking differs from our normal approach, which is through language. We think with words; that's our common practice. If we add thinking with images, we gain another way to generate ideas.

Among the most famous of all visual thinkers was Albert Einstein, who often thought pictorially. Ideas came to Einstein in images that he later converted to words, diagrams, and mathematical formulas. Other scientists who made discoveries through visual means include William Harvey, who envisioned the heart as a pump while watching the exposed heart of a live fish. They include Niels Bohr, the physicist, who envisioned an atom in terms of the solar system, and Sir Isaac Newton, who saw in an instant that the moon's gravitational pull and an apple's fall were the same. Among the most famous of these scientific discoveries occurred when the chemist August Kekulé dreamed of a snake swallowing its tail, which inspired his discovery of the chemical structure of benzene. The molecular structure of DNA was discovered by James Watson and Francis Crick when they realized visually its double helix shape.

The geographer Alfred Wegener recognized how the west coast of Africa fit neatly into the east coast of South America, seeing that all the continents were once part of a single large land mass. The artist Man Ray, in *Le Violon d'Ingres*, envisioned a woman's torso as the body of a violin. (You can find this work on the Internet.)

A second "rethink your thinking" strategy is this: "Don't assume boundaries that aren't there." You might be surprised at how often your thinking is constrained because you assume and set unnecessary limits and restrictions. Suppose you are asked to plant four trees equidistant from one another. The instinct of most people is to assume that the trees are to be planted on a level piece of land— a two-dimensional surface. And when you try to plot a solution on paper, it simply does not work. However, if you break through the limiting assumption of planting the trees on the same plane, you solve the problem: one tree is placed on a higher plane, on top of a hill, with the other three placed equidistant on the sides.

Yet a third "rethink your thinking" strategy is to set yourself some limits. Now that sounds like a contradiction of what we were just saying about not assuming constraints that aren't stipulated. But this time we are deciding to play a different game—the game of working within a set of boundaries. We play tennis with the net up.

We play basketball on a court with boundaries. Football and base-ball fields have lines drawn that suggest in and out of bounds, fair and foul grounds. Boundaries matter; they make the game more interesting and challenging.

Limitation often spurs imagination. A poet writing a sonnet within a prescribed meter and rhyming pattern can surprise her-self with verbal solutions that would not have emerged without the constraints of the sonnet form. Leonardo da Vinci noted that "small rooms discipline the mind," and the great jazz musician, composer, and bandleader, Duke Ellington said that "it's good to have limits," while writing music for specific instrument combina-tions and for particular players of those instruments. And Robert Frost once compared writing free verse (poetry without formal rules) to playing tennis with the net down. The net is necessary for the game to be a challenge, in fact, to be the game of tennis as we know it. Rules and constraints and boundaries stimulate cre-ative play, whatever the nature of the game.

Break the rules

In the previous guideline, setting limits, we spoke of the struc-ture of the sonnet, and how that structure provides enabling con-straints. Now we'll say that sometimes you may want to break out of those constraints by breaking the rules of the game—in this case, writing sonnets. Robert Frost wrote a number of con-ventional sonnets, adhering now to the Shakespearean, or English pattern, and now to the Petrarchan, or Italian form. Sometimes, however, Frost combined the two different sonnet forms in a single hybrid structure. For example, on occasion, he kept the meter and number of lines of the "regular" sonnet, but rhymed in unconven-tional ways. Sometimes he wrote sonnets with slightly shorter line lengths; sometimes he wrote sonnets a line longer than the 14-line standard, and sometimes a line shorter. Although purists might claim that these longer and shorter than the standard poems are not really sonnets (because a sonnet must have fourteen lines), it is clear that Frost is playing with and breaking the rules of the tra-ditional sonnet, though not abandoning those rules entirely (not "playing tennis with the net down").

Jack Foster presents a list of rule-breakers that includes a num-ber of the following examples:

- Vincent van Gogh broke the rules on how to paint a flower.
- Pablo Picasso broke the rules on what a woman's face could look like.
- Pete Gogolak broke the rules on how to kick a football (he kicked it soccer style).
- Ludwig van Beethoven broke the rules for writing a symphony—by adding a chorus to the movement of his ninth symphony (among other things).
- Niccolò Macchiavelli broke the rules about how a prince should behave toward his constituents.
- Thomas More, in his *Utopia*, broke the rules about how a society should be organized.
- e.e. cummings broke the rules on how poems should be punctuated and how author's names should be printed.
- Louis Pasteur broke the rules on how to treat diseases.
- David Ogilvy broke the rules on how advertising copy should sound.
- Igor Stravinsky broke the rules on how ballet music should sound.
- Charlie Parker broke the rules for jazz by playing "forbidden" notes over fast tempo chord changes.
- Bobby McFerrin broke the rules for singing, by persuasively imitating the sounds of various musical instruments with his voice.
- The Beatles broke the rules on what a music "album" should be.
- Four Seasons Hotels broke the rules about what hotel service can be.
- Apple broke the rules about how music should be delivered and sold—and what a retail store might be.
- Twitter broke the rules about how frequently communication can occur.

Creative Whacks

One of the best things that can happen to you as a thinker, suggests Roger von Oech, is to get "a whack on the side of the head." You need these whacks, he says, because your mind is locked into various kinds of ruts. A good "whack" can jolt you into thinking along fresh paths. He identifies ten mental locks that interfere with creative thinking:

1. The right answer
2. Being logical
3. Following rules
4. Being practical
5. Not being playful
6. Limiting your territory
7. Being afraid of foolishness
8. Avoiding ambiguity
9. Being afraid of error
10. Thinking you're not creative

To break these mental locks you need a variety of tactics and strategies (creative "whacks"). A "whack" that jolts you out of your routine patterns of behavior and your habitual ways of thinking, however, can be painful; it might come as a problem or failure, like losing a job, failing an exam, blowing an interview, or mismanaging a project at work. Often, however, you need to find ways to give yourself such a metaphorical "whack" as a way to rethink your situation and to ask questions that lead to better answers. We will sample a few strategies for putting ourselves into a more creative mode of thinking.

As a prelude to the first creative "whack," do the following:

1. Turn the Roman numeral six (VI) into a seven by adding a single line. Turn it into a four by moving a single line.
2. Turn the Roman number nine (IX) into an eleven by moving a line and twelve by adding one.
3. Turn it into a six by adding a single line.

What happened as you made those number conversions? The first two were pretty simple, right? 6 to 7 = VI to VII; 6 to 4 = VI to IV; 9 to 11 = IX to XI; 11 to 12 = XI to XII. But what about turning the nine into a six? The IX becomes ... what?

To solve this problem, you need a whack on the side of the head. Why? Because you have been locked into a pattern of moving a single line (I) or adding one line. You have also been locked into the pattern of "Roman numerals." And if you stay locked within those patterns, there is simply no way to add a line to the Roman number representing nine (IX) to convert it to a 6 (VI). If the direction were to move two lines you might solve the problem by moving the I after the X to get XI and then taking the X apart and moving the left side over further to the left to make a V and thus get VI. But that was not the challenge.

Instead, the challenge here is to add a single line to IX. And so, you need, as Edward de Bono might say, to stop digging the Roman numeral hole deeper, and instead begin digging a new whole, or as Roger von Oech says, to "do something different."

You need a "shift" of attention—a redirection away from the locked-in concept of "ROMAN" numerals to something else. You can get there any number of ways, but one of them is simply to think of what, in English, Roman numbers are. They're letters, aren't they?— I and X and V (and also C and D and M). Now try to use that fact as a lever to think differently, to think in a new direction, to think in another way about what IX can be. What ELSE can it be?

If the Roman numeral nine is composed of the letters I and X (or i and x), suppose you add an "S" in front to make "SIX," or "six."

Now you might want to say—"But wait. You said to add a line, and I was not thinking of a line that curves. I was thinking of lines like the ones used for the Roman numeral we were adding and moving in the first examples." Those were straight lines.

But an "S" is a line, too, isn't it? It's just a curving line. What you probably did in your thinking was to make an assumption that the line could not curve. In this case, you added a constraint when that constraint was not warranted. And so you were locked into two patterns: the pattern of Roman numerals and the pattern of non-curving lines. And both of those "locks" needed opening to get from IX, as a Roman number composed of straight lines, to SIX (or six), as English letters (with one curvy line). To solve the problem, you needed a creative whack to go in a different thinking direction—from numbers to letters, and from straight to curved lines.

Another way to think about what you very likely did in the process of working through the previous exercises with Roman numerals is that you created an artificial barrier through making an unwarranted assumption. In *Think Like a Freak*, Steven D. Levitt and Stephen J. Dubner suggest ways out of this kind of impasse. They advise a reframing of the problem and a complete ignoring of any artificial barriers.

They describe an international hot-dog eating contest in which a Japanese contestant "reframed" the challenge from "How do I eat more hot dogs?" to "How do I make hot dogs easier to eat?" For most people, eating hot dogs involves eating the hot dog in a hot dog bun, eating the buns being a requirement of the contest along with eating the hot dogs. The Japanese contestant Takeru Kobayashi decided to eat the buns separately from eating the hot dogs. That's one of his reframing elements. Another is that he looked at the contest less as a contest than as a serious "sport." He rethought the challenge by considering it as something that requires the preparation, practice, and serious analytical work of getting ready for a serious athletic competition and not just a competition in which you eat hot dogs in the everyday manner. He thus developed a serious regimen of physical training to prepare himself for the "sport" of speeded hot-dog eating.

These two reframing aspects were accompanied by Kobayashi's refusal to see the previous record as a barrier or limit that he might surpass. Had he done that, he would have set himself the goal of eating perhaps one or two more hot dogs than the previous champion. By ignoring that "artificial barrier," and instead simply focusing on eating as many hot dogs and buns (separately) as he could, Kobayashi was able to smash the record decisively by eating almost twice as many hot dogs as the previous record holder.

The right answer

Let's take this a step further by considering more than a single possible right answer. Rather than being satisfied with your first solution to the IX to six (or 6) problem, consider the value of searching for alternatives. What might you discover in the process of looking for more than one solution?

Let's consider some other ways to convert IX to six (or 6). Suppose you write it this way: Ix or: I x? Or suppose you do it like this: I x ? = 6. That should lead to I x 6 or I X 6, "one times six." In this case, we have rethought the meaning of X yet again. Previously, X meant the number 10; thus, XI = 11 and IX = 9. Then we considered X as a letter, as in SIX. But now we want X to

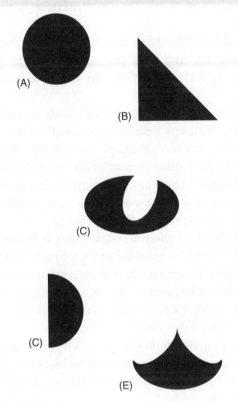

Figure 5.2   Odd shapes

mean something else– "times"—the multiplication sign, "x." We have changed the "context" of X to make it mean different things: a Roman numeral, an English letter, and now a symbol meaning to multiply. In the process you have been exercising both your critical and creative thinking capacities. You have been engaging your imagination, playfully.

Here's another challenge—this one strictly visual. From the five figures of odd shapes (Figure 5.2), select the one that's different from the other figures. Explain how it differs. Then compare your explanation with the answers and explanations of others.

Did you select figure B? Is that correct? Is that the right answer? Why? But what if you chose figure C. Is that also correct? Is that the right answer, too? Why? And what if you chose figure D. Is that the correct answer, as well? How about A—and E? In fact, they are all correct; they are all "the right answer"—or rather right

151

answers. Plural. And that's the point. There is more than one "right answer."

We are conditioned to think that one answer is the right answer, or the best answer. And that can be the case in some circumstances. But in this instance, there are multiple equally valid correct answers.

You might find some of the "right" answers more interesting than the others, perhaps because you didn't think of them first, perhaps because you didn't think of them at all—because you quit after finding the first (and presumably) the only correct answer. Perhaps you found one or another explanation more compelling for why this figure or that one was also correct. In this context, consider the French philosopher Emile Chartier, who wrote: "Nothing is more dangerous than an idea when it is the only one we have." Why? Well, you may come to love your idea too much; you may think it's the best approach, maybe even the only really worthwhile approach—in large part, perhaps, because it's *your* idea. In reality, though, to have a good idea, it's wise to have a lot of ideas to choose from. What is needed is prolific thinking, fertile thinking, fluent thinking to generate many ideas. The more ideas generated, the greater the chance a good one will be discovered.

It is often useful to approach a problem or question from multiple directions.

Consider, for example, how each one of the following sports—baseball, cricket, golf, ice hockey, and soccer—might be least like the other four. Let's take these sports one at a time, beginning with baseball. One way that baseball differs from the other sports is that it has no true world or international championship, as its World Series takes place among teams from the United States. The game itself has something in common with cricket in terms of the pace at which it is played and in terms of pitchers (or bowlers in cricket) throwing a ball that a batter or batsman attempts to hit into a field of defending players. Both cricket and baseball differ from the other sports in significant ways, though both are like golf, a highly individual sport, in that like ice hockey as well, each employs a stick or stick-like object to hit a ball or puck.

Other differences include golf's emphasis on mental rather than physical action as compared with the other sports—though there are plenty of opportunities for mental effort being expended in each of the other sports. How, for example, do baseball and cricket require mental effort? In what ways does that mental effort compare with and differ from the mental work expended in soccer and ice hockey?

We could go on to catalogue other ways in which each of the sports differs from the other four—in terms of playing surface, time of year in which the sport is most frequently played; in terms of the amount of physical contact permitted and the number of players on the field or playing surface; in terms of how scoring works and how the game is "timed" or otherwise structured. The important thing is to acquire the habit of considering a variety of approaches, to see the problem or question in various ways, as there are, clearly, many "right answers."

Being Practical/What Iffing

Practicality is the bane of creative thinking. "Be practical," we are admonished. "Be realistic." "You can't do it that way." "That won't work." Our response to these inter-related "don'ts" and "can'ts" should be, "Why not?" "Who says?" and "What if"?

Of course, there are times when being practical, taking "reality" into account is necessary. There is certainly value in being practical, and there is often a need to be realistic. However, there is also a time and place for ignoring those constraints, when you are trying to "think differently," when you are attempting to generate some new ideas.

Considering "What if" is necessary to challenge conventional thinking. "What if" questions are an easy and effective way to get your creative juices flowing. "What if" questions are playful and often enjoyable to consider. Having fun, enjoying what you are doing, is a major element of doing it successfully, whatever "it" is—including thinking.

Here are some "What if" questions that Roger von Oech provides:

- What if animals became more intelligent than human beings?
- What if men also had babies?
- What if politicians were elected by lottery?
- What if pigs had wings?
- What if human life expectancy exceeded 200 years?

- What if people had to spend every third year living in a different country?
- What if people didn't need to sleep?
- What if there was a country where all leaders and rulers were women?
- What if there was a "war of the worlds" between humans and creatures from outer space?

Each of these "what if" questions is an idea generator. Each pushes thinking in new directions, imagining alternatives to customary realities of the familiar.

The "what if" habit is such a crucial one to develop that we extend it a bit further with Michael Michalko's (2006) particular spin. In his book *Thinkertoys*, he suggests that we need "what iff-ing" as a technique to transcend the possible. It's a playful and nonthreatening way to develop the habit of imaginative thinking, a step toward creativity and innovation.

Here are some of the "what if questions" Michael Michalko proposes:

- What if you had eyes in the back of your head as well as the front?
- What if trees could produce large amounts of petroleum?
- What if people slept 23 hours a day and were awake for only 1?
- What if each US adult worker had to adopt and care for a homeless person for a lifetime?

And then a few others:

- What if United States senators and members of the House of Representatives (along with the President, Vice President and Cabinet) were required to send their children to public schools?
- What if a pill could be taken to counteract prejudice and bigotry?
- What if as you aged you became younger, living your life backwards?

(This "what if" serves as the premise for a short story by F. Scott Fitzgerald that inspired the movie, *The Curious Case of Benjamin Button*.)

The "what if" approach can take your thinking in new directions. In thinking of a particular person, perhaps someone you know, perhaps a figure from history, even a fictional character, you might imagine how that individual would respond to a problem you are confronting. Some candidates: Machiavelli, the Pope, the Dali Lama, Socrates, Confucius, Buddha, Martin Luther King, Jr., Freud, Mozart, Oprah, the Beatles, Mother Theresa, the Three Stooges, Julius Caesar, Joan of Arc, your mother, uncle, cousin, fifth-grade teacher, your best friend. Winston Churchill, Spider Man, Attila the Hun. Huckleberry Finn, Ahab, Holden Caulfield, Hamlet, Lady Macbeth, Romeo or Juliet, Madonna, Beyoncé, Lady Gaga, Justin Bieber, Ice-T, Jay-Z.

John Medina (2008), in *Brain Rules,* uses "what if" questions in conjunction with basic knowledge of how the brain functions optimally, with particular emphasis on teaching and learning. Noting how the increased emphasis on state testing in some school districts limits physical education and opportunities for students to engage in physical activity generally, he argues that this is exactly the wrong approach. Research shows that reducing physical exercise diminishes cognitive performance. And so we might ask, "what if a school district inserted regular rather than occasional exercise into the normal curriculum on a regular basis, even twice a day?" We might expect that students' academic performance would increase, with aerobic exercise supplying increased oxygen to their brains. And to go just a bit further, "what if" students didn't sit at desks for so much of the day? What if they had a math lesson or a history lesson walking around the room or while walking on treadmills?

Or consider that there is much research to support the value of sleep for learning and for productive work. Lack of sleep—and many students (and teachers) are sleep deprived—reduces effective learning and interferes with productivity. It has long been known that teenagers don't function well in the early morning hours, yet high school schedules typically begin at 8 am or even earlier. And the 3-hour plus SAT test is routinely given early on Saturday mornings.

It is also known that significant fatigue sets in for adults even more than for teenagers in the mid-afternoon. And so John Medina asks "what if" schools and businesses took this information seriously? What if there were opportunities for students and teachers to regenerate with a quick 20-minute power nap? What if the school day began later? To what extent might such changes improve productive and effective teaching and learning? If, as he argues, the loss of sleep diminishes attention, decreases memory, impairs mood, dexterity, logical reasoning, and quantitative analysis, why wouldn't school administrators find ways to counter those negativities? And, on the other side—to what extent might moving the school day start time later simply result in students simply being at school later and staying up later? "What if" these considerations were taken seriously?

Combining Things

In *Where Good Ideas Come From: The Natural History of Innovation*, Steven Johnson (2011) claims that all new ideas are combinations of former ideas, and that all inventions are based on aspects, elements, and components of things that already exist. Ideas are typically networks of other ideas; we take the ideas we've found and combine them into some new form. The secret to innovation involves combining odds and ends, tinkering with what's available, with what's already around, to make something new.

Making connections, seeing relationships, linking things, as we have noted earlier, is at the heart of all thinking, both critical and creative. We combine objects to make something new, phones with cameras and electronic calendars and Web browsers and email access and on and on. We combine ideas, as with the notion of freedom within structure, which yields among many possibilities, various poetic forms, such as the sonnet and the villanelle. We combine subjects from different intellectual domains, such as the creation of social psychology from sociology and psychology, or bioengineering from biology and engineering. Gregor Mendel developed the laws of heredity by combining the fields of biology and mathematics to create the then new field of genetics.

Using the analogy of two chemicals creating a new compound—hydrogen and oxygen forming water for example—we can catalyze creative thinking by looking for cross-pollinating opportunities. Einstein's famous equation $E = mc^2$ combined the concepts of energy, mass, and the speed of light into a new set of relationships. He called his mode of thinking "combinatory play," a telling term,

Figure 5.3   Rabbit/duck. © Fine Art Images/Superstock

indeed. Closer to home, Fred Smith combined three observations and concepts: (1) a speedy messenger service; (2) discounted jets for sale; and (3) empty skies at night. Putting them together led him to create Federal Express, or FedEx.

Using Paradox

A paradox is an apparent contradiction that upon closer inspection turns out to reveal an interesting truth. In *Creative Thinkering*, Michael Michalko (2011) gives the example of the following statement as uttered by a man from Crete: "All Cretans are liars." What are we to make of this contradictory provocation? If the man is telling the truth, then all Cretans, indeed, are liars. But this includes him, too, since he is from Crete. In that case, then, the statement is false because he is lying, as all Cretans do. If he is being truthful, then he is lying; if he is lying, then he is telling the truth; hence, the paradox.

A visual example occurs in Figure 5.3 (Rabbit/duck), which depicts simultaneously a rabbit and duck.

The rabbit looks to your right and the duck to your left. So which is it, rabbit or duck? The answer, of course, as you have seen, is both. Not either–or, but both–and. Michael Michalko contends that when we think about paradoxes, we transcend ordinary logical thinking. In suspending logic, we create new ideas, which the "swirling of opposites" stimulates. He gives an example of a paradox in which a person wants to make a lot of money but is lazy

157

and lacks ambition. One solution is to take a vacation to an exotic locale and then write a book about it. (Of course, the book will involve some work; but that work should have some pleasure associated with it because of the topic—the exotic vacation—with the prospect of more, if the concept of vacationing and writing takes hold effectively.)

Another solution to this kind of problem is presented in Mark Twain's novel *The Adventures of Tom Sawyer*. You may remember that Tom had to paint a fence. In this case, his need to have the fence painted conflicted with his desire to avoid the work of actually doing it. His solution: begin painting the fence and pretend that it's a lot of fun. When his friends ask to join in the fun, he resists for a while, but he finally relents and lets them do the work—by themselves. What Tom didn't realize, however, is that sometimes after beginning to do something you didn't initially want to do, you discover that it can be fun, or perhaps that you can find a way to make it fun.

Paradox is a powerful provocation to thinking. Consider the paradox in the following poem by Emily Dickinson:

Much Madness is divinest Sense—
To a discerning eye—
Much Sense—the starkest madness—
'Tis the Majority
In this, as All, prevail—
Assent—and you are sane—
Demur—you're straightway dangerous—
And handled with a Chain—

The first three lines of Dickinson's poem present a paradox, a literary device that describes an apparent contradiction. In a paradox, the apparent contradiction disappears with a shift of perspective. So, for example, from the standpoint of worldly wisdom, sacrificing everything else in life for money or power may be very sensible. From a religious standpoint, however, such as from the perspective of Buddhism, Islam, or Christianity, such behavior is a form of madness.

The paradoxical idea is that madness is really "sense" and sense "madness"—the "starkest" madness. But in order to perceive the sense in madness and the madness in sense, we need to have a "discerning eye." Not everyone can see these opposite conditions—sense in madness and madness in sense, in the manner of a yin-yang pairing. Not everyone can see how something that appears mad or crazy might really be quite sensible, and conversely, how something that may appear sane and sensible, on closer inspection, or from another perspective, reveals, instead, a kind of madness.

The poem's opening lines do not assert or insist that madness is always sane or sensibleness always crazy. The lines don't insist that what appears to be madness never is, or that what appears sensible is never so. But when "Madness" is "Sense," it is "divinest" sense—a special, extraordinary kind of meaningfulness, a sense that might require seeing things from a very different (perhaps spiritual) perspective. Note the superlative in both "divinest" Sense and "starkest" Madness. When something is fundamentally mad that appears sane, that madness is stark, basic, mad to the core, fundamentally and intensely so.

Paradox is a staple of mathematics as well as of language. Consider the extraordinary idea that a series of numerical subsets—all odd numbers, all even numbers, and all prime numbers (those that can only be divided by themselves) is equal to the totality of *all* natural numbers. This flies in the face of logic and reason. For how can the total of *all* cardinal numbers, which includes odd numbers and even numbers, be *equal* to the total number of odd number or the total of even numbers, alone? And yet, the nineteenth-century mathematician George Cantor proved just this paradoxical mathematical concept—that, as Daniel Tammet (2012) explains in *Thinking in Numbers*, "parts of the collection (subsets) as great as the whole (set) really do exist." Paradoxically, there are as many even (or odd, or prime) numbers as all the numbers taken together.

A different kind of paradoxical example comes from Malcolm Gladwell's (2013) book *David and Goliath*. You will remember the story from the Bible of how the Israelite teenage shepherd David, engaged in battle with the Philistine enemy giant Goliath. Goliath was decked out in his heavy armor and gigantic sword and shield while David confronted him on the battlefield naked of armor with a slingshot and five stones. The story is told to celebrate how David slew Goliath by slinging a stone at his forehead, which felled the giant, whereupon David ran up to him, unsheathed Goliath's sword and decapitated him.

This story is typically read as a celebration of how the weak can overcome the strong, of how when the odds are stacked against you, you can still prevail by virtue of courage, ingenuity, skill, and some assistance from divinity. Malcolm Gladwell, however, flips this traditional explanation, and suggests that David, not Goliath, had the advantage in their battle. Why? Goliath was weighed down by his heavy armor. He could move only slowly and with difficulty. David, by contrast, was nimble and quick, and he used this advantage to sling his stone at Goliath's forehead with speed and accuracy before Goliath knew what was happening. David's appearance, moreover, as a smooth-skinned youth of no apparent threat, undermined Goliath's ability to recognize David as an opponent worthy of respect or of fear. Goliath underestimated David's capabilities.

In addition, at the time this ancient battle was fought, every army had expert slingers who were recognized as a significant military threat feared by enemy forces. From this perspective, David is not the underdog at all. David has every advantage—of surprise, of youth, of speed, of the feared and dangerous slingshot—such that Goliath with his heavy armor and his arrogant attitude hardly has a chance against him. Paradoxically the apparent disadvantaged individual possesses the real advantages, and the apparently advantaged individual is hampered by his size and weaponry, which are really disadvantages that result in his defeat and death.

Thinking the Unthinkable

In *Creative Thinkering*, Michael Michalko argues that creativity is enhanced when we attempt to think the unthinkable. He suggests that we need ways to "unstructure our imaginations" in order to go beyond the common approaches to thinking. There are a number of ways to do this, most of which involve freeing ourselves to allow for "crazy or fantastical ideas." One example he offers was developed by a Red Cross director in the state of Washington who wanted to think of activities for children of soldiers deployed to war zones to keep the kids connected in some way with their dads. One suggestion was to hire actors to play the role of the fathers.

The idea was considered laughable. But the director thought about its underlying concept—that of a father substitute. This concept reminded her of a program she heard that was based on a children's book, *Flat Stanley*, in which a character's picture travels around the world in stamped envelopes. This concept then led the director to ask for pictures of the fathers along with their jacket sizes. She had the pictures blown up to life-size, backed them with foam cardboard, and then distributed the pictures to the children at a party. The idea was a big hit with the kids, who enjoyed keeping their "Flat Daddies" with them.

Michael Michalko proposes consciously generating a list of outrageous, crazy ideas about a subject. If you are designing a new office space, a new building, a new ad campaign; if you are planning a party for a child, organizing a dinner for friends, creating a new recipe—for these and many other tasks and challenges, you can start by listing some fanciful, outlandish ideas. These ideas serve as starting points, as thought stimuli. They lead to other more usable ideas by means of extracting their essential notion or concept—as with the concept of "substitute fathers" in the previous example. Putting down randomly a number of far-fetched ideas allows also for unusual combinations, things that might not normally be considered together and that can lead to fresh thinking.

Applications

5-1. Think of a time in your life when your imagination was stifled or at least constrained—by a parent, a teacher, a counselor, a friend. How did that limiting of your imagination affect you? How did you respond?

5-2. Identify two examples of how imagination spurred creativity and innovation in one of the following fields—and add two additional examples.
   1. Professional sports: baseball, football, basketball, tennis, golf, cycling, etc.
   2. Industry: life insurance, health care, banking, electronics, food production, etc.
   3. Popular music (including country, blues, rock, hip-hop, etc.)
   4. Classical music or jazz

5. The arts of drawing, painting, sculpture, ceramics, print-making

6. Architecture and/or engineering

7. Theatre and/or dance

8. Film and/or comics

9. An academic field: mathematics, economics, psychology, history, etc.

10. A public service: transportation, safety, sanitation, water, electricity, etc.

5-3. Which of the Lincoln Center Education capacities seem new—perhaps even unusual—to you? Which are similar to ideas and strategies you have seen and heard before? Which of these capacities do you think can be most useful to you? How?

5-4. To what extent do you agree with Edmundson about the potential "perils" of imagination? To what extent do you think that the dangers of imagination he identifies can be redressed and checked in the ways he describes?

5-5. To what extent do you agree with Foster that having fun breeds ideas, often good ideas? To what extent is this borne out in your own experience, or in what you know of the experience of others? Provide an example of a time when having fun enhanced your creativity.

5-6. Think of a good joke that puts together two things not normally expected to exist together. Explain where the surprise of the joke lies. That is, identify its incongruity. Provide two ideas for how you can have more fun at work or at home or school—or wherever else fun might be useful.

5-7. Add three questions of your own to those that follow:
- Why are milk cartons square?
- Why don't kitchen faucets have foot pedals?
- Why is the moon round?
- Why is grass green?
- Why are squirrels grey (and brown and white and black?)
- Why do we have dreams?

5-8. Think of something you could do at work or in your personal life in which being like a child—perhaps acting like a child—can help generate interest, curiosity, and excitement for thinking and learning. Think about some ways to let the child in you come out—and play. Ask yourself how you might approach one of your projects if you were in the fifth grade. Think like a child. Be silly. Have fun.

5-9. Try to visualize one or more images for the following products that need to be advertised: master locks; company leadership; solar heat panels; a college or university; a hospital; an insurance company. Ask yourself what the problem or challenge looks like. Try to think in pictures first and in words second.

5-10. Add two people who broke the rules to Foster's list. Explain what rules they broke, and what resulted from breaking them.

5-11. Think of a sport that you know well or have a serious interest in. If you know the history of this sport, you can answer the following questions—and if you don't, you can do a bit of research. How has this sport changed in the past few years or decades—or in the past century (if it's old enough)? What pattern of rules were broken or challenged? Think not only of the game itself, but also of equipment, playing locations and surfaces, attire. Some candidates for consideration: baseball, basketball, football, softball, soccer, swimming, tennis, golf, volleyball, downhill skiing, snowboarding, figure-skating.

5-12. Think of a time when you were either forced or shown how to consider alternatives to an idea—a single dominating idea to which you were wedded. What happened to your original idea? What was the result of considering alternative ideas—whether you came up with them yourself, were persuaded to consider them, or were forced to do so?

5-13. Where else have you encountered the importance of exploring multiple possibilities before? Why is it important not to be satisfied with the first solution to a problem you find, or the first idea for a project you come up with? What are the benefits of considering alternatives?

5-14. Choose one "what if" scenario each from Roger von Oech, Michael Michalko, and John Medina, and play out the consequences for each of them. Add two of your own "what ifs," and explore their implications. This exercise benefits from partnering with one or two other colleagues.

5-15. Select two candidates from among the various people mentioned earlier to see a problem from their point of view. Focus on a problem or challenge you are dealing with and consider how they would approach it. What assumptions would they make? What special wrinkle would they see? What expertise would they add? What perspective would they bring? What changes might they suggest? What questions might they ask?

5-16. Explain how you might go about resolving the contradictions implicit in the following paradoxes. How can you begin to make sense of them intellectually? What might you do with them, or from them, in terms of action?
1. Lead by following
2. Win by losing
3. Create order while allowing freedom
4. Build a cohesive team but welcome conflict
5. Reward team effort while encouraging individual achievement

5-17. How do you respond to Malcolm Gladwell's paradoxical reinterpretation of the story of David and Goliath. To what extent do you agree that a disadvantage can really be an advantage, and correspondingly, that an apparent advantage can be a disadvantage? Might a woman's beauty, for example, exemplify this kind of paradoxical complexity?

5-18. Do you agree with Michael Michalko about the value of "thinking the unthinkable?" Why or why not?

References

Alchin, Nicholas and Carolyn P. Henly. 2014. *Theory of Knowledge*, 3rd edn. London: Hodder Education.

Carson, Shelley. 2012. *Your Creative Brain*. San Francisco: Jossey-Bass.

Dyer, Jeff, Hal Gregersen, and Clayton M. Christensen. 2011. *The Innovator's DNA*. Cambridge, MA: Harvard Business Review Press.

Edmundson, Mark. 2012. "Imagination: Powers & Perils." *Raritan*, 32, Fall: 144-158.

Foster, Jack. 2007. *How to Get Ideas*. San Francisco: Berrett-Koehler.

Gladwell, Malcolm. 2013. *David and Goliath*. Boston: Little Brown.

Huizinga, John. 1971. *Homo Ludens*. Boston: Beacon.

Johnson, Steven. 2011. *Where Good Ideas Come From*. New York: Riverside.

Lang, Amanda. 2012. *The Power of Why*. Toronto: HarperCollins.

Le Guin, Ursula. 1969. *The Left Hand of Darkness*. New York: Penguin Putnam, Ace.

Le Guin, Ursula K. 2014. "Where Do You Get Your Ideas From." In *The World Split Apart*. Portland, OR: Tin House Books.

Levitt, Stephen D. and Steven J. Dubner. 2014. *Think Like a Freak*. New York: William Morrow.

Liu, Eric and Scott Noppe-Brandon. 2011. *Imagination First!* San Francisco: Jossey-Bass.

Medina, John. *Brain Rules*. 2008. Seattle: Pear Press.

Michalko, Michael. 2006. *Thinkertoys*. Berkeley: Ten Speed Press.

Michalko, Michael. 2011. *Creative Thinkering*. San Francisco: New World Library.

Nussbaum, Bruce. 2013. *Creative Intelligence*. New York: Harper Business.

Tammet, Daniel. 2012. *Thinking in Numbers*. Boston: Little, Brown.

Thomas, Douglas and John Seely Brown. 2011. *A New Culture of Learning: Cultivating the Imagination for a World of Constant Change*. CreateSpace.

Von Oech, Roger. 2008. *A Whack on the Side of the Head*. New York: Business Plus.

Web site for Roger von Oech: http://www.creativethink.com, accessed March 28, 2015.

Web site for Michael Michalko: http://www.creativethinking.net, accessed March 28, 2015.

Zukav, Gary. 2001. *The Dancing Wu-Li Masters*. New York: Harper Collins.

Interchapter 5

Combining Connections

Combining things in new ways is a key to innovation. We make new things from old ones, as innovation results from combining existing things in previously unexpected ways. Combining a human and a lion yields a sphinx, a human and a horse, a centaur. Less imaginary couplings range from putting a rag on a broom handle to make a mop, to combining free Wi-Fi, a comfortable environment, and quality coffee (Starbucks). Successful Internet companies combine ideas from different domains, resulting in services such as Amazon, Twitter, Instagram, and YouTube.

Another kind of combination occurs when you make something by putting together things you have at hand. In *Where Good Ideas Come From*, Steven Johnson (2009) describes how incubators were made out of spare automobile parts in a developing world country so that when the incubators broke down they could be fixed locally by car mechanics.

Other combinatory ideas include sandals made from automobile tires, a form of cheap footwear available from something no longer useful in its present form. Johnson notes that these early-stage, or first-order, examples of innovation open the door to other potential innovations. The limits of such improvised creativity are those of available parts, objects, and circumstances. Even with these limitations, "the adjacent possible" reminds us to explore the environment around us—to look at its borders and edges to see what combinations might be interesting and potentially useful. The French have a term for ad hoc improvisatory innovation with at-hand materials: *bricolage*. The improvising individual adept at *bricolage* is a *bricoleur*.

One way to explore the adjacent possible is to expose yourself to varied environments. The goal is to encounter a variety of "spare parts," things lying around, that you might put to use. Nurturing varied friendships is one way to do this in the social realm. Reading books and magazines from different fields is a way to do it in the intellectual realm. Having a storehouse of varied parts— of toys, machines, tools, and the like—is a way to do it in the hands-on physical realm. Exposing yourself to a wide range of perspectives stimulates fresh thinking that combines things normally unrelated.

As Michael Gelb (2009) has noted, Leonardo da Vinci was constantly looking for connections among disparate aspects of the natural world. One of Leonardo's grand themes is how the energy of life manifests itself in both the human and natural worlds. Leonardo loved the flow of water; he saw it as a harmonious interplay of natural and human forces. Leonardo's fascination with the natural world was inextricably linked with his interest in human beings. He wrote, "A human being can be understood only by turning toward nature." The interplay among these considerations led Leonardo to make a multitude of connections between science and art, nature and humanity, body and soul, heart and mind, heaven and earth.

Leonardo's fascination with water, its movement and flow, stimulated his thinking about energy and pattern. He made analogies between swimming and flying, noting, "swimming in water teaches men how birds fly upon the air." He saw a relationship between the movement on the surface of water and that of air. And he drew inspiration for thinking from the way a stone in striking the water's surface, creates a rippling effect, leading him to consider that sound travels in waves.

The ripple effect of the stone in water might be taken, as well, for the rippling effect of thought—an idea dropped into the mind, spreading out to encompass further implications, complications, applications. Leonardo's notebooks contain a further example of his rippling thought where the water's ripples suggest the voice of an echo, rays of light, the force of percussion, the lines of a magnet, and the traveling movement of an odor. Analogy and play are two strategies Leonardo used repeatedly to stimulate his imagination—an imagination that was an engine for recombinant, or combinatory, play.

Among his most important analogies are those between the human body and the larger map of a city, and between the human body as a system and the cosmos as a system. His notebooks contain the following elaboration of this micro/macro-cosmic analogy:

> The ancients called man the *microcosmos*, and surely the term was well chosen: for just as man is composed of earth, water, air, and fire, so is the body of the earth. As man has bones as support and framework for flesh, so the earth has rocks as support for the soil; as man carries a lake of blood in which the lungs inflate and deflate in respiration, so the body of the earth has the ocean which waxes and wanes every six hours in a cosmic respiration; as the veins emanate from the lake of blood and are ramified throughout the human body, in the same way, the ocean fills the body of the earth with an infinity of veins of water.

Applications

1. Think about the origins of something you value—a piece of jewelry, a special gift, a book or letter, a musical instrument or special piece of clothing. Imagine where its materials or parts or elements came from, how they got combined or made, and how they found their way to you as an object of value.

2. Think of a time when you improvised something that you needed to make or something you had to accomplish. Consider what items or elements you had at hand that you put to a new use or put together in a new way to meet a challenge or solve a problem.

3. Identify two modern products or inventions that were developed or made by combining different things. Explain how the original things are combined in the new product or device.

4. Watch the scene from the movie Apollo 13, in which the astronauts work together with the ground crew in Houston to improvise a solution to a life-threatening situation, working with materials at hand.

References

Gelb, Michael. 2000. *How to Think Like Leonardo da Vinci*. New York: Dell.

Johnson, Steven. 2009. *Where Good Ideas Come From*. New York: Riverhead.

Part Three

Applying Critical and Creative Thinking

6

Decision Thinking
Making Critical Decisions

Figure 6.1 This way, that way. © Brian A. Jackson/Shutterstock

The sign of a good decision is the multiplicity of reasons for it.
—Mary Doria Russell

You are defined by the decisions you make.

—Benjamin Bayani

Critical and Creative Thinking: A Brief Guide for Teachers, First Edition. Robert DiYanni.
© 2016 John Wiley & Sons, Inc. Published 2016 by John Wiley & Sons, Inc.

Making Decisions

Jonah Lehrer (2009) begins his book *How We Decide* by describing a scene in which a pilot is trying to avoid crashing a jumbo jet that has just taken off, but which has developed a fire in one of its engines. As the plane sways out of control, the pilot has to decide whether to increase the throttle in an attempt to gain altitude and speed, or circle the runway in an attempt to stabilize the aircraft. Fearing that the plane's second engine might not be able to handle the strain of such a maneuver, the pilot considers steepening his descent, which might allow him to avoid stalling the plane and sending it into free-fall. He has only moments to decide. What should he do?

Lehrer's little story is not about an actual flight with a real pilot, but rather about himself as pilot attempting to control a plane via a flight simulator. The decisions he had to make, however, felt to him every bit as real as they would to a real pilot in an actual flight situation—the kind of situation Chesley "Sully" Sullenberger found himself in as he approached New York City's LaGuardia airport on January 15, 2009, when his plane lost thrust from both engines after a flock of geese was sucked into them. The pilot cut off his engines and glided his plane into the Hudson River to a safe landing with no casualties. An overnight celebrity, Sully wrote a book about the experience, with his landing dubbed "the miracle on the Hudson."

Lehrer's simulated crisis and Sullenberger's real one lead to a number of questions about making decisions. First, how do we make decisions—what are our minds doing in the process of decision-making? And second, how might we make better decisions—what can we do to increase the chances that our minds will guide us to the right decisions?

Lehrer suggests that making good decisions requires the use of very different mental aspects—the rational and the irrational, the analytical and the emotional, the logical and the intuitive. Sometimes we need to think through options, reasoning carefully and deliberately about them. Other times, however, we need to follow our gut, listen to our feelings, attend to our instincts. Knowing when to use each style of thinking and knowing how to deploy these differing styles of thinking effectively is the challenge for successful decision thinking. Also critical is recognizing the power emotion has on our more deliberate analytical reasoning.

Intuitions and rationalizations

In *The Righteous Mind*, Jonathan Haidt (2012) argues that our thinking, typically, develops after-the-fact explanations— rationalizations primarily—for our beliefs. He suggests that this kind of post hoc justification for beliefs prevails in all kinds of thinking. We use thinking to confirm our beliefs and our intuitions rather than to consider them rationally; our reasoning and decision-making, in short, are motivated by self-justification. Evidence that confirms what we believe, we accept; evidence that contradicts what we believe, we reject. We decide things based on what we believe, and we believe what suits us.

Jonathan Haidt suggests that the prominence we give reason in our own thinking and the thinking of others is misinformed, even delusional. Fair-minded analysis and careful exploration of beliefs, ideas, and evidence is rare. More often than not, thinking tends to confirm our beliefs by rationalizing our point of view. This seems to be the case almost without exception when moral issues and questions are at stake.

We are not, of course, always in error about our ideas. And it is not necessarily wrong to follow intuition. The point, simply, is that reason does not drive our thinking; emotion does. The psychological studies Haidt cites, and those he himself has conducted, provide evidence that intuition comes first and reason follows it. We justify our beliefs and our decisions, basing them on intuition, rather than on rational analysis.

Intuition is a form of cognition, one that differs from reasoning but which is a form of cognitive activity nonetheless. Think, for example, how often in considering your beliefs, you ask yourself whether you "can" believe something (something you want to believe or already believe) as opposed to something you think you "ought" to believe (but which you don't want to believe). In the first case, you seek confirmation and accept as evidence examples and studies that support your ideas and beliefs; in the second, you look for evidence that contradicts what you don't want to believe. Or you simply find ways to reject contradictory examples and studies as being somehow flawed, outdated, biased, or otherwise inadequate. This kind of confirmation bias lies at the heart of much decision thinking.

Support for a de-emphasis on rational decision thinking is provided by Leonard Mlodinow (2012) in *Subliminal: How Your Unconscious Mind Rules Your Behavior*, whose subtitle identifies its central claim. He argues that in being aware only of conscious influences for your behavior, you are at a disadvantage. Conscious understanding provides only part of what motivates your actions. Rational decision-making, he contends, is a chimera—a false and misleading fantasy, as your unconscious mind is equally if not more influential than your conscious mind.

Leonard Mlodinow suggests that any picture either of the world outside yourself or of your own actions is misleadingly incomplete. The theories you possess about both physical and psychological "reality" are only approximations—models that provide potentially useful but inevitably limited descriptions of how things really are in the external world and in your own consciousness. The inaccuracies of sensory perceptions, moreover, are further compounded by inaccurate memories, which deceive us with conjurings of things that did not happen, or that did happen, but not in the ways we believe them to have occurred.

The decisions we all make are often based upon such mistaken remembrances, erroneous ideas, and misrepresentations of external reality. Those decisions, clearly, serve us not nearly as well as decisions based on more accurate memories, ideas, and representations of reality.

We have then, two systems for thinking— an intuitive, emotional decision-making system, which he refers to as "fast" thinking; and a rational, deliberate, decision-making system, which Daniel Kahneman (2011) in *Thinking, Fast and Slow* (2011), calls "slow" thinking. Both systems of decision thinking are useful and valuable. Kahneman explains our thinking processes as the operation of these two parallel mental systems. The first of these, "System I," operates quickly and automatically, even effortlessly. The other, "System II," involves effort and thought; it takes time and involves concentration, judgment and analysis. We operate mostly with our System I thinking habits in full force. We prefer the cognitive ease of this kind of thinking, as it is nearly effortless. That's why we default to the quick, instinctive "blink" and avoid the cognitive strain of the more arduous, slower "think." "Just stop and think about it," we sometimes have to tell ourselves, when we are ready to make a decision. Or we ask, "Have I really thought this through"? In such instances, we acknowledge "System II" thinking. We need both of these thinking systems, along with their strengths and weakness, the uses and the limitations of each system—of thinking fast, and of thinking slow.

One of the real challenges for making decisions is that we almost always do not have all the information we need or we might wish to have when a decision must be made. Four-star general and former US Secretary of State Colin Powell maintained that he would not make a major decision unless he had an estimated 70% of the information he needed. But that still leaves nearly one-third of what would help to ensure a good decision out of the equation and left to guesswork. And we might ask just how Powell knew when he had that 70%.

Daniel Kahneman calls the incompleteness of information for decision-making WYSIATI, or "What You See Is All There Is." This is a variant on Powell's notion. Where Powell was confident that he could make the right decision most of the time with only 70% of the needed information, he suggests that most people assume they are making good decisions when they do not really know how little information they actually have. They believe that they have all the information they need because what they see is all that they think there is to see. This, of course, is erroneous. Believing WYSIATI leads to bad decisions because those decisions are based on woefully incomplete information.

When we believe WYSIATI, we are likely to make judgments and decisions on insufficient information, on a too-small sample, on inadequate evidence. When we do that, we often make mistakes. WYSIATI errors are related to overconfidence that the pattern we detect in the information and evidence we have is a pattern of value and importance. We also tend to believe that the pattern we detect allows for accurate predictions about what will happen next. But this is less a matter of fact than a matter of faith. In addition, our faith in WYSIATI often confirms what we want to believe, what we hope for, rather than what might actually be the case. WYSIATI confirms our biases.

The fundamental problem we have about knowing how things really are and what we might predict from them is that we don't really know what we don't know. As Khaneman puts it, we're "blind to our own blindness."

In a book about the failure of prediction and forecasting, *The Signal and the Noise*, Nate Silver (2012) offers three common reasons for the persistence of these kinds of errors. First, we focus on signals—information and details—that convey a story or embody a picture of the world less as it is, than as we believe it to be. Second, we exaggerate positive potential outcomes for ourselves while wildly downplaying risks, all the while ignoring the risks that are hardest to measure. And third, the assumptions we make about "reality"—the world as it is—are typically far rougher and cruder than we realize. We have a distaste for uncertainty and ambiguity, even when—especially when—ambiguity and uncertainty are an inescapable and intractable part of what we are trying to understand—earthquakes or economic behavior, for example, or the irrational exuberance people feel when they gamble. All these mistakes about thinking lead to bad decisions, decisions based on erroneous information.

As Daniel Levitin (2014) points out in *The Organized Mind*, decision-making is difficult because it consistently involves uncertainty. We can't know decisions we make are the right decisions, whether they will lead to the outcomes we hope for, and whether those outcomes are necessarily the best possible outcomes for us. Bad decisions sap our confidence and diminish our physical and psychic energy. Levitin suggests that we can increase our chances of making good decisions if we develop strategies to organize our minds and our lives.

One suggestion related specifically to making decisions in an organized way is to sort the many decisions large and small that confront us, using the following categories:

1. Decisions we can make immediately; these are obvious cases.
2. Decisions we can delegate to someone who has more knowledge, experience, expertise—someone we trust and respect.
3. Decisions we must make ourselves but for which we lack the time needed to process the information we have. These decisions require time for us to digest and process that information.
4. Decisions for which we need additional information.

Levitin provides a handy four-step process to deal with these decision categories.

He proposes that we act in one of the following ways for each decision confronting us.

1. Do it.
2. Delegate it.
3. Defer it.
4. Drop it.

Levitin warns that even when we use a hierarchical structure such as his recommended organized approach to making decisions, we often make our decisions less rationally than we think we do. Our rational decision thinking, he says, "is partly illusory." This is so because emotion affects our decisions, with decision-making often "lying outside our conscious control."

Choice, self-justification, and decisions

Psychologists have been studying for decades the ways in which we rationalize our decisions and justify our choices, whatever those choices might be. In *Mistakes Were Made (but not by me)*, Carol Tavris and Elliot Aronson (2007) provide many examples of how the process of self-justification occurs. The authors explain that the basis for self-justificatory explanations of our decisions is rooted in our difficulty in accepting "cognitive dissonance," a conflicting set of facts that confuse and upset our desire for consistency in belief and attitude. To take the most general of examples, when we idolize someone—a figure from history, religion, the arts—or when we admire someone close to us—a relative, friend, or mentor—and then discover that he or she did something that does not fit our mental model of them, we tend to discredit that information, to deny its validity, or to explain away its seriousness and importance. We simply are not comfortable with that dissonance, and thus, seek a way to eliminate the conflict it generates within us.

Or to take a different kind of example, if we have a strong desire to go on an expensive vacation, such that we will not be able to use the money for other more practical purposes, such as buying a much-needed new home appliance, or getting necessary dental care, we tend to justify our decision by minimizing the value of the appliance and the dental care and maximizing the value of the vacation. We might tell ourselves that the vacation will enhance our overall state of health both physical and mental, that it will provide our spouse with a highly deserved chance to relax, that it will refresh us such that when we return to work, we will be more creative and productive—and the like. On the other side, we tell ourselves that the appliance can wait, the dental work is not really necessary, and that we are far better off with the decision we made.

Movies often provide provocative examples of critical decision-making, decisions that affect people's lives in significant ways. Daniel Gilbert (2006) discusses one noteworthy example in *Stumbling Upon Happiness*, where he references the famous ending of the classic film *Casablanca*, starring Humphrey Bogart and Ingrid Bergman. At the end of the film, the Ingrid Bergman character has to decide whether to remain in Morocco with the Bogart character, or to return to her Nazi-fighting husband. Bogart tells her that she should go back to her husband and that if she doesn't, she will regret it—"maybe not today, maybe not tomorrow, but soon, and for the rest of your life." She decides to leave Bogart and return to her husband. Was this the right decision for her? Gilbert suggests that it was. And he suggests further that she can justify the decision so that she can live with it.

Yet, what if she would have made the opposite decision and remained in Morocco with Bogart? That decision, too, would have been the correct one for the Ingrid Bergman character. Why? Because in either case—in both cases—she would find reasons to justify her choice, reasons that would outweigh the choice she did not make, no matter what choice it was. She would invent reasons that would support either decision such that she could salve her conscience and live comfortably with her choice. That way of thinking is what most of us do most of the time. It is a way we learn to live with the decisions we make, especially the big decisions, those affecting our future happiness and well-being.

Affective Forecasting

The ability to predict how a decision made now will affect our future happiness is known as "affective forecasting." Economic decisions and decisions about money generally are examples of affective forecasts that we regularly make. Economists usually explain such decisions in terms of how people generally attempt to "maximize utility," a process in which rationality and logical analysis yield the best decision option. Psychologists, on the other hand, tend to explain these decisions in more subjective terms, with an emphasis less on a rational process of decision-making than on a feeling or intuition about what we believe will make us happiest in the future.

In "Affective Forecasting ... Or ... The Big Wombassa" (2013), Daniel Gilbert argues that we are not very good at determining our future happiness. He suggests that we tend to overestimate the ways future events will impact our lives, for better or worse. Losing a lover and losing a job certainly have a negative impact on the lives of most of us. However, when we experience such a misfortune, our present selves tend to vastly overestimate the amount of pain and the degree of lasting distress it will cause us. He and his colleagues have done considerable research to show that "impact bias," as they name this process, tends to make us overestimate the effect of such losses, while downplaying or neglecting the resilience and compensatory mechanisms we have to help us survive them and get on with our lives.

An interesting corollary to "impact bias," is our ability in hindsight to explain why a job or lover we have lost was actually a good thing. We might, acknowledge, for example, how the job was really physically harming us through stress, or the lover was limiting our capacity for self-development. On one hand, we might consider these ex-post-facto explanations as delusional "justifications," or "rationalizations," that we use to comfort ourselves and diminish the pain of those losses. Daniel Gilbert suggests that changing our view, retrospectively, in this way, is not necessarily a bad thing. Perhaps, he suggests, we might actually be recognizing destructive aspects about that previous job and lover that we were previously unable to acknowledge. When Shakespeare wrote "'Tis nothing either good or bad, but thinking makes it so," he hit on this aspect of our psychological makeup. Changing our response to something that happens to us—seeing it in a way that helps us accept adversity, for example—is actually a survival mechanism, one that long before Shakespeare was alive and well in the philosophy of the Stoics, in ancient Rome. The Stoics contended that although we can't change what happens to us, as circumstances are often beyond our control, we can change how we understand and respond to them.

Marriage decisions

One experience affected by affective forecasting involves one of life's major decisions: whether or not to get married. A related corollary, of course, once you decide whether to marry is whom to wed. And should you lose a spouse to death or divorce, those related questions arise again.

Charles Darwin approached the problem analytically, making a list of reasons for and against marriage for himself. Here, from Darwin's autobiography (1969) is what his list includes:

Marry

Children—(if it please God—Constant Companion, (& friend in old age) who will Feel interested in one, object to be beloved and played with —better than a dog anyhow— Homer, and someone to take care of house—Charms of music and female chit-chat. These things good for one's health. Forced to visit and receive relations *but terrible loss of time.* My God, it is intolerable to think of spending one's whole life, like a neuter bee, working, working, and nothing after all.—No, no won't do.—Imagine living all one's day solitary in smoky dirty London house.—Only picture to yourself nice soft wife on a sofa with good fire, and books and music perhaps—compare this vision with the dingy reality of Grt Marlboro's St.

Not marry

No children, (no second life) no one to take care for one in old age... Freedom to go where one liked—Choice of Society and *little of it.* Conversation of clever men at clubs—Not forced to visit relatives, and to bend in every trifle—to have the expense and anxiety of Children— perhaps quarreling. Loss of time—cannot read in the evenings—fatness and idleness —anxiety and responsibility— less money for books etc—if many children forced to gain one's bread.—(But then it is very bad for one's health to work so much) Perhaps my wife won't like London; then the sentence is banishment and degradation with indolent idle fool.

Darwin decided to marry, writing under the left column: "Marry—Marry—Marry Q.E.D." However, he also added a note: "There is many a happy slave." In his book *Risk Savvy*, Gerd Gigerenzer (2014) speculates that Darwin may have had two basic ways to make his decision to marry: "maximizing" and "rules of thumb." Maximizing involves estimating what each of the pros for marriage is worth (its utility), estimating the probabilities that those good things will actually happen, then multiplying those probabilities by the utilities and adding up the numbers. This would be done, as well, for the cons to avoid marrying. Then the numbers would be compared and the choice would be made based on the alternative with the highest number. As Gigerenzer points out, this method, called "the maximization of subjective expected utility" is taught in universities as the essence of rational choice. It is based on the assumption that risks can be estimated, understood, and calculated.

That assumption, however, is unreasonable. The calculation is meaningless because the probabilities are purely speculative; they are not at all based on authentic knowledge, but rather on guesswork. For situations in which uncertainty reigns, it is better to use a "rule of thumb," a simple clear guideline for decision-making: "*Find the most important reason and ignore the rest*," Gerd Gigerenzer advises. He speculates that this may have been what Darwin did when he imagined himself on a sofa with his wife, a fire going and books and music to accompany their conversation. Here, the power of visualization is not to be underestimated.

Deciding to marry is one consideration; a related decision concerns whom to marry. A similar kind of calculus could be used to weigh the relative merits of different partners, with many of the same pitfalls associated with an attempt to put a number on the mate value resulting from such an analysis. However, because this decision is also based on uncertainties rather than on knowledge, on things that can't be predicted about the future, this kind of decision, too, might be better approached with rules of thumb. Different people will have different rules of thumb to guide them in making the choice of a life-partner. For some it might be finding the richest partner, for others the most beautiful or the most intelligent, the most compliant, or the most compatible. It might involve finding someone with the same core values, someone who comes from the same racial or ethnic background, someone with a similar level of education, socio-economic background, sense of humor. Whatever the rules of thumb used, they are mostly based on feeling, on intuition, rather than on complex analytical procedures.

A year after making his list of pros and cons, and perhaps trusting his instinct as much as his reason, Darwin married his cousin Emma Wedgwood with whom he had ten children.

Achieving Insights that Affect Decisions

How we achieve and sustain insights is another factor in decision-making. In *Seeing What Others Don't*, Gary Klein (2013) analyzes ways that we can develop insights—and also ways that insights might be prevented from developing. He suggests that insight is related to intuition in being unexpected, but that it differs from intuition in the radical shift of understanding that accompanies insight. Intuition relies on previously learned patterns; insight discovers new patterns. We achieve insight in the search for better, more accurate, and more comprehensive explanations— stories that explain what we were previously unable to understand. Insights are disruptive; they change our understanding, our feelings, and sometimes even our perspective or beliefs.

Gary Klein suggests that we gain insights in four ways, through: (1) making connections; (2) following our curiosity; (3) observing coincidences; and (4) noticing contradictions. Most often, two or three of these ways of achieving insight occur together, so that noticing a coincidence arouses our curiosity, which leads us to ask questions, investigate further, and so follow an enticing lead. Or we might make a connection between two things we had not previously put together, and wonder what further connections, led by our curiosity, we might make. The key is to notice the coincidence, connection, or contradiction, and then to take action by following up and through with further questioning, noticing, investigating. We need to be decisive in making connections and taking action.

An additional path toward insight is something Klein calls "creative desperation." This path or trigger for intuition differs from the others in being more dramatic and more ingenious. He provides a number of examples, the most dramatic of which is the way a smokejumper firefighter, Wagner Dodge, in 1949, saved his life by starting a small fire that encircled him and then diving headfirst into its ashes. Dodge had barely a minute in which to make this life-or-death decision. A raging forest fire was rapidly approaching him and his men as it jumped across a gulch, its flames rapidly ascending the walls of a canyon the men were themselves ascending toward safety at the top. Dodge realized that neither he nor his men could outrun the fire. At that moment he decided to stand still, light a match and start his own small fire, igniting the grass in front of him so that its flames would move away and up the mountain. He then wet his handkerchief, clutched it to his mouth and lay down in the embers of this fire. He had effectively created a little buffer of burned land that would serve as his safe haven. Within minutes the gigantic fire roared past him. He had enough oxygen to breathe and was barely singed by the fire. His men, who tried to outrun the fire, were incinerated. The only firefighter who managed to outrun the fire died of severe burns a few days afterwards.

What saved Wagner Dodge's life was his quick but rational thinking. Under the influence of emotion, one's instinct is to run—as fast as possible away from a raging fire. Dodge, however, had the benefit of experience—he had seen fires like this one before; he knew there was no chance of outrunning it. The speed at which the fire was racing up the walls of the canyon consuming the tinder-ready dry grass made that impossible. Dodge's counter-intuitive but logical decision saved his life. Ever since, this strategy of lighting an "escape fire," has been used by firefighters the world over.

To improve our chances to gain insights and make better decisions, Klein suggests that we tune our thinking and behavior differently for each of the insight paths. In noticing contradictions, we need to be willing to be surprised, even shocked by the unexpected. We need to take contradictions seriously even if they violate our normal patterns of belief and understanding. In making connections, we need to be open to new possibilities and ready to explore the unfamiliar. Creative desperation necessitates that we examine our assumptions and act in a way that might violate our usual patterns of behavior.

An insight is a jump—an imaginative leap—to a different way of understanding how things work. It surprises us in that it is not the result of deliberation, analysis, or conscious thought. The changes in ourselves that insights provoke can sometimes be difficult to

185

Table 6.1 Decision thinking aspects

Experiencing intuitions and rationalizations
Thinking fast and slow
Being limited to WYSIATI
Self-justifying choices
Acknowledging affective forecasting
Achieving insights

accept. But when we accept them, we alter how we understand things. As a result, we may shift not only our way of thinking, but our way of believing and behaving, and our way of making decisions.

In an essay, "Insight," Gary Klein (2013) adds another wrinkle to these arguments, suggesting that intuition in the form of expertise and tacit knowledge drives decisions, often very good decisions. He distinguishes between explicit knowledge of factual information, on the one hand, and implicit or tacit knowledge, such as pattern recognition, on the other. Other aspects of tacit knowledge that are factors in quick decision-making include the mental models we have of the world, the stories we tell ourselves about the world, and the sense of typicality we have about things we know a lot about. In those instances, when something is awry, or off-the-mark, we know it intuitively; we make intuitive judgments not through analysis of factual details and information, but through instinctive sense-making, sizing things up (see Table 6.1).

Institutional Decisions

Among the most important decision-making challenges people confront are those that involve institutions and the people who lead them. Large-scale public projects and complex procedures often require a network of shared responsibility for decisions, especially in designing effective approaches. Urban planners confront such challenges as a matter of course. So, too, do those entrusted with the responsibility of designing and re-designing transportation systems; taxation, banking regulations, and other financial systems; public health directives; educational policies and other large-scale provisions with significant social implications. Each of these kinds of responsibilities is riddled with challenging, high-impact decisions.

Pension reform, social security, automotive fuel efficiency, sanitation, global warming, and other international problems—all require decision thinking at the institutional level, the governmental level, and beyond. These and other large-scale challenges require practical, creative resolution (and compromise) in addressing, if not always or even often resolving, intractable human problems. And they require political will, whether exercised through democratic or authoritarian principles.

Richard Thaler and Cass Sunstein (2009) provide one approach in their book *Nudge*, in which they detail a set of suggestions for structuring social policies to influence people's behavior. In Richard Thaler's words, they aim to influence the "design of policies in both the public and private sector that make people better off," without coercion. These authors present a series of ideas for the practice of structuring choices in such areas as energy conservation, investing, insurance, marketing, politics, health care delivery, and more.

One example is their suggestion that employers make 401k savings plans automatic—the "default"—which employees can opt out of, if they wish. The way such plans are typically structured now is that people must sign up for them; they have to opt in. They argue that it is good for us to have these plans as protection for our future, and that more of us will use them if they are the default, rather than an option. Another example is the way organ donations are made in different countries. When you renew your driver's license in the United States, you have the option of enrolling in an organ donor program by checking a box on the form. Opting out is the default. In some other countries, including Poland and France, you have to check a box to opt out; participation is the default. These examples "nudge" people in the direction of policies regarded by many as socially beneficial.

Some people, however, libertarians among them, think these nudges are dangerous because they allow others to decide things for us. Such nudges, say these critics, are a form of social engineering, with government bureaucrats making decisions that we should make for ourselves.

Incentives and Decisions

People make decisions based on incentives. You've heard the expression "It's like giving candy to a baby." The baby, perhaps a toddler, is crying; you give the child some M&Ms or other sweet treat, and he stops crying. In the same way, you are motivated to do something—or not to do it—based on various kinds of incentives, including threats as well as rewards to elicit a particular desired behavior.

Different kinds of incentives motivate people to behave in different ways. Among the most common incentives, of course, is money; it's a powerful incentive because it allows us to satisfy a wide range of desires and to pursue many types of goals. Money is a reward that allows for various kinds of personal satisfaction.

You expect to be paid for your work as a teacher or administrator. And you expect that your school's secretaries and custodians, its bus drivers and guidance counselors, technology support staff, consultants and the like need to be paid. It's their reward for the work they do. And yet students aren't paid for their work in schools.

With the incentive of money, size matters. When you have the opportunity to earn more money doing similar work in similar circumstances, you tend to take it. And yet money is not the only incentive. If you have to give up autonomy, or if you have to give up working in a pleasant environment where you are comfortable with your colleagues for work in a less favorable set of circumstances, with reduced autonomy and friction among colleagues, the allure of more money will likely not be sufficiently seductive for you to give up one job for another. Size does matter, but only up to a point.

Other incentives matter, besides money, as Daniel Pink (2009) notes in his book, *Drive*. These include autonomy, along with the desire to do productive work—work that matters to you, work you value and that you believe contributes to the public good. Public servants of all stripes sacrifice the opportunity to earn more money for the satisfaction of doing meaningful work that achieves goals they believe are purposeful and important.

A third incentive is mastery. If you are like many people, you want to get better at what you do. And you want to have the opportunity to grow and develop, to achieve mastery and the satisfactions that derive from it.

These three incentives—autonomy, mastery, and meaning—provide alternatives to financial incentives. So, too, do the incentives to contribute to the public good, along with other types of social incentives, including appearing well in the eyes of others. And so, again, if you are like others, you want to do what they are doing, not all the time of course, while preserving your individual specialness.

And to these incentives should be added those of legality and morality. Most people, most of the time, obey the law. More people obey the law more strictly when they know they are being watched. Think of your driving habits when a police car comes into view. Moral codes also guide behavior; people make choices according to their sense of and their beliefs about right and wrong. Being ethical, believing yourself to be an ethical person, also affects decisions you make about your behavior. We take up ethical decision-making in the next chapter. For now, it's enough to note that various kinds of incentives—financial, social, legal, and moral—among others are implicated in the act of making decisions and in the kinds of decisions made.

Decisiveness

In their book *Decisive*, Chip Heath and Dan Heath (2013), provide a model for decision-making composed of four major elements:

- Widening our options
- Reality-testing our assumptions
- Attaining distance from our problem
- Preparing to be wrong

For each of these elements, the Heaths offer specific suggestions and illustrate these with case studies.

For widening our options, they recommend the following: (1) avoiding a narrow frame for your problem; (2) multi-tracking; and (3) finding someone who has solved your problem.

For reality-testing your assumptions, they advise (1) considering the opposite; (2) zooming out and then in on the problem; and (3) "ooching," or dipping a toe in, going small at first before investing too much too fast.

To attain distance before making a decision, they encourage (1) overcoming short-term emotion; and (2) honoring core priorities.

To prepare to be wrong, the Heath brothers advocate (1) book-ending the future; and (2) setting a tripwire.

Let's consider their suggestions by identifying some questions we might ask about making an important decision.

Imagine that you have an important choice to make about a career matter, a personal situation, or an academic issue. Let's take the example of whether or not to pursue a second master's degree from a particular institution. We can ask ourselves the following questions:

- How can I expand my set of options so as not to frame my choice too narrowly? (*Strategy*: Develop at least three options to seriously consider. Alternatively, have two or three friends or coworkers suggest the other options. These might be alternative programs to the one being considered, or alternatives to earning the second masters.)
- How can I avoid gathering only confirmatory information? (*Strategy*: Talk to people who graduated from the program who found it wanting in some respect. Research outcomes of those who selected other alternatives to a second masters. Look deliberately for criticism of the program and/or of the idea of doing a second masters.)
- How can I collect trustworthy information to reality-check my assumptions? (*Strategy*: Consider the source of the information; go beyond the school and program Web site, for example. Look for inconsistencies and contradictions in the information you gather. Follow up on initial research.)
- How can I avoid allowing emotion to drive me to the wrong choice? (*Strategy*: Acknowledge the fact that emotion plays a strong part in making any decision; give emotion its due recognition. Then imagine Mr. Spock analyzing the data gathered and questioning the decision being contemplated.)
- How can I avoid becoming overconfident about the rightness of my decision? And: How can I avoid being overconfident about the future prospects of my choice? (*Strategy*: Imagine a future scenario in which the decision leads to "worst-case scenario"

Table 6.2 Making better decisions

Widen options
Reality-test assumptions
Attain distance
Expect errors

outcomes. Consider the implications of those outcomes and what might have been done to minimize or avoid the damage incurred.)

Developing multiple options minimizes the chance that we will indulge our egos in a single choice option. It maximizes the chance to consider all options seriously. There is, of course, the danger that considering too many options at once can create option paralysis. The paradox of choice is that with too many choices available it is more rather than less difficult to make a decision. One study, for example, offered buyers the option of twenty-four different choices of jam flavors. Confronted with that many options, very few people bought any jam. When the choices were reduced to six jam flavors, ten times more people selected one of the six for purchase.

Sometimes, options are not presented honestly, and are not really the only options available. Former US Secretary of State Henry Kissinger once offered the options of staying with the then current policy of planning for nuclear war, or of surrendering. Clearly, Kissinger was slanting the options, limiting them to two completely unpalatable possibilities (nuclear war or surrender) in order to drive the decision to remain with the then-current policy.

An additional consideration in evaluating options is to move back and forth between prevention and promotion mindsets. A prevention mindset avoids negative outcomes; a promotion mindset pursues positive possibilities. It is wise to toggle between these prevention and promotion mindsets rather than becoming locked in to only one of them. Let "and" be the option-generating and considering motto rather than "or." Instead of "either" this "or" only that, make it "both this and that." Table 6.2 presents techniques for making better decisions.

Avoiding confirmation bias: considering the opposite

One of the strongest impediments to successful thinking and decision-making is "confirmation bias," a notion mentioned in earlier chapters. Confirmation bias refers to our tendency to see only the evidence that supports our way of thinking while avoiding any and all evidence that contradicts it. When we buy a new car or are considering buying one, and we are emotionally attracted to a particular brand and model, we look for those features that garner positive evaluations and ignore those features that receive less than positive acclaim. Once we have made our purchase, we tend to look only at those aspects of our purchase that satisfy us—for example, at its smooth ride, its attractive appearance, its great stereo system—while downplaying the car's mediocre safety record, its poor gas mileage, and its high cost. Confirmation bias goes hand in hand with self-justification.

In order to avoid the trap of confirmation bias, hunt for information that runs counter to what you believe and want to believe about the choice you are making. Look for contradictory information, and in organizations, seek constructive disagreement. Ask what the Heaths call "disconfirming questions," that is, questions that might unsettle your easy confidence in the decision you are about to make. With our second Master's program example, seek out people who chose not to apply to that school or program, or who dropped out. Ask why they decided to do what they did—in the face of the direct opposite decision you are contemplating.

We should seek extreme disconfirmation to consider the opposite of our instincts and inclination. This is a way of "seeing the other side," of allowing that what appears to us in a negative light, might be seen by someone else more positively. In each of these ways, we need to make a concerted and concentrated effort to seek counter-evidence, an opposite perspective, a more variegated set of possibilities, if we are to make wise and sound decisions.

Making Tough Decisions

In her book *The Power of Mindful Learning* (1997), Ellen J. Langer describes the situation of a female colleague who had to decide whether to remain at a university where no woman had been tenured in her department and where no one in her field had been tenured for fifteen years. The professor's friends suggested she seek another job because, given the base rates for the two applicable dimensions, the odds were decidedly against her receiving tenure.

Without denying the discouraging statistics, Ellen Langer reframed the problem and asked her friend how often she had been successful in her professional pursuits. She also asked her how many people in her university received tenure having earned their degrees at the prestigious institution where she earned her doctorate. Those questions yielded a rather different base rate, one that was much more encouraging about a positive tenure decision. Langer suggests that when making an important decision, we broaden the base for how we analyze various prospects and outcomes.

In addition, we should also factor in our own intuition, our feelings, and our sense of what is right for us. Making decisions solely on the basis of group aggregated data, however accurate, omits an important personal element that we ought to include. Using both the broad group data and our own personal instincts allows for what Langer describes as "mindful" decision-making.

In *How Good People Make How Tough Choices*, Rushworth M. Kidder (2009) develops a framework for how people can make tough choices responsibly and effectively. Although many of the examples he discusses reflect difficult moral or ethical decisions, his model for decision-making can be applied more broadly to any type of difficult decision, personal or professional, individual or social.

The process is driven by what he calls "energetic self-reflection" grounded in a clearly defined set of personal values. To make tough choices with the goal of getting those choices right rather than simply getting over and through them requires courage. Consider the example of a librarian who fields phone questions from a caller and is overhead by a police officer who demands to know with whom she has been speaking. It seems that the officer has some grounds for suspecting that the caller committed a rape the previous night. The librarian has to decide whether to weigh more heavily her obligation to protect the caller's confidentiality or her obligation as a member of the community to help safeguard it from further danger and violence. This kind of dilemma is a choice between "right versus right" since there is good reason for the librarian to decide either way.

And now consider a second example of a recently installed plant manager who learns that a major Hollywood television company annually shot a scene for one of its television shows in the plant parking lot on a weekend. The company's corporate headquarters allowed the filming to be done free of charge. When the new plant manager is offered a $500 payment, he does not want to accept it, even though his predecessor had done just that. He could justify taking the payment since he did spend a full day of his own time at the filming. However, if he accepts the check made out to the company and sends it on to corporate headquarters, he will very likely get his predecessor in trouble, since the company has had no prior knowledge of such arrangements and payments. The plant manager has a tough choice to wrestle with, considered in light of his own strongly held beliefs and values, one that requires courage to make.

In the cases of both the librarian and the plant manager, the core values of the individual making the decision are critical. Those core values, along with the courage required to apply them, impinge on matters of morality and ethics. We discuss those kinds of questions more thoroughly in the following chapter.

Making Group Decisions

In *Wiser*, a book about how to improve the thinking of groups, Cass Sunstein and Reid Hastie (2015) describe the difficulties involved with group decision-making. Among the common obstacles to successful group decisions, the authors identify groupthink and happy talk. Groupthink precludes diversity of perspectives; happy talk avoids contentious ideas. Both groupthink and happy talk create a sense of complacency. They suppress thinking that cuts against the optimistic grain of the majority consensus thinking. As a result, important information that could lead to better decisions isn't brought forward.

Sunstein and Hastie suggest that when groups fail to correct the errors of their majority members, they actually amplify those errors, making matters worse by intensifying and extending bad ideas put forward by individuals. And because those who speak first and strongest tend to influence those who speak later, group thinking cascades into herd thinking. Like-minded individuals confirm each other's thinking, pushing it toward more extreme forms. In addition, the shared information confirmed through groupthink and happy talk increases a group's confidence about its decisions. Disturbing information remains unshared even when that information is vital to effective decision-making, largely because individuals fear being criticized, ostracized, and devalued when bringing unpopular ideas or disruptive information into group discussions.

For effective group decision-making, cognitive diversity and opportunities for dissent are essential. So, too, is avoiding various kinds of biases, especially biases towards status. Leaders, thus, should listen rather than speak during group discussions. Their views should not be voiced early, if at all. Leaders and other influencers need to silence themselves so that a diverse set of views can be identified and considered. For successful group decisions, new and different ideas should be encouraged, contrarian perspectives voiced, and disruptive potentialities identified.

Applications

6-1. To what extent do you think Jonathan Haidt is right in his claim that our thinking is more confirmatory than exploratory, and that we react with intuition and feelings that we subsequently seek to justify? To what extent are you ready to accept his point about "after-the-fact" decision-making?

6-2. To what extent do you agree with Leonard Mlodinow that your unconscious rules your behavior?

6-3. Do you think it is easier to convince someone to change his or her mind by logical reasoning or by considering intuitions and beliefs? What happens mostly in political discussions when you dispute, criticize, attack, correct, or otherwise attempt to change someone's position or perspective? To what extent do you think Jonathan Haidt's theory of thinking explains this behavior?

6-4. What relationship exists between the ideas of Leonard Mlodinow and those of Jonathan Haidt? What might we do to mitigate or minimize the potential dangers they describe?

6-5. What benefits can we take away from Daniel Kahneman's analysis of our propensity to overestimate our knowledge and our ability to predict what will happen in the future? How useful do you find his discussion of WYSIATI—of his idea that we are "blind to our own blindness?" When might you find this concept useful?

6-6. What does Nate Silver add to your understanding of the challenges that confront us as we attempt to understand how things work in the world? How do you respond to Colin Powell's 70% rule for making decisions?

6-7. How might you use Daniel Levitin's approach to decision-making today to organize your approach to decisions that confront you?

6-8. To what extent do you agree with Carol Tavris and Elliott Aronson that our ex-post-facto explanations are forms of self-delusional compensations that avoid the truths of difficult situations? To what extent do you agree with Daniel Gilbert that such justifications are a necessary response in adjusting to complicated and painful circumstances? Is there any way to negotiate productively between their competing views and judgments?

6-9. What do you think of the choice that Ingrid Bergman makes at the end of *Casablanca*? To what extent do you find Daniel Gilbert's explanation of the choice she made, and the hypothetical case of her having made a different choice, persuasive?

6-10. What are some of your favorite movies in which a character has to make an important choice that will have a significant effect on his or her life? Do you think the character made the right choice in each situation? Why or why not? And do you think the character believes that he or she made the right choice, thus confirming Gilbert's theory.

6-11. To what extent do you agree with Daniel Gilbert's explanation of "affective forecasting?" Do you find yourself misjudging your ability to adjust to difficult and challenging circumstances? Or is this something you are good at?

6-12. To what extent do you make important life decisions in the way Charles Darwin went about deciding whether to marry? What are the merits and pitfalls of a completely analytical approach to making major life decisions?

6-13. Do you think Gerd Gigerenzer is right to emphasize the importance of gut instinct for making significant decisions in both personal and professional life? What do you think of the examples he provides?

6-14. When you gain an insight, an "aha" moment of understanding—how, for you, does it occur? Does one of the pathways identified by Gary Klein, more than the others, seem to capture how you achieve insights? Or is there, perhaps, some other explanation for how they occur for you?

6-15. How do you respond to the story of Wagner Dodge and his counter-intuitive decision to "fight fire with fire"? What were the ingredients or elements that led Dodge to his decision? To what extent can you extrapolate from Dodge's decision-making and apply it to a situation of your own? And, how do you use "tacit knowledge" to make decisions?

6-16. Who should be responsible for the development and implementation of principles of "institutional design?" To what extent should institutional design be the primary or even the sole responsibility of institutional leaders? To what extent should institutional design practicalities be shared with and distributed among various stakeholder and participant constituencies?

6-17. Give an example of an institution with which you are familiar—in terms of shaping its future direction, purpose, goals, and strategies for achieving them. Explain what might be done to encourage better decision-making in that institution.

6-18. Do you agree with the strategies for creating "default" positions advocated by Richard Thaler and Cass Sunstein with regard to shaping public policy decisions? Do you think that your decision-making capacity is being limited by the kinds of nudging they advocate? Why or why not?

6-19. Should the incentive of paying students for achieving good grades or for achieving a particular level of score on national tests be introduced in places where schools and students are performing poorly—below the national average, for example? Steven D. Levitt and Stephen J. Dubner (2014), in their book *Think Like a Freak*, suggest that paying students sizable amounts of money for excellent performance (thousands of dollars for an A, for example) would dramatically increase the numbers of students on the honor roll around the country. What do you think about this?

6-20. Which of Dan and Chip Heath's four major categories of advice for decision-making resonates most immediately for you, and why?

6-21. Identify a personal, professional, or academic situation in which you need to make an important decision. Use the Heath brothers' suggestions for widening your options in order to avoid a narrow frame of reference and avoid confirmation bias by considering the opposite. Then apply their strategies for "reality-testing your assumptions."

6-22. Now apply the strategies the Heath brothers suggest for "attaining distance," and "preparing to be wrong."

6-23. In Rushworth's Kidder's scenario about the librarian, what do you think she should do? Is her responsibility toward her caller more important than her responsibility to provide information to the police officer?

6-24. In Rushworth Kidder's scenario about the plant manager, what should he do with respect to the offer of the $500 payment? What is your reasoning for that decision?

6-25. Identify a situation involving a particular group making one or more decisions in school or at work. What forces make or made that group decision less rather than more effective. What would need to be done, specifically, for better decisions to be made by this group.

References

Darwin, Charles. 1969. Nora Barlow, ed. *The Autobiography of Charles Darwin*. Norton.

Gigerenzer, Gerd. 2014. *Risk Savvy*. New York: Viking.

Gilbert, Daniel. 2006. *Stumbling Upon Happiness*. New York: Knopf.

Gilbert, Daniel. 2013. "Affective Forecasting ... Or ... The Big Wombassa: What You Think You're Going to Get, and What You Don't Get, When You Get What You Want." In *Thinking*. Ed. John Brockman. New York: Harper.

Haidt, Jonathan. 2012. *The Righteous Mind*. New York: Pantheon.

Heath, Chip and Dan Heath. 2013. *Decisive*. New York: Crown Business.

Kahneman, Daniel. 2011. *Thinking, Fast and Slow*. New York: Farrar, Straus and Giroux.

Kidder, Rushworth M. 2009. *How Good People Make Tough Choices*, rev. edn. New York: Harper Perennial.

Klein, Gary. 2013. "Insight." In *Thinking*. Ed. John Brockman. New York: Harper.

Klein, Gary. 2013. *Seeing What Others Don't*. New York: Public Affairs.

Langer, Ellen J. 1997. *The Power of Mindful Learning*. New York: Da Capo Press/Perseus Books.

Lehrer, Jonah. 2009. *How We Decide*. Boston: Houghton Mifflin.

Levitin, Daniel. 2014. *The Organized Mind*. Toronto: Penguin Canada.

Levitt, Steven D. and Stephen J. Dubner. 2014. *Think Like a Freak*. New York: Harper Collins.

Mlodinow, Leonard. 2012. *Subliminal*. New York: Random House, Vintage.

Pink, Daniel. 2009. *Drive*. New York: Riverhead.

Tavris, Carol and Elliot Aronson. 2007. *Mistakes Were Made (but not by me)*. New York: Harcourt.

Thaler, Richard and Cass Sunstein. 2009. *Nudge*. New York: Penguin.

Silver, Nate. 2012. *The Signal and the Noise*. New York: Penguin.

Sunstein, Cass and Reid Hastie. 2015. *Wiser: Getting Beyond Groupthink to Make Groups Smarter*. Boston: Harvard Business Review Press.

Interchapter 6

Embracing Ambiguity

Ambiguity is one type of complexity in which meaning is unclear or inexact. Ambiguous images can be read in two ways simultaneously. The famous images of the rabbit/duck and of the goblet/faces you saw earlier are ambiguous.

Ambiguity is often troubling because its inherent indeterminacy frustrates our desire to understand. Ambiguity is the enemy of clarity, which it obscures and obfuscates. The world of ambiguity is the world of shadows; it is the place where you literally don't know what is going on. It's a place where you are unsure, uncertain, and often uncomfortable.

Ambiguity in language can be troubling, offering multiple meanings for something that is spoken or written. For example, if you say that you will "give someone a ring," does that mean you will call him or her on the phone or give her a piece of jewelry? Consider the following ambiguous sentence: "I cannot recommend this person too highly." Does this mean that you wish to recommend the individual very highly, or does it mean that you can't recommend the person highly at all?

Jay Leno, the retired late night talk host, once compiled a set of ambiguous newspaper headlines. Here are a few of them.

"Drought Turns Coyotes to Watermelons."
"Red Tape Holds Up New Bridges."
"Police Begin Campaign to Run Down Jaywalkers."

Critical and Creative Thinking: A Brief Guide for Teachers, First Edition. Robert DiYanni.
© 2016 John Wiley & Sons, Inc. Published 2016 by John Wiley & Sons, Inc.

These comic examples suggest that some individuals were not paying attention to their language.

Ambiguity is not always a problem. Some types of ambiguity are unavoidable, even desirable. Poets frequently complicate a poem with ambiguity intentionally to enrich what it suggests.

Consider the opening line of John Keats' "Ode on a Grecian Urn":

Thou still unravisht bride of quietness.

The word "still" here can mean both not moving and also "yet." The ancient urn is both at once.

Or, for a slightly longer example, consider William Blake's "The Sick Rose":

> O Rose thou art sick.
> The invisible worm,
> That flies in the night
> In the howling storm:
> Has found out thy bed
> Of crimson joy;
> And his dark secret love
> Does thy life destroy.

This ominous sounding poem contains a number of ambiguities, including the word "bed," which refers simultaneously to the bed of roses in which the "Rose" is found and the "bed" in which love is made. The word "Rose" names both a flower and a woman.

Ambiguity, as Michael Gelb (2000) suggests, can be demonstrated visually with Leonardo's famous "sfumato" style of painting. *Sfumato* refers to smokiness or cloudiness. It suggests a balance and blend of light and shadow that conceals as much as it reveals. For Leonardo, *sfumato* implies mysteriousness, even secrecy; it is illustrated most famously in the smile of his *Mona Lisa* (Figure 6.2). Leonardo embraced ambiguity by means of *sfumato;* his use light and shadow allowed for a complex portrayal of human faces.

Sfumato suggests intellectual dispositions that can help develop your capacity for critical and creative thinking. These include both ambiguity and uncertainty, along with an open-mindedness that accepts complexity and the indeterminate. *Sfumato* also includes a willingness to look for ways in which opposite qualities and characteristics can be balanced, blended, and harmonized.

Figure 6.2 *Mona Lisa*, Leonardo da Vinci. © Gianni Dagli Ortis/Corbis

Figure 6.3 *St. John the Baptist,* Leonardo da Vinci. © Photo Scala, Florence

Look for example at Leonardo's *St. John the Baptist* (Figure 6.3) for another example of *sfumato*'s ambiguity. Notice how the saint's face, similar to that of the *Mona Lisa,* balances highly lit portions with others that are shadowed and shaded. Notice the figure's smile—and how Leonardo creates that smile through blending light and shadow, a contrast echoed in the lit figure and dark background.

Another provocative aspect of the painting is the figure's stance, with its curved arm and its hand and index finger pointing upward. What are we to make of this gesture? Where is St. John pointing and why?

Applications

1. Explain the ambiguity in the following sentences—an ambiguity created by punctuation: (a) Woman without her man is nothing. (b) Woman: without her, man is nothing. (c) Woman, without her man, is nothing.
2. What is ambiguous about these sentences?
    A friend in need is a friend in deed.
    A friend in need is a friend indeed.
3. Leonardo wrote, "every part is disposed to unite with the whole, that it may thereby escape from its own incompleteness." Provide an example from your own experience to which this insight applies.

Reference

Gelb, Michael. 2000. *How to Think Like Leonardo da Vinci*. New York: Dell.

7

Ethical Thinking
Making Ethical Decisions

Figure 7.1   Ethical decisions. © Stuart Miles/Fotolia

The first step in the evolution of ethics is a sense of solidarity with other human beings.

—Albert Schweitzer

An ethical person ought to do more than he's required to do and less than he's allowed to do.

—Bertrand Russell

Ethical decisions ensure that everyone's best interest is protected.

—Harvey Mackay

Critical and Creative Thinking: A Brief Guide for Teachers, First Edition. Robert DiYanni.
© 2016 John Wiley & Sons, Inc. Published 2016 by John Wiley & Sons, Inc.

Basic Ethical Concepts

Not a day goes by that we don't hear and read in the news about some violation of rules governing stock trading practices; new guidelines for banking regulations; new legal strictures governing political campaign donations; new rules in baseball about crashing into the catcher at home plate, or in football regarding helmet to helmet contact. While all these examples do not, strictly speaking, involve ethics and moral choices, they all involve things, within their respective frames of reference, that should and should not be done. Ethics pervades our lives; there is no escape from questions that require moral choice and ethical decision-making.

Ethics is concerned with matters of right and wrong, responsible and irresponsible behavior. As a branch of moral philosophy, ethics investigates questions involving appropriate and inappropriate action and behavior, making it a very practical branch of philosophy. Ethics and moral philosophy involve an attempt to think critically and reflectively about good and bad, right and wrong in small matters, such as gossiping about people, and in larger ones, such as global poverty, environmental destruction, racial justice, assisted suicide, animal rights, and many other complex issues.

Some thinkers, Julian Baggini (2012) among them, differentiate morality from ethics. They suggest that morality involves adhering to conventional rules whereas ethics concerns a broader attempt to "do the right thing." From this standpoint, morality impinges on acting in ways that particular moral codes either encourage or prohibit. Ethics, by contrast, is concerned more with living a good life, one that goes well for oneself and for one's relations with others. That being said, the most serious ethical questions tend to be rooted in moral concerns in that they involve not only ourselves, but also the impact our actions can have on others. Moral values serve as guidelines, as rules governing ethical behavior. Morals involve principles; ethics involves actions.

Even when we agree on moral rules or laws, we may disagree on how to apply or uphold those moral principles in practice. In practical ethics we consider whether particular actions are right or wrong. Is killing another individual ever justifiable? Is aborting a fetus right or wrong? Is euthanasia ever permissible? Is it allowable, ever, to tell a lie? Is it ethical to misrepresent yourself on the

Internet? On a resume? In a situation where you are seeking help, advice, advancement?

A second way to think about ethics involves developing general theories or principles, which we can then apply in practical situations. This more normative ethics develops general principles or norms for use in specific instances. A third approach considers the very ideas of good and evil, right and wrong, as concepts in and of themselves. This more abstract and speculative approach to ethics is called "meta" ethics. In this chapter, we emphasize the practical questions raised by ethics, while also considering some fundamental ethical principles.

Among ethical concerns are questions of morality, whether there are absolute or universal ethical principles and values, or whether ethical behavior is situational or contextual. The famous principle of the "golden rule" (to treat others as you wish to be treated) is an example of a guiding principle of ethical behavior—and one that appears in many cultures throughout history.

The golden rule finds expression in different religious and philosophical traditions, offering variations on its basic theme. It is found in the Christian scriptures in the gospel of Matthew: "Do unto others as you would have them do unto you." Other New Testament versions include one from the gospel of Mark: "Love your neighbor as yourself." These biblical injunctions are anticipated and echoed by those from other cultures, including those shown in Table 7.1.

One question we might ask about these varied expressions of the golden rule is whether there is any real difference between those stated positively and those stated negatively. Is a negative version somewhat more passive than an active positive version of the rule? Julian Baggini, in his book *Ethics,* argues that positive and negative versions ultimately come down to the same fundamental value. The differences in tone and expression are not significant. In theory, he suggests, the negative version seems to demand less of us—to minimize harm to others—while the positive versions demand this and also that we maximize the welfare of others. And yet, he contends, the spirit of the golden rule boils down to what he calls "an ethos of reciprocal demand." This suggests that whether we are "doing" or "not doing" something to or for others, it should be just what we would want done or not done to us.

Table 7.1 The golden rule across cultures, philosophies, and religions

- What you do not wish done to yourself, do not do to others. (Confucius, *Analects*).
- What is hateful to you, do not do to your neighbor. This is the whole Torah; all the rest is commentary. (Hillel, *Talmud*, Shabbat)
- To those who are good to me, I am good; to those who are not good to me, I am also good." (Lao-Tzu, *Tao Te Ching*)
- Hurt not others in ways you would find hurtful yourself. (Buddha, *Dhammapada*).
- Do naught unto others which would cause pain if done to you. (Hindu, *Mahabharata*)
- No one of you is a believer until he desires for his brother that which he desires for himself. (*Hadith*, Islamic teachings)
- Avoid doing what you would blame others for doing. (Thales, pre-Socratic Greek philosopher)
- Do not do unto others whatever is injurious to yourself. (Zoroastrianism, *Shayast-na-Shayast*)

The good life

What does it mean to lead "a good life" in terms of ethics? According to the ancient Greeks, what makes a life go well for us are good health, friends, useful and productive work, honor and respect, and integrity. Things that make for a less-than-good life include poverty, isolation, a lack of useful and productive work, a lack of friends, and a general sense of purposelessness.

To what extent, we might ask, does "the good life" involve going outside of ourselves to attend to the needs and concerns of others? To what extent does the good life make demands on us, such that we are honest in our dealings with others, fair in our treatment of them, and perhaps even gracious and generous in our behavior toward them? Many virtue ethicists would argue that a good life requires more than an egotistical approach to living, and that there is more to it than the attitude that "if I don't hurt anyone, why shouldn't I simply satisfy all the desires for myself that I can?" These virtue ethicists would counter that a focus on the self as supreme goal limits one's ethical development and diminishes one's real and deep joy in living. And they would argue further that for a life to go well in the long run, there is a need to develop one's character and to perfect such virtues as loyalty and stead-fastness grounded in a personal code of integrity. And further that these character traits need to be developed over time and through repeated practice, reinforced by repetition, custom, and habit.

Ethics, Values, and Virtues

Ethics is based on values, which ground ethical decision-making. We justify our ethical decisions by appealing to values. Those values, in turn, are most often based upon universal principles, such as that taking human life and stealing another's property are wrongful acts and should be condemned. When those values and those principles conflict, however, we experience what might be called ethical confusion or ethical distress. In such instances, all ethical values cannot be honored either because the underlying principles are in conflict, or because the conflicting values are given different priorities.

A classic example comes from Greek drama as exemplified by Sophocles' play *Antigone*. When one of Antigone's brothers leaves Thebes to fight against his home city-state and is killed, the king, Creon, announces an edict that forbids burial of such a traitor. Betrayal of the state violates an ethical norm; that violation entails serious consequences, including denial of a proper burial. Competing against this set of patriotic values, however, in the mind of Antigone, the play's title character, are values associated with her responsibility to honor her brother and fulfill the obligation decreed by the gods to bury one's family members. The conflict, thus, is between the demands of the state, enacted in law, and the ethical demands of conscience, required by adherence to religious practice.

Other examples of ethical conflict can be taken from history. For example, during the rule of Adolf Hitler, harboring Jews was against the law. Yet ethical principles, derived from religious beliefs and from common human values suggest that protecting Jews during Hitler's "final solution" to exterminate them was the right thing to do. Similarly, staging civil disobedient protests against racial oppression and racist behavior allowed by law in the southern United States in its earlier history reveals conflicting values rooted in radically different ideologies. The right thing to do, in such instances, pits ethically normed values that respect basic human rights against laws on the books in particular places at particular times, laws that violate basic ethical principals grounded in a respect for human life.

Associated with any discussion of ethical values is the notion of trust. Trust is essential for ethical behavior and ethical decision-making. Violations of trust are, essentially, ethical violations, whether or not the broken trust involves the breaking of laws. In her book *The Ethical Canary*, Canadian philosopher Margaret Somerville (2001) asks a number of questions relating to trust in its relation to ethics, among them the following: (1) How many people do we need to trust that the foods we eat are safe? (2) What do we expect of scientific research with regard to trust? (3) To what extent do we have "blind trust" in doctors and the medical profession? (4) How much trust do we have in banks, in global companies with regard to their services and products? (5) How do food growers, processors, and purveyors; doctors, dentists, pharmacists, nurses; researchers, technicians, educators; and those with responsible positions in business and law, for example, earn and maintain our trust?

In addition to trust, another factor related to ethics is risk. Risk is a centrally important ethical matter. When any of us undergoes a medical procedure, a triple cardiac bypass operation, for example, we need to know the various risks involved. For example, what percentage of bypass patients die as a result of the operation, either directly or indirectly as a result of postoperative complications? What other less drastic risk factors are associated with the procedure? To what extent is diminished cognitive capacity a potential risk—and how serious a risk might it be? How do one surgeon's and hospital's rates of post-operative complications, such as infection rates, including mortality, compare with those of other hospitals? What kinds of risks, that is, beyond those directly associated with the operation itself, need to be honestly assessed? What are the ethical obligations of doctors and hospitals to make these risks known to patients?

A recent example of risk is that associated with the banking crisis and the housing bubble that occurred in the United States in 2008, and the consequences for financial distress across many sectors in the following years. There is no question that ethical norms were violated, as dishonest risk assessments were provided by banks to government agencies and to investors. Honesty and good faith—the bedrock upon which trust is built—were violated repeatedly in the deceptive risk analyses that were routinely provided, while the real risk factors were intentionally hidden. Further complicating matters and additionally violating ethical norms was the shunting of risk from the banks that made subpar loans and packaged them in complex and difficult to understand portfolios to those least able to bear the costs when the bubble burst.

Margaret Somerville recognizes six ethical virtues: (1) honesty, (2) courage, (3) fidelity (4) restraint, (5) tolerance, and (6) forgiveness. Without honesty, we destroy trust and truth, both of which are essential for the functioning of human society. Courage enables us to act with integrity and to say no to what should not be, when we need to exercise restraint. Fidelity to ethical principles requires consistency in their application. Tolerance is essential in recognizing the validity of others' perspectives, and forgiveness for excusing our own mistakes and those of others.

Other virtues derive from various religious and philosophical traditions and focus largely on the state of one's soul. Advocates of Hinduism and Buddhism honor renunciation and detachment; advocates of Christianity, charity and obedience; advocates of the Greek philosophical tradition, self-knowledge and the search for truth; Confucian adherents, benevolence and respect for elders, among other virtues for everyday living.

Jonathan Haidt (2012) considers such virtues social skills, character traits that are needed for exemplary living. "Virtue theories," he notes, however, "are messy" because in affirming them one gives up the hope of finding a single principle upon which all of morality can be built. Ethical pluralism is the inevitable result of virtue ethics.

In *The Righteous Mind,* Jonathan Haidt compares the mind to a rider on an elephant. The elephant's rider represents reason, the conscious and controlled deliberative process of analytical thinking. This conscious rational rider represents a mere 1% of our actual thinking process. The other 99% is the elephant, which represents unconscious, automatic thinking. Virtue theories are primarily about developing habits both of behavior and perception. So, for example, in order to develop the virtues of tolerance and of kindness, one needs to have a strong sensitivity to other people's needs. It requires learning to feel compassion and empathy;

it involves learning when and how to offer appropriate assistance in times of need.

He suggests that the moral mind turns on a set of binary moral "taste" receptors: care/harm, fairness/cheating, loyalty/betrayal, authority/subversion, and sanctity/degradation. Moral systems, he suggests, are analogous to "cuisine[s] that are constructed from local elements to please these [moral] receptors."

Joshua D. Greene *et al.* (2013) agrees up to a point with Haidt's metaphor of moral "tastes," but believes that it needs to be supplemented by another analogy—that of the camera. Greene contests the implicit intuitive emphasis of Jonathan Haidt's decision ethics. While acknowledging the efficiency of his approach, Joshua Greene claims that it lacks flexibility. For quick ethical decision-making, he uses the analogy of a camera with automatic settings that are quick and easy to use but that lack the refinements of manual controls. (Think point-and-shoot cameras versus those whose settings you establish, adjust, and control yourself.) While acknowledging that our moral sense can operate on a kind of "I like this and dislike that," and "this I approve and this I deplore" setting, he argues that we have the ability to think more fully, consciously, and deliberately about moral problems. This, he calls "the brain's manual mode."

The automatic settings for ethical decisions are good for situations where proper training has been provided. However, something more complex is needed for confronting fundamentally new and unanticipated problems, for which generic ethical training has not been (and perhaps cannot be) provided. These more complex new problems are often moral problems relating to new technologies. One example is our ability to bomb people on the other side of the world, whether by means of intercontinental ballistic missiles or with drones. Another challenging problem that requires a less-than-automatic kind of ethical decision response results from cultural variation and diversity. Intercultural contact that transcends getting along with people in our own cultural group, dealing with strongly differentiated cultural moral values requires nuanced toleration and tact, an ability to negotiate the rocks and shoals of wildly different cultural, norms, principles, expectations, and behaviors. These more complex problems require a manual camera mode, one that allows us to make adjustments and refinements, one that permits us to reflect and choose rather than to default to a quick, instinctive ethical response.

Another aspect of virtue ethics is developed by Kwame Anthony Appiah (2008) in his *Experiments in Ethics,* in which he explains that, from the perspective of "virtue ethics," a virtuous act is the kind of act "done by a virtuous person for the kinds of reasons a virtuous person would do it." Although somewhat circular, this definition highlights the centrality of character for virtue ethics, which is complemented by a corollary idea: that a virtuous life is a better life. Virtues are "intrinsically worth having"; being virtuous "makes life worthwhile." Appiah cites the essential theoretical aspects of virtue ethics as outlined by Rosalind Hursthouse (2002) in her book *On Virtue Ethics* (2002):

1. The right thing to do is what a virtuous agent would do in the circumstances.
2. A virtuous person is one who has and exercises the virtues.
3. A virtue is a character trait that a person needs in order to...live a good life.

For virtue ethics, doing the right thing, though necessary, is not sufficient. What is also needed is that the right thing is done for the right reasons. That condition is also necessary.

Complicating matters a bit more involves considering how a virtuous person becomes virtuous, how a virtuous person decides what is necessary to exercise honesty, for example, across a wide range of situations. Some heuristics or guiding principles are needed; these heuristics provide a standard by which to measure virtuous and non-virtuous actions. Such standards were developed by a number of philosophers in the western tradition, beginning with the ancient Greeks.

Ethical Imagination

In *The Ethical Imagination,* Margaret Somerville (2008) invites us to consider ways that ethical controversies "go to the very roots of what it means to be human, how we relate to others and our world, and how we find meaning in life." She suggests that when we think as ethicists, we confront two kinds of challenges: first, the ethical challenges of a particular situation, and second, the ethical responsibility that comes with the exercise of power.

Somerville suggests that we can develop our ethical imagination by doing the following things:

1. recognizing guiding moral principles;
2. maintaining respect for persons even if not for their beliefs;
3. valuing other ways of knowing beyond the cognitive and rational; and
4. respecting all life, but in particular human life, including human dignity and the human spirit.

In elaborating on these ideas, Somerville explains what she means by a "shared ethics," where we can agree in practice even though not agreeing entirely on ethical principles. She suggests that maintaining and promoting the good of humanity should be a broad ethical goal. This goal could be promoted by ensuring a respect for individuals and their relationships to others, for life. It could be promoted with the recognition of a shared desire to live fully human lives. It would include obligations to fulfill the needs of others, to respect their freedom, and not harm the deep human need for imagination, creativity, and play.

One domain in which such a set of ethical responsibilities plays out is politics. Another is business. Respect for individuals requires that they be treated not as means to an end but as ends in themselves. And it involves a sense of empathy and fairness. Walt Whitman's ethic hinged on his saying that "Whoever degrades another degrades me." Degradation of others violates his basic ethical norm. Akin is Abraham Lincoln's remark: As I would not be a slave, so I would not be a master." In this Kantian formulation, Lincoln suggests that as he would not wish to be enslaved by another, so he would not enslave another person.

Somerville sees ethics as boiling down to four basic presumptions, from which to begin an ethical analysis. These four presumptions serve as a starting point on which to build an ethical argument. They are:

"*No*: we must not do this."
"*Yes*: there are no restrictions or conditions on what we want to do."

"*No, unless*: no, we must not do it unless we can justify it, and these are the requirements for justification."

"*Yes, but*: yes, we may do it, but not if certain circumstances prevail."

The first of these conditions imply that there is a set of ethical standards, principles, or norms in play that simply cannot be violated. No, for example, one must not commit adultery, for it violates our basic moral convictions—not only because it is a guiding commandment of one's religion, but also because it degrades one's spouse.

The second situation suggests that ethical norms are not in play; there are no morally based reasons to prevent one from, for example, participating in a culling of the deer population.

Somerville's third and fourth guidelines require either that one is able to defend the action about to be taken in principle, philosophically, or that it is acceptable under a set of particular circumstances that need to be identified or defined.

It matters whether or not we begin from these principles. It makes a difference when considering the issue of human cloning whether we begin with the technology that could someday permit it, or whether we begin with ethical guidelines that inform our thinking about complex ethical questions. Starting with the technology privileges it; beginning with the guidelines subjects the technology to more stringent and critical analysis (see Tables 7.2 and 7.3).

Table 7.2   Ethical virtues

Honesty	Restraint
Courage	Tolerance
Fidelity	Forgiveness

Table 7.3   Ethical behaviors

Recognize guiding moral principles
Maintain respect for other people
Value other ways of knowing
Respect all forms of life

In *The Ethical Canary*, Somerville argues that ethics is grounded in a fundamental respect for human life. She suggests that anything that fails to show respect for life, especially human life, is "inherently wrong." Equally wrong, she suggests, is anything that "puts at risk or harms the human spirit." Appropriating a term from religion without recourse to the supernatural, Somerville advocates the concept of the "secular sacred," which postulates that some things, life among them, deserve "the utmost respect." She illustrates the concept of the secular sacred with our relationship to the earth and suggests that we should assess our actions with reference to the potential benefit and harm they cause not only to the physical realities of our world but to metaphysical ones, including our values. Ethics, in this sense, involves exploring our moral universe in the manner that science explores the physical universe.

Who decides what is ethical and what is not? Traditionally, this function has been grounded in religious belief. To take but one example, the ten commandments of Judaism and Christianity function as guidelines to right and wrong, what to do and what to avoid doing. Islam, too, has its commands and prohibitions, as do the other religions of the world. But what is the ground of ethics for the non-religious, for those who do not subscribe to any particular religion? If what is ethical, or moral, for the religious is enshrined in their commandments and religious beliefs, what grounds ethics for the non-religious?

Simon Blackburn (2011), in his *Ethics*, discusses what he calls an "ethical climate," a particular kind of philosophical environment grounded in ethical norms, even networks of ethical norms. The ethical climate includes a set of ideas about how to live, especially ideas that determine our conceptions of "what is due us, and what is due from us, as we relate to others." Somerville would concur, arguing that Blackburn's notion of duty, or what is due, is essentially respect for life. His ethical climate also determines our conception of when things are going well and when they are going badly—all based on a set of standards, which, as Blackburn suggests, are often invisible.

Michael Sandel (2010) suggests that justice is a key concept upon which to evaluate ethical claims. In his book *Justice*, Michael Sandel asks to what extent we can reason our way through ethical questions involving justice and injustice, equality and inequality, and how we might go about doing so. He suggests that in considering difficult moral questions we begin with a view, an opinion, a conviction about "the right thing to do." He asks that you imagine that you see a driverless trolley speeding down a track when you notice five workers up ahead directly in its path. You assume that if the trolley crashes into them they will be killed. You observe a switch that allows the trolley to be diverted onto a side track. If you pull the switch to divert the trolley, five lives will be spared. However, one individual on this track will be killed. Should you do this? If you say, "yes," what assumptions have you made about human life? What position are you deciding from?

But suppose a slightly different scenario. You are now an onlooker from a bridge above the track, and there is no side-track. A train is speeding toward those five workers and there is no one to driver to stop it. You notice standing nearby a large man, whom, if you pushed onto the track, could stop the trolley before it hit the five workers. What would you do? Why? What is the difference between these two difficult moral dilemma scenarios? How do you decide what would be the right thing to do in either case?

In the many studies that have evolved out of the original trolley scenarios, which date from the 1970s, and the variations played upon them, people consistently agree that it is ethically acceptable to pull the switch to divert the train toward a single victim, thus saving five lives. However, those same people would not physically push the fat man onto the track to stop the train to save those same five lives. It seems that the act of physically pushing someone to his death violates our ethical norms; we see it as "murder," as a form of killing and not just an expedient way to save lives by means of a mechanical maneuver.

A variant on these two options is to imagine a trapdoor upon which the fat man is standing. Instead of pushing him over the railing and onto the tracks, all you need do is pull a release to open the trap door, and drop the man onto the track in front of the oncoming train. Could you imagine doing this; is it the "right" thing to do, or not? How does this compare with the options of pulling the switch to divert the train and pushing the man onto the track?

In a different set of ethical, challenges, we might consider the tendency of financial markets to expand into spheres of life that were traditionally governed by other principles and forces, by

217

"non-market norms." Applying capitalist assumptions and practices, such as outsourcing military operations with mercenaries fighting for your country or interrogating enemy prisoners; buying and selling body parts on the open market; offering money to students for their performance on standardized tests; selling US citizenship for a $100,000 fee are some examples.

These and other suggestions and practices involve what Sandel calls "utility and consent." But they also involve questions of how we value important social practices, such as military service, education, criminal punishment, the conferring of citizenship, and the like. Since these and similar market based social practices may degrade their defining norms, it is important to think about which social practices should be protected from market driven practices.

Cosmopolitanism and Global Ethics

In his book *Cosmopolitanism*, Kwame Anthony Appiah (2007), develops an ethics for global citizenship in which he lays out two major intertwining strands of thinking. The first is that "we have obligations to others … that stretch beyond those to whom we are related." The second is that "we take seriously the value not just of human life but of particular human lives." Two corollary notions are (1) that there is much to learn from the differences among people; and (2) that we can do this through conversation and association with one another openly, honestly, and patiently.

Appiah argues that it is practices and not principles that enable us to live together and work together toward solving challenging social and political problems. He makes an analogy between reading imaginative literature and engaging in serious conversation across boundaries of race and religion, creed and culture, ethnicity and identity. He uses "conversation" in the larger metaphorical sense of engagement with the ideas, values, and experiences of others. The goal of such imaginative engagement is not to come to an agreement, largely because principles deter that agreement. Instead of consensus about values and principles, the goal of imaginative engagement through conversation is to become accustomed to other people's ways of seeing and understanding, to get to know them as individuals and as members of the groups that shape their identities. In the process we come to value their different points of view, even when we can't agree with either their principles or their viewpoints.

One of the great challenges of understanding, appreciating, and working with others who differ from ourselves in significant ways is that we can mean very different things by the same terms. What is "courage" to one person might be "foolhardiness" to another; one person's "cruelty" is another's "discipline." Terms of value tend to be what philosophers call "open-textured." That is, they are open to multiple interpretations and meanings. They are "essentially contestable," to use another term from social philosophy. And so even people who share a vocabulary have much to disagree about due to the open-textured, contestable nature of evaluative terms.

Cosmopolitanism involves a commitment to pluralism.

British philosopher Isaiah Berlin recognized the need to acknowledge the plurality of values that motivate and animate the beliefs and behaviors of different peoples. In the same way that some individuals prefer isolation and quiet contemplation to a gregarious sociality, so, too do some cultures value individualism over social cohesion, restraint and reserve over an outgoing and hedonistic pursuit of personal pleasure. Yet this recognition of different values and valuations does not help us distinguish between what is right and wrong—what ought and ought not to be and to be done. Berlin suggests that recognizing different cultural values does not amount to a moral or ethical relativism. Pluralism, in his view, is not relativism. And even though values can clash both between and within cultures and civilizations, there are ways to negotiate their contradictory and conflicting aspects.

One familiar example is the extent to which we pursue individual agendas and the extent to which we share in larger communal enterprises. How do we find a balance between individual freedom and satisfactions and a commitment to larger common social and communal purposes? Each represents a real value; each demands a modicum of attention and recognition. Yet rather than seeing them in absolute conflict and contradiction, we seek ways to balance and blend their needs and purposes. We look for and find ways to harmonize, integrate, and otherwise negotiate their relevant and valuable differing claims.

There are many values worth living by, and they don't all agree with one another. There needs to be, thus, an acceptance that there can be alternative values of equal merit, that different people and societies will embody varied values, all of which are worthy of respect. A second aspect of cosmopolitanism includes the notion that our knowledge is provisional, tentative, imperfect, and subject to change and revision. We don't have all the answers all the time. And the answers we do have are incomplete, partial truths in both senses of the word "partial," both limited and biased. The consequence of these notions is that cosmopolitanism requires that we interact "on terms of respect with those who see the world differently than we do."

Technology and Ethics

A number of developments in technology raise profoundly important moral and ethical issues. Among them are scientific discoveries that have enabled animals to be cloned, human beings to be kept alive on respirators, the transplantation of body parts from animals to humans, and the mapping of genes onto chromosomes. Each of these, along with a variety of other technological developments, has been accompanied by questions about whether certain things should be done at all, even if the technology to accomplish them has become or will soon become available. Cloning human beings is one prominent example. Replacing people with robots is another.

In *The Ethical Imagination*, Margaret Somerville discusses a series of important ethical questions related to technology. One of her ideas is that developments in the fields of artificial intelligence and robotics challenge our traditional concepts of what "being," is, what a "creature" is, and what kinds and degrees of respect we owe to other forms of life besides the human. She asks how we would characterize a composite creature composed of half human and half robotic elements. She asks, too, whether we should use technological advances in robotics and artificial intelligence to enhance ourselves, in the process making our human selves more machine-like. And if such an eventuality does occur, would people who are enhanced technologically become more important and more powerful than those not so artificially improved? Following such a trajectory of events, would "unmodified (natural) humans" become less desirable and perhaps eventually obsolete?

Margaret Somerville mentions a device developed for the military that allows soldiers to receive signals to their brains from cameras and sonar equipment mounted on their helmets. Something called a "Brain Port" links the soldiers' helmets with their tongues, with signals traveling to the brain. She surmises that one day we will be faced with the decision of whether or not to implant such a device in humans' brains rather than in their helmets. She asks whether it is ethical to create "human techno-warriors."

And further, if we were to take the developments in robotics and artificial intelligence, add those in genetics and nanotechnology already underway, and factor in other technologies yet unknown, we would need, she suggests, to consider the possibility of homo sapiens morphing into "techno sapiens" and what the consequences of that would be for humanity. Developments in technology keep coming; they continue on a pace faster than our ability to absorb them and fully understand their implications and consequences. That's one reason it remains important to have people like Margaret Somerville asking questions about how the new technologies will be used and what kinds of checks and balances should be developed for them.

Current developments in machine automation and robot technology raise thorny questions about ethical choices robots and other human-substitution machines will inevitably need to make. As Nicholas Carr (2014) notes in *The Glass Cage*, in some cases involving the rapid computation of probabilities, the quick sorting of multiple options, robots may be very good indeed at making fair and rational choices. In more complex situations, where no clear rational choice is the right one, such as those involving life and death, automated decision-making involving ethical choices by means of pure numerical analysis will almost surely lead to morally repugnant less than salutary decisions.

Further complicating automated decision-making in ethically challenging situations is the question of who decides how the robot is to be programmed. Who determines just what the best or right action should be? Who designs the robot's, or other automated machine's, decision-making capacity? There is no algorithm for moral choice, no set of clear-cut calculations leading to unambiguous ethically appropriate choices. The forms of artificial intelligence devised for automated decision-making lack consciousness. They simply do not possess the human equivalent of a moral conscience.

Autonomous machines are already entering the arena of moral action. But they do so unprepared to make moral decisions based on anything resembling human feeling. Moral codes, as Carr suggests, will need to be translated into computer codes.

Alone together

A set of related questions about robots is raised by Sherry Turkle (2011) in her book *Alone Together*. Examining the implications of robots on human relationships, she describes a series of research studies in which people interact with a variety of robot creatures not just as functional aids for cleaning floors, lifting heavy objects, or washing clothes, but as friends, confidants, even romantic partners. Turkle suggests that technology has become "the architect of our intimacies," with robots only the latest, most fashionable, and most extreme example. She believes that we are at a "robotic moment," when we need to decide just how far we want to allow our relationship with robots to develop. How far is far enough, and how far is too far, she wonders?

Turkle argues that it is not simply a matter of whether or not we can build the robots with sufficient artificial intelligence to assume the roles of friend and lover, caretaker for children and aging parents, and even substitute for children, parents, and friends. Her questions and concerns relate more to whether and to what extent we are ready for robots to assume these roles in our lives. She believes that we are coming to the point where we actually want robots as friends and companions, as romantic partners and caregivers. Why? Because it's easier that way. A robot boyfriend or girlfriend, husband or wife, doesn't make demands on us, doesn't challenge or question us, doesn't have its own set of needs, worries, and concerns. Sociable robots, she contends, allow us to avoid conflicts about intimacy, and they also reveal a desire for relationships with limits, a way to be, as she notes, "both together and alone."

The Ethics of Information

In *Information: A Very Short Introduction*, Luciano Floridi (2010) has developed a model of information in which the infosophere, or the domain in which information is manifested, requires careful "ecological management" in order to sustain its well-being. In this model, information is conceived under three aspects: (1) the aspect of resource; (2) the aspect of product; and (3) the aspect of target. As a resource, information is valued as something that can be used to advance personal improvement and collective progress. As a product, information is something that can be consumed. Information as resource is information as input; information as product is information as output. Information as a target involves considerations of the uses and misuses of information, the managing of one's information environment.

Luciano Floridi's model of information as "resource," "product," and "target" implies not only an ecology, but also an ethics of information. The ethics of information as resource involves issues such as fair treatment, informed consent, the protection of anonymity, and offering unbiased evaluations. Information ethics involves such things as deciding when to access information and when to avoid accessing information one does not have a right to know. Under the aspect of information as resource, information ethics includes the availability, accessibility, and accuracy of information.

The ethics of information as product involves issues such as accountability, liability, plagiarism, propaganda, misinformation, and other practical rules of communication. Lying and secrecy are two major issues considered under the ethics of information as product. Telling the truth—or not—in advertising is one notable area of interest and concern.

The ethics of information as target involves issues such as privacy and confidentiality. Hacking, piracy, vandalism, filtering, and censorship exemplify some specific aspects of its application. All three aspects of information touch on issues of monitoring and controlling information; they raise questions about who owns information, and how it should be used fairly, along with legislative concerns such as copyright and patent—legal issues, which are becoming increasingly complex in the digital age. Implications of such a theoretical model of information raise further questions about what it means to be a citizen in the "infosphere." What are the rights and responsibilities of a citizen of the infosphere?

Technologies that allow for easy file sharing and swapping, that make copying anything easy, lead to charges of piracy, and theft of property. Rapid technological developments, however, have also pushed the discussion of ownership and property to considerations of collective ownership. The issue cuts across not only physical property rights and intellectual property debates, but also involves environmental issues, scientific questions, technological innovations, historical precedents and procedures, as well as artistic, social, cultural, and religious values.

Ethical Decisions

In *The Organized Mind* (2014), Daniel Levitin suggests that ethical decision-making involves different regions of the brain than economic decision thinking. The challenge for us is to switch between the criteria we use in making economic and ethical decisions; especially difficult for us is making decisions that include both economic and ethical dimensions. We need to decide which aspect—the economic or the ethical—is foremost when both elements are present in a difficult choice we need to make.

Such decision-conflicts frequently arise in corporate decision-making situations. What's good for a company isn't necessarily good for the larger community. Analogously what advances our individual economic needs might be at the expense of others. Small-scale situations like not paying for company provided breakfast foods when a suggested amount is expected saves us money but undermines the goal of each person paying a fair and equal amount, with the company subsidizing the rest. Larger-scale situations such as companies finding loopholes to avoid paying their fair share of taxes hurts the larger community of taxpayers, who have to shoulder a bigger tax burden.

Levitin argues that it is difficult for individuals and companies to consider the larger community in making decisions involving a combination of economic and ethical aspects because other individuals and companies may appear to be getting away with decisions that favor their own interests at the expense of others. But we might ask whether individuals and companies that take the larger community into account in making decisions involving ethics and economics may actually do better for themselves and the larger community in the long run. They build trust and gain respect for their consideration of others in their actions.

Ethical Provocations

Bank error in your favor

Imagine that you go to an ATM and request $100 with a receipt. Instead, the machine gives you $10,000 and a receipt for only $100. You get home and check your account online and sure enough it's only been debited $100. You think that the bank will catch the mistake, but decide to hold onto the money and put it in a safe place—but not in that bank account. After a couple of months, you decide it's time to buy a new car. You convince yourself that you didn't steal the money; it was given to you. You didn't rob anyone; no one else would be hurt. And the bank's loss was infinitesimal given the volume of money they deal with daily. The bank is insured against all kinds of losses, anyway. Besides, it was the bank's fault—their mistake and your good luck.

And yet, given this scenario, we have qualms, don't we, that the money doesn't really belong to us, and that we should return it. If a cashier returned you $20 in change instead of $10, would you keep it? Or would you identify the mistake, so it wouldn't come out of his or her earnings when the mistake was later found.

The principle at work is fairness; it's not fair to take advantage of someone's mistake, especially if they are going to be hurt by it. Furthermore, if we deal with this individual from time to time, we would feel guilty in taking advantage of their mistake even more. But that might not be the case with a "faceless" large corporation, like a bank.

If you think that keeping the money is justified on the basis that the bank won't really "feel" the loss, you might also justify shoplifting items from stores, using the same argument. But somehow that doesn't seem right; it certainly involves your doing something yourself actively—going into the store and actually "stealing" merchandise. In the case of the ATM error, it kind of just happened. That money just kept coming out of the machine; it's as if you won the lottery. Or is it? What is the right, or ethical, thing to do in this situation?

Whose ball is it?

For a number of years, the *New York Times Sunday Magazine,* carried a column under the heading "The Ethicist." In these weekly columns, Randy Cohen, the ethicist, presents two or three short letters he has received, each of which focuses on an ethical dilemma. In his capacity as ethicist, Randy Cohen responds to the articles with something like Margaret Somerville's four presumptions, "No; Yes; No, unless; or Yes, but."

We will consider one such letter that Cohen received and raise some ethical questions about the situation it describes. "The Ethicist" received the following letter from a woman whose husband and son had attended a Boston Red Sox baseball game. Here's her description of the situation:

> My husband and our 11-year-old son attended a Red Sox game last season at which our son coaxed a player to toss him a ball. A man sitting nearby offered him $30 for the ball to give to his own son. My husband told our son to ask for $50. They settled on $40, and all parties were pleased. My husband said it was a good lesson in "supply and demand," but I am uncomfortable with the transaction. What do you think?

The first question to ask about this scenario is whether there is an ethical issue at stake here at all. What do you think?

The second question is whether you agree with the boy's father about the lesson taught and learned regarding "supply and demand." Are there any other "lessons" being taught and learned in this little scenario? If so, what are they?

A third consideration is to look closely at the text of the letter. What inferences do you make based on the details provided? Do you infer that it was a foul ball that was tossed into the stands? What do you infer from the word "coaxed"? What did the 11-year-old boy do to get the Red Sox player (or was it a player from the opposing team?) to toss him the ball? And what inference can we make about the player as he tossed the ball to the boy in the stands? To what extent do the inferences you make about these matters affect your judgment about the father's and boy's action to sell the ball. Does it make any difference what price they sold the ball for? Why or why not?

What arguments would you make in support of the father's (and son's) action? What arguments would you make to support the mother's feelings of uneasiness at the transaction?

Ethics and dating Web sites

Web sites, such as Facebook, Google, and YouTube all wrestle with what is allowable and what is forbidden as site content. Dating Web sites, in particular, have come under scrutiny for not only the kinds of information they gather about their users but for how they use that information. The dating site OKCupid, for example, conducted experiments in which it hid information from its users' profiles to see how users' personality ratings would be affected. They also experimented by misleading users that they were a better or worse match with others than the site's software indicated.

At issue in such experiments with user data is whether, in fact, those experiments violate ethical norms—whether, for example, the intrusiveness and the dishonesty involved should have required prior consent or ex-post-facto disclosures of what OKCupid had done. Users who have been advised of how their information is disseminated, manipulated, and sold are frequently angered by what they learn. Companies like Facebook and OKCupid argue that the studies they are conducting with users' data is advancing the knowledge of human behavior, which, in the long run, will benefit everyone.

Applications

7-1. Why do you think "the golden rule" has been such an influential idea across many different religions? To what extent do you think the golden rule is actually practiced?

7-2. The following humorous take on the golden rule, one that serves as a provocation to thinking about its limits, is given by Thomas Cathcart and Daniel Klein in their book *Plato and a Platypus Walk Into a Bar*. They suggest that "a sadist is a masochist who follows the golden rule." By inflicting pain on others, the masochist follows the golden rule—doing what he would like done to him.

To what extent do you think the masochist/sadist example illustrates "the golden rule?" How would you respond to this application of the golden rule?

7-3. To what extent do you find the approach of "virtue ethics" helpful? How do you understand the relationship between virtues and values?

7-4. What do you believe are your ethical responsibilities—your obligations and duties to others? Why? What do you think it might mean to have an "ethical imagination?"

7-5. Is lying ever ethically justified? What about social lies, "white lies," lies involving desperation, as for example, telling a crazed person with an axe that your children are visiting a relative when they are sleeping upstairs?

7-6. Is it ever ethical to sell shoddy products—tainted meat, for example, or flimsy furniture that breaks after minimal use, or insurance plans with so much fine print that they provide insurance against virtually nothing? What ethical issues are at stake in these and similar examples, as for example, Oscar Schindler producing shoddy products for his Nazi clients?

7-7. Consider how to go about responding to the following challenge presented by Margaret Somerville: How can we hold in creative tension safeguarding individual rights and liberties while also protecting the community? Think of one area or domain where this challenge needs to be addressed—with the dissemination (and control) of information, for example; or with the rights and responsibilities of medical practitioners and their patients; or with freedom on speech or the right of assembly—and so on.

7-8. Use Margaret Somerville's ethical presumptions on an ethical dilemma that interests you. It could be a small-scale local, even personal issue. Or it could be a large-scale global ethical dilemma or challenge.

7-9. Identify a time when you engaged in just such a kind of conversation, an imaginative engagement, with someone whose way of understanding and explaining the world differed significantly from yours. What did you learn from participating in that conversation? What challenges did you have to deal with to remain part of that conversation? To what extent was it of value to you?

7-10. To what extent can a cosmopolitan perspective be used to address the following complex international ethical challenge: An international group of religious leaders drafted a "universal declaration of a global ethic." Included were these statements: (1) "We must not commit any kind of sexual immorality"; (2) "We must put behind us all forms of domination and abuse"; (3) "We must strive for a just social and economic order." Choose one of the three statements, and explain how people from different parts of the world, with different religious beliefs and different cultural traditions might interpret it. Explain how a cosmopolitan approach might be used to begin an imaginatively engaged conversation about the statement.

7-11. Whatever you decide in the trolley scenarios, to what extent would you want to discuss the moral implications of your decision with others? To what extent might such a discussion be a political discussion? A religious discussion? How would we go about deciding with others what principles should underlie our decision about "the right thing to do" in such complex circumstances?

7-12. Which kinds of things do you think should be immune from buying and selling? Sex? Babies? Human Organs? What other examples of social norms do you think should be debated from this standpoint? Why?

7-13. A couple of years ago, the CEO with the highest compensation was Larry Ellison of Oracle, who was compensated in cash and stock more than $90 million. The second highest paid CEO less than half that—a mere $45 million. As reported by *The New York Times* on June 8, 2014, Ellison's pay dropped to approximately $78.5 million, exceeded by that of Mario Gabelli of Gamco Investors ($85 million) and Charif Souki of Cheniere Energy, at a whopping $141.9 million. Rounding at the top ten were CEOs who were paid, respectively, $65.6 million, $64.2 million, $57.8 million, $55.3 million, $49.1 million, $39.0 million, $38.2 million, and $37.2 million. The average compensation of these CEO's, excluding the highest earner, is around $70 million. Not all of these companies had profitable years. Can these compensation numbers be ethically justified?

7-14. Consider that as reported by the Institute for Policy Studies the 25 public universities with the highest-paid presidents had student debt at their universities that increased at a faster rate than the average at state universities overall from 2005 to 2012. And at the same universities during these years, there was an increase in the use of part-time adjunct faculty instead of full-time tenured faculty. Is there an ethical issue here?

7-15. What do you think of the fact that many hospital administrators routinely make more than doctors who work at their hospitals, sometimes much more? And that college football and basketball coaches make more than college presidents?

7-16. Identify one or more ethical issues in each of the following broad areas:

(1) politics; (2) business; (3) academia; (4) media; (5) environment; (6) science; (7) medicine; (8) sports; (9) armed conflict; (10) social networking.

7-17. Identify two recent technological developments that have had or are about to have a significant impact on human life and experience. Consider the extent of their impact on social, cultural, and intellectual life. You might consider, for example, the use of neural implants, such as those that help victims of stroke learn to walk, or the hearing impaired hear, but which could also be used to help an athlete focus on perfecting the swing of a tennis racket or baseball bat, or hit perfect basketball free throws or jump shots.

7-18. Do you think that machines will ever be capable of making moral decisions, that they will one day be able to make ethical calculations as well as or better than human beings? Why or why not?

7-19. What do you think of the use of robots as friends, companions, or lovers? What about their use as caretakers of children and aging parents? How about their use as parent substitutes? Do you think, for example, that a robot might be programmed to give you better advice about important matters than a parent or a friend? To what extent do you think that virtual social experience degrades our actual social experience?

7-20. To what extent do you find Floridi's notion of an "infosphere" useful? To what extent do you think we inhabit an "infosphere?" What are some ecological implications of living in an "infosphere?"

7-21. Cite an example or situation in which the ethics of information revolved around information as a resource. To what extent might this be an issue with credit reporting agencies? With reporting of grades at school, evaluations at work, medical records? Have you ever been the victim of one of the violations of information as target—have you ever had your identity stolen, had yourself misrepresented, been a victim of a hacker? What were the consequences?

7-22. To what extent do you find Daniel Levitin's distinction between economic decision and ethical making helpful. Do you think knowing about the different brain regions affected in making these different kinds of decisions can help when you have to make decisions of each type?

7-23. What do you think of the way Facebook and some data Web sites like OKCupid experiment with user information? To what extent do you think that users need to be advised either before or after such experimental uses of their information is developed? To what extent do you think that such experiments with user information are beneficial for humankind in general?

References

Appiah, Kwame Anthony. 2007. *Cosmopolitanism*. New York: Norton.

Appiah, Kwame Anthony. 2008. *Experiments in Ethics*. Cambridge, MA: Harvard University Press.

Baggini. Julian. 2012. *Ethics*. London: Quercus Publishing.

Blackburn, Simon. 2011. *Ethics*. Oxford: Oxford University Press.

Carr, Nicholas. 2014. *The Glass Cage*. New York: Norton.

Floridi, Luciano. 2010. *Information: A Very Short Introduction*. Oxford: Oxford University Press.

Greene, Joshua *et al.* 2013. "The New Science of Morality." In *Thinking*. Ed. John Brockman. New York: Harper.

Haidt, Jonathan. 2012. *The Righteous Mind*. New York: Pantheon.

Hursthouse, Rosalind. 2002. *On Virtue Ethics*. Oxford: Oxford University Press.
Levitin, Daniel. 2014. *The Organized Mind*. Toronto: Penguin Canada.
Sandel, Michael. 2010. *Justice*. Farrar, Straus and Giroux.
Somerville, Margaret. 2001. *The Ethical Canary*. Toronto: McGill-Queens University Press.
Somerville, Margaret. 2008. *The Ethical Imagination*. Toronto: McGill-Queens University Press.
Turkle, Sherry. 2011. *Alone Together*. New York: Basic Books.

Index

accidents 80–1
Adams, James L. 8
adaptation (SCAMPER thinking
    strategy) 45
affective forecasting 180–4
Alchin, Nicholas 137
Alexander, Stephon H. 89
alternatives 38–40
ambiguity 4
  decision-making 178
  embracing 81, 200–4
  figure ground 18
  tolerance of 11
  and understanding 25
analogy 42, 80
  arguments 114–16
  innovation through 78–9
  Leonardo da Vinci 168
Anthony, Susan B. 86
anxiety, as block to thinking 11
Appiah, Kwame Anthony 213, 218
Apple 89, 147
Arbesman, Samuel 15, 26
arguments
  analogical 114–16
  assumptions 102–3

authority 113–14
causality 116–20
claims 102–3
enthymemes 112–13
evidence 102–3, 105–6
and implication 103–4
inductive and deductive
    reasoning 106–8
nature 102
syllogisms 112, 113
Arnheim, Rudolf 16
Aronson, Elliot 179
art and science, blending 130–1
artificial intelligence 220–2
Asimov, Isaac 142
assumptions 102–4
attention
  focus 83–4
  illusion 20
  shifting 42–3, 149
authorities, and arguments
    113–14
autonomy 7, 66
  as incentive 188, 189
  machines 222
Avatar 136

Critical and Creative Thinking: A Brief Guide for Teachers, First Edition. Robert DiYanni.
© 2016 John Wiley & Sons, Inc. Published 2016 by John Wiley & Sons, Inc.

backing for an argument 105
Baggett, David 111
Baggini, Julian 108, 206, 207
bank errors 225
banking crisis 210–11
Beatles, the 50, 86, 147
Beethoven, Ludwig van 50, 147
belief perseverance 26
Bell Labs 38
Bergen, Benjamin 75–6
Berlin, Isaiah 219
Blackburn, Simon 216
Blake, William 131, 201
Bohr, Niels 145
boundaries 145–6
boxes for creative projects 47
bricolage 167
Brockman, John 87, 89
Brook, Timothy 119
Brooks, David 7–8
Brown, John Seely 134
Bryant, Kobe 51
Burke, Kenneth 75
butterfly effect 15

Cain, Susan 85–6
Cameron, James 136
Cantor, George 159
Carr, Nicholas 99, 221–2
Carson, Shelly 142
Casablanca 180
categories 39
   conceptual 15–16
Catmull, Ed 48–9, 144
causality 122–3
   argument 116–20
   coincidence and correlation
      120–2
   inexactness 25
   reverse 121–2
Chabris, Christopher 19–20
change blindness 26
character, intellectual 7
Chartier, Emile 152
childlike behavior 81, 143–4

choices 179–80, 191
Christensen, Clayton M. 53–4, 138
Church, Mark 55
claims 102–4, 105–6
Clark, Sir Kenneth 61, 131
cognition 38
cognitive dissonance 179
cognitive flexibility 39
cognitive tools, concepts as 87–90
Cohen, Randy 226
coincidences 120–2, 184
collaborative (interdependent)
   thinking 7, 8
combinations 45, 156–7, 166–8
complexity 81
computers 99
Conan Doyle, Sir Arthur/Sherlock
   Holmes 109–12
concentration 111
conceptual framework for
   understanding 32
confidence, creative 48–9
confirmation bias 25, 176, 192
confusion, tolerance of 11
connections 81, 184, 185
connotations
   language and thought 67
   reports, inferences, and
      judgments 72, 73
consciousness, bodily act of 98
constraints 38, 149
   avoiding 81
   rethinking your thinking 145–6
continued learning, openness to 4,
   6, 143
contradictions 184, 185
Coppola, Francis Ford 50–1
correlation 120–2
cosmopolitanism 218–20
courage
   critical thinking 66
   intellectual 7, 8
creative confidence 48–9
creative crime 51–2
creative desperation 184–5

creative DNA 47
creative habit 46–7
creative questions 52–5
creative theft 49–51
creative thinking
  becoming a creative thinker
    79–80
  guidelines 80
  nature of 37–8
  strategies 44–6
  tools and techniques 80, 81
creative whacks 147–53
Crick, Francis 145
crime, creative 51–2
critical thinking
  becoming a critical thinker 66
  competencies 4
  essential questions 4–5
  guiding questions 5
  intellectual standards as
    guidelines for 67
  model 13
  nature of 4–5
cross-fertilization 42, 80
culture 38
  blocks to thinking 10, 13
  language 69
  perception 20–3
cummings, e.e. 147
curiosity 81
  children 143, 144
  developing and sustaining 7,
    60–2
  insights 184
Curious Case of Benjamin Button,
  The 154

Darwin, Charles 61, 79, 85, 182–4
Das, Satyajit 25
data 32
dating Web sites 227
David and Goliath 159–60
de Beauvoir, Simone 86
de Bono, Edward 84, 85, 90, 148
deadlines 48

decisions
  affective forecasting 180–4
  aspects of decision thinking 186
  better 191
  ethical *see* ethics
  group 194–5
  and incentives 188–9
  insights 184–6
  institutional 186–7
  making 174–80
  marriage 182–4
  tough 192–4
decisiveness 189–92
deductive reasoning 106–9
  Holmes, Sherlock 109, 110
  syllogisms 112
denial of the negative 43–6
descriptive questions 53–4
desperation, creative 184–5
Deutscher, Guy 68
Dewey, John 6, 37, 135
Diamond, Jared 118
Dickinson, Emily 158–9
disruptive questions 53–4
Dobelli, Rolf 20
Dodge, Wagner 184–5
Donoghue, Denis 75
dualities 89–90
Dubner, Stephen J. 143–4, 150
Dyer, Jeff 53–4, 138

Edison, Thomas 6
Edmundson, Mark 136
Einstein, Albert 145, 156
Elder, Linda 5, 66, 67
elimination (SCAMPER thinking
  strategy) 45
Ellington, Duke 146
emotion
  as block to thinking 11–12, 13
  decision-making 175, 179, 184,
    185, 190
empathy 66
empirical knowledge 14, 34
enthymemes 105, 112–13

Epley, Nicholas 26, 99
Erlanger, Steven 119
error-blindness 23
errors 37
  being wrong 11, 23–5
  data and information 32
  ethics 225
  and intellectual development
    11
  models 14–15
  persistence 25–7
ethical climate 216
ethics 224–5
  concepts 206–9
  global 218–20
  good life 208–9
  imagination 213–18
  as incentive 189
  of information 222–4
  provocations 225–7
  technology 220–2
  tough decisions 193–4
  values and virtues 209–13
evaluation 4
evidence 102–4, 105–6, 109
expectation 18–20
experience
  embodying 96–9
  Holmes, Sherlock 110
  knowledge from 14, 34

facts
  change over time 15
  claims 106
  creative questions 52–3
  knowledge 32–4
  reports, inferences, and
    judgments 69, 70, 71
factual inertia 26
failure 38, 82
  children 143
  embracing 6
  fear of 49
  willingness to fail 6, 8

fairness 225
fear
  as block to thinking 11
  of failure 49
Federal Express 157
Feynman, Richard 33
figure ground 17–18, 19
financial incentives 188, 189
firmness 7
Fitzgerald, F. Scott 154
Florida, Richard 37
Floridi, Luciano 222–3
flow 81
focus 83–5
  Holmes, Sherlock 111
Ford, Henry 79
forecasting
  affective 180–4
  errors 25, 178
Fosl, Peter S. 108
Foster, Jack 140–1, 143, 146
Four Seasons Hotels 147
Freud, Sigmund 23, 24
Frost, Robert 96–7, 146
fun 81, 141–3, 144

Gawande, Atul 43
Gefter, Amanda 89–90
Gelb, Michael 33, 62, 167, 201
gender
  language 69
  as perceptual filter 23
general area focus 84
General Electric (GE) 81
generosity 7–8
Genovese, Kitty 71–4
Gigerenzer, Gerd 183
Gilbert, Daniel 180, 181
Gladwell, Malcolm 159–60
global ethics 218–20
Gneezy, Uri 120–1
Goethe, Johann von 49
Gogolak, Pete 147
golden rule 207–8

Gombrich, E. H. 15
good life 208–9
Greene, Joshua D. 212
Gregersen, Hal 53–4, 138
group creativity 85–7
group decisions 194–5
groupthink 194–5

habits of mind 5–8, 80–3
  creative habit 46–7
Haidt, Jonathan 175, 211–12
happy talk 194–5
Harvard University 54–5
Harvey, William 145
Hastie, Reid 194
Hayakawa, S. I. 69, 70
hearing 16
Heath, Chip and Dan 189, 192
Henly, Carolyn P. 137
hindsight 24, 181
Hitler, Adolf 209
Holmes, Sherlock 109–12
Huizinga, John 141
humility 8, 66
humor 142
Hursthouse, Rosalind 213

ideas
  combinations 156
  generation 140–7
  importance 139–40
  and metaphor 75–6
illusions 17, 18, 20
imagination 37, 134–9
  capacities 137–9
  cognitive vs. sensory 137
  constraints 38
  creative whacks 151
  creativity and innovation 135–6
  cross-fertilization 42
  ethical 213–18
  Holmes, Sherlock 110
  Leonardo da Vinci 168
  limits 136–7

reading 77
  releasing your 80
imitation 50–1
impact bias 181
implications 103–4
inborn knowledge 14
incentives 188–9
incongruity 142
independent thinking 7
inductive reasoning 106–9
  analogical argument 114–16
  authority 114
  causal arguments 118
  Holmes, Sherlock 109, 110
inexactness 25
inferences 69–74
  Holmes, Sherlock 109, 110
information 32
  ethics 222–4
information technology 99
  Internet 34, 85
innate knowledge 14
innovation
  through analogy 78–9
  combinations 156, 166–6
  curiosity 61
  facts and knowledge 34
  ideas 140, 141
  imagination 135–6
  independent and interdependent
    thinking 7
  promoters vs. inhibitors 130
  questioning 53
insights in decision-making 184–6
Institute for Habits of Mind 5
institutional decisions 186–7
integrity 66
intellectual blocks to thinking
    10–11, 13
intellectual character 7
intellectual courage 7, 8
intellectual risk taking 6, 8
intellectual standards 67
interdependent thinking 7, 8

Internet 34, 85
intuition
  decision-making 175–9, 184,
    186, 193
  Holmes, Sherlock 109
  and insight, comparison between
    184
intuitive knowledge 14
Ioannidis, John 26

James, William 16
Jobs, Steve 79, 89
Johnson, Mark 74
Johnson, Steven 122–3, 156, 166
judgments 70–4
justice 216–17

Kahneman, Daniel 24, 176–7, 178
Kearney, Richard 99
Keats, John, "Ode on a Grecian
  Urn" 201
Kekulé, August 145
Kelley, Tom and David 48
Kidder, Rushworth M. 193
Kirstein, Lincoln 97
Kissinger, Henry 191
Klein, Gary 184, 185, 186
Kleon, Austin 49
knowledge
  application to new situations 6
  change over time 15
  explicit vs. implicit 186
  facts 32–4
  how you know what you know 14
  intellectual blocks to thinking
    10–11
  and perception 15–23
  as pillar of observation 9
  thirst for 61
Kobayashi, Takeru 150
Konnikova, Maria 109
Kovach, Bill 33

Lakoff, George 74
Lang, Amanda 143

Langer, Ellen J. 192–3
language
  ambiguity 200–1
  Orwell on 115–16
  paradox 159
  thinking through 145
  and thought 67–9
  see also metaphors
Lawrence, D. H. "The Blind Man"
  97
Le Guin, Ursula K. 134, 136
learning 14
  attitude toward 8
  creative questions 53
  curiosity 7, 60
  facts 34
  through imitation 50
  interdependent thinking 8
  and the Internet 34
  Leonardo da Vinci 34
  from mistakes and failures 37,
    49
  through observation 9
  openness to continued 4, 6, 143
  from others 14
  from reading 77
  through reflection 6
legality, as incentive 189
Lehrer, Jonah 174
Lennon, John 50, 86
Leno, Jay 200
Leonardo da Vinci
  ambiguity 201–4
  art and science, blending 131
  combinations 167–8
  curiosity 7, 61, 62
  embodied experience 97, 98
  facts and knowledge 33–4
  limitation 146
  Mona Lisa 201, 202
  St. John the Baptist 203–4
Leslie, Ian 60
Levitin, Daniel 25, 83, 178–9, 224
Levitt, Steven D. 143–4, 149–50
Lewis, C. S. 86

limitations *see* constraints
Lincoln, Abraham 214
Lincoln Center Education 137–8,
 141
List, John A. 120–1
listening 111
Liu, Eric 135, 140–1
logic
 causality 117
 Holmes, Sherlock 109–12
long run 83

Machiavelli, Niccolò 147
magnification (SCAMPER
 thinking strategy) 45
Magritte, René, *Les Valeurs
 Personnelles* 134–5
Malthus, Thomas 61, 85
marriage decisions 182–4
mastery, as incentive 188–9
Matisse, Henri 86
maximization of subjective
 expected utility 181, 183
McCartney, Paul 50, 86
McFerrin, Bobby 147
McWhorter, John 69
meaning, as incentive 188, 189
Medina, John 155
memory 47
Mendel, Gregor 156
mental virtues 7–8
meta ethics 207
metaphors 42, 67–8, 74–8
 and ideas 75–6
 of reading 76–7
 of teaching 77–8
Michalko, Michael 42–4, 154, 157,
 160, 161
Michelangelo, *David* 41
milestones 48
Milton, John 50
minimization (SCAMPER thinking
 strategy) 45
mirror neurons 99
Missimer, Connie 103

mistakes *see* errors
Mlodinow, Leonard 176
models 13
 errors 14–15
monetary incentives 188, 189
Monopoly 85
moral enterprise, critical thinking
 as 8
morality 206
 see also ethics
More, Thomas 147
Morrison, Karin 55
multi-tasking 83–4
muscle memory 47

navigation skills 99
necessary conditions 117
negative, denying the 43–6
Newton, Sir Isaac 145
Noe, Alva 98
Noppe-Brandon, Scott 135, 140–1
normative ethics 207
noticing deeply 137, 138–9
Nuland, Sherwin 131
Nussbaum, Bruce 38, 142

observation 8–9, 16
 Holmes, Sherlock 109, 110
 inductive reasoning 106–7, 109
 Leonardo da Vinci 33
obstacles to thinking, overcoming
 8–13
Ogilvy, David 147
OKCupid 227
omitted variable bias 122
originality 49
Orwell, George, "Politics and the
 English Language" 115–16

paradox 157–60
Pareto principle 88–9, 90
Parker, Charlie 147
Pasteur, Louis 147
pattern identification 81
Paul, Richard 5, 66, 67

perception
  blocks to thinking 8–9, 13
  broadening your 80
  culture 20–3
  expectation 18–20
  figure ground 17–18, 19
  illusions 17, 18
  and knowledge 15–23
perceptual positions 43
perseverance 66
perspective 17, 18
  child vs. adult 144
  by incongruity 75
Petit, Philippe 51–2
Piaget, Jean 143
Picasso, Pablo 9, 86, 147
Pink, Daniel 188
Planck, Max 26
play 141–3
  combinatory 156
  creative whacks 151
  Leonardo da Vinci 168
pluralism 219
polarizing blocks to thinking 12–13
policy, claims of 106
Pollack, John 79
possibilities
  pursuing 43, 44
  seeking 38–40, 80
Postman, Neil 52, 143
Powell, Colin 177
practicality 153–6
preconceptions 143–4
predictions, errors in 25, 178
preparation 46–7
prevention mindset 191
problems, identifying 6
Project Zero program, Harvard
  University 54–5
promotion mindset 191
public good, as incentive 189
purpose focus 84–5
putting ideas to other uses
  (SCAMPER thinking strategy)
  45

qualifiers 106
questioning routines 54–5
questions 52–5, 81
  for analyzing authorities 114
  curiosity 62
  essential critical thinking
    questions 4–5
  guiding questions for critical
    thinking 5
  Holmes, Sherlock 110–11
  idea generation 143
  posing 6

Rabbit-Proof Fence 120
race, as perceptual filter 23
rationalizations 175–9, 181, 183,
  184
Ray, Man, *Le Violon d'Ingres* 145
reading, metaphors of 76–7
rearranging (SCAMPER thinking
  strategy) 46
reasoning 14
  see also deductive reasoning;
    inductive reasoning
rebuttals 106
recursive structure 89, 90
relationship reversal 41
religion 10, 23, 123, 158
  ethics 207, 208, 209, 211, 215,
    216
reports 69, 70–4
reservations 106
rethinking your thinking 144–6
reversal
  relationships 41
  SCAMPER thinking strategy 46
reverse causality 121–2
right answers 150–3
risk, and ethics 210–11
risk taking
  creativity 38
  intellectual 6, 8
Ritchhart, Ron 7, 55
rituals 46–7, 80
robotics 220–2

Rockwell, Norman, *Triple Self-Portrait* 50
Roman Empire, fall of the 118–19
Rosenstiel, Tom 33
rules
  breaking the 81, 146–7
  of thumb 183–4

Sandel, Michael 216–18
Sartre, Jean-Paul 86
Sawyer, Keith 85
SCAMPER thinking strategy 44–6
Schulz, Kathryn 23
science and art, blending 130–1
scientific method 109
scratching, as creative habit 47
Searle, John 68
secular sacred 216
self-direction 4
self-justification 179–80, 192
sfumato 201–3
Shakespeare, William 50, 181
Shenk, Joshua Wolf 86
sight 8–9, 15–16
Silver, Nate 14, 25, 178
Simons, Daniel 20
Sister Act 78
skills, and creative thinking 82
Smith, Fred 157
social dynamics of creativity 38
Socrates 6, 111
solo creativity 85–7
Somerville, Margaret 210, 211, 213–16, 220–1, 226
Sophocles 209
spine, and creative thinking 81–2
standards, intellectual 67
Stanton, Elizabeth Cady 86
Stravinsky, Igor 147
substitution (SCAMPER thinking strategy) 44
sufficient conditions 117
Sullenberger, Chesley "Sully" 174
Sunstein, Cass 187, 194
support for an argument 105

support network 48
syllogisms 112, 113
System I and System II thinking 24, 176

Tallon, Philip 111
Tammet, Daniel 159
Tata, Ratan 138–9
Tavris, Carol 179
teaching, metaphors of 77–8
technology
  ethics 220–2, 224
  see also information technology
testimony 114
Thaler, Richard 187
Tharp, Twyla 46–7, 80–1, 82, 83
theft, creative 49–51
thinking the unthinkable 160–1
Thomas, Douglas 134
Titanic 136
tobacco use, effects of 119
Tolkien, J. R. R. 86
Toulmin, Stephen 105, 106
trust, and ethics 210, 211, 225
Turkle, Sherry 222
Twain, Mark, *The Adventures of Tom Sawyer* 158
Twitter 147

uncertainty
  decision-making 178
  embracing 81, 201
  tolerating 11
  and understanding 25
unconscious mind 176
unintended consequences, law of 119–20
unthinkable, thinking the 160–1
utility maximization 181, 183

Valéry, Paul 142
value
  claims of 106
  ethics 209–13, 218–20
van de Lagemaat, Richard 13, 14

van Gogh, Theo 86
van Gogh, Vincent 86, 147
Vasari, Giorgio 97
virtual memory 47
virtues/virtue ethics 208–13, 215
visual thinking 145
von Oech, Roger 21, 147, 148,
    153

Wagner, Tony 130
warrants 105–6
Watson, James 145
Wegener, Alfred 145

whacks, creative 147–53
what iffing 153–6
Wheelan, Charles 121
White, E. B. 11–12
Whitman, Walt 214
Willingham, Daniel T. 33
World War I, consequences 119
Wright, Wilbur and Orville 79, 86
wrong, being 11, 23–5
    see also errors
WYSIATI 24–5, 177

Zukav, Gary 143